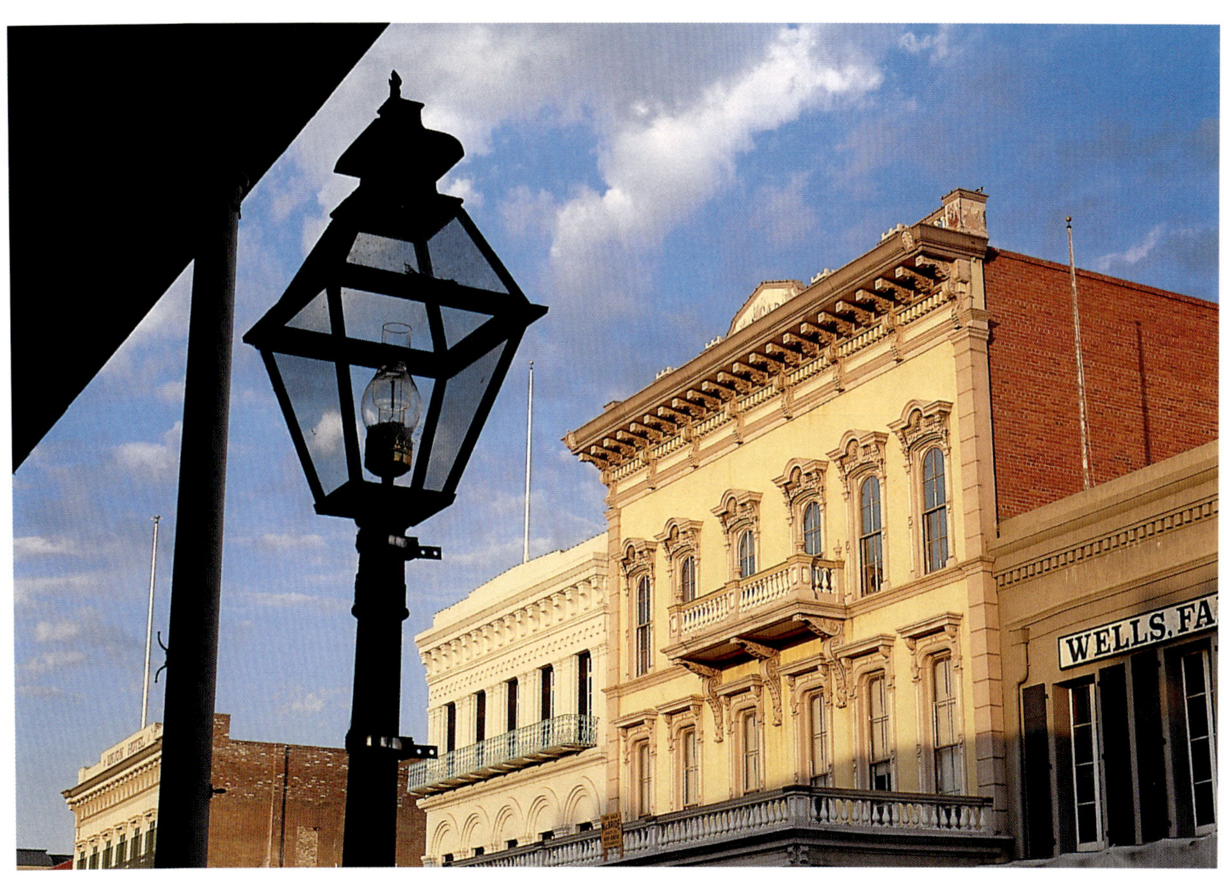
WELLS, FA

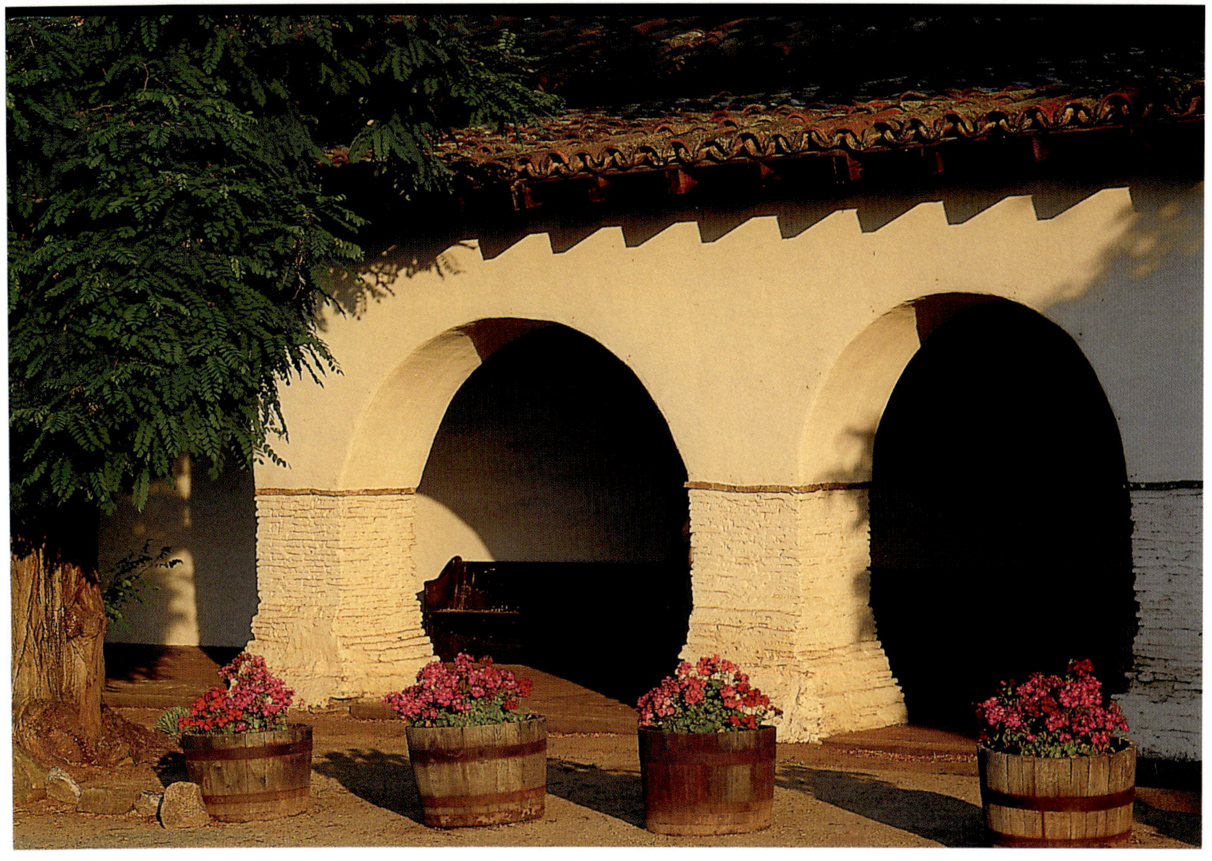

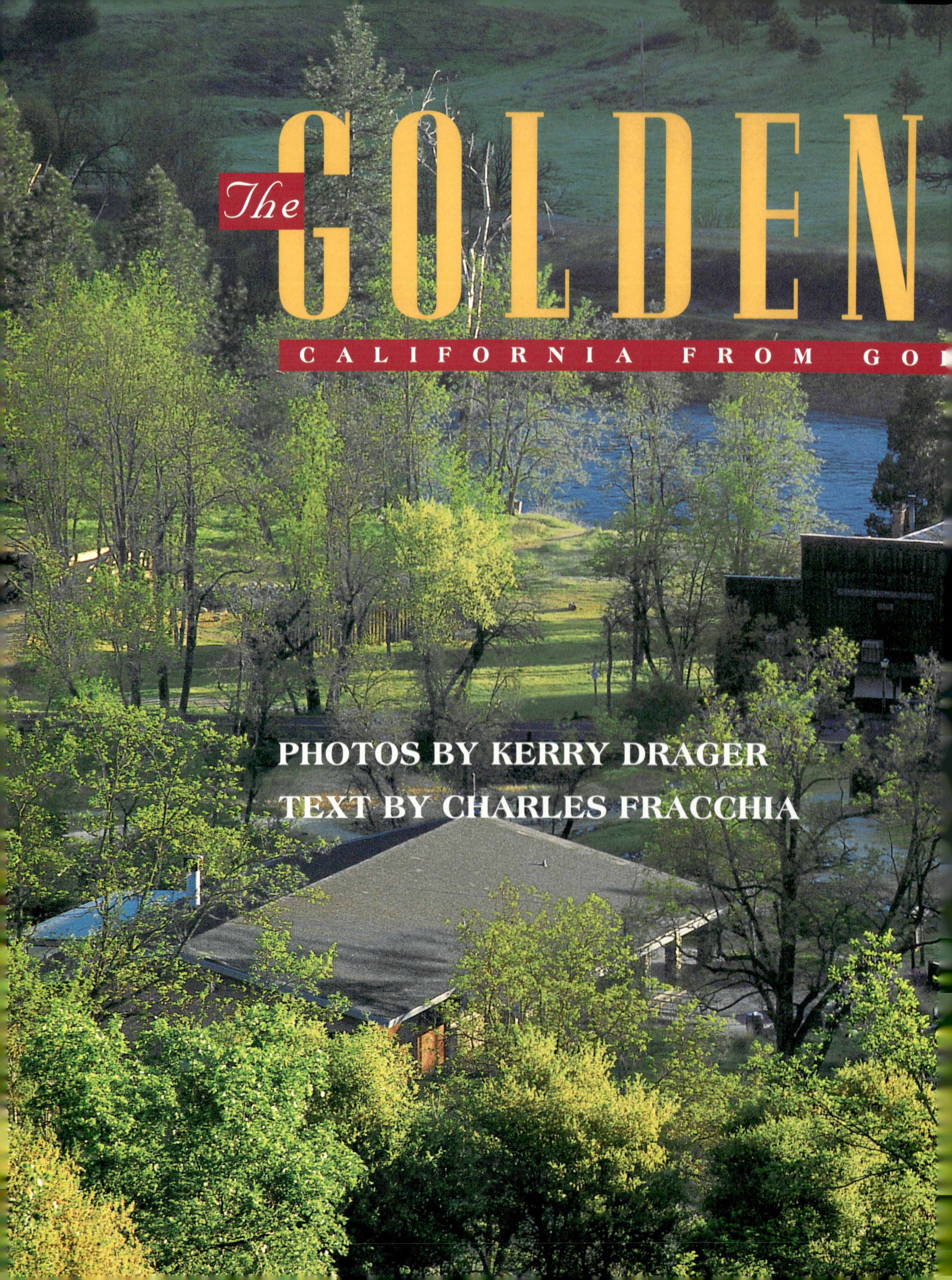

The GOLDEN
CALIFORNIA FROM GO[LD]
PHOTOS BY KERRY DRAGER
TEXT BY CHARLES FRACCHIA

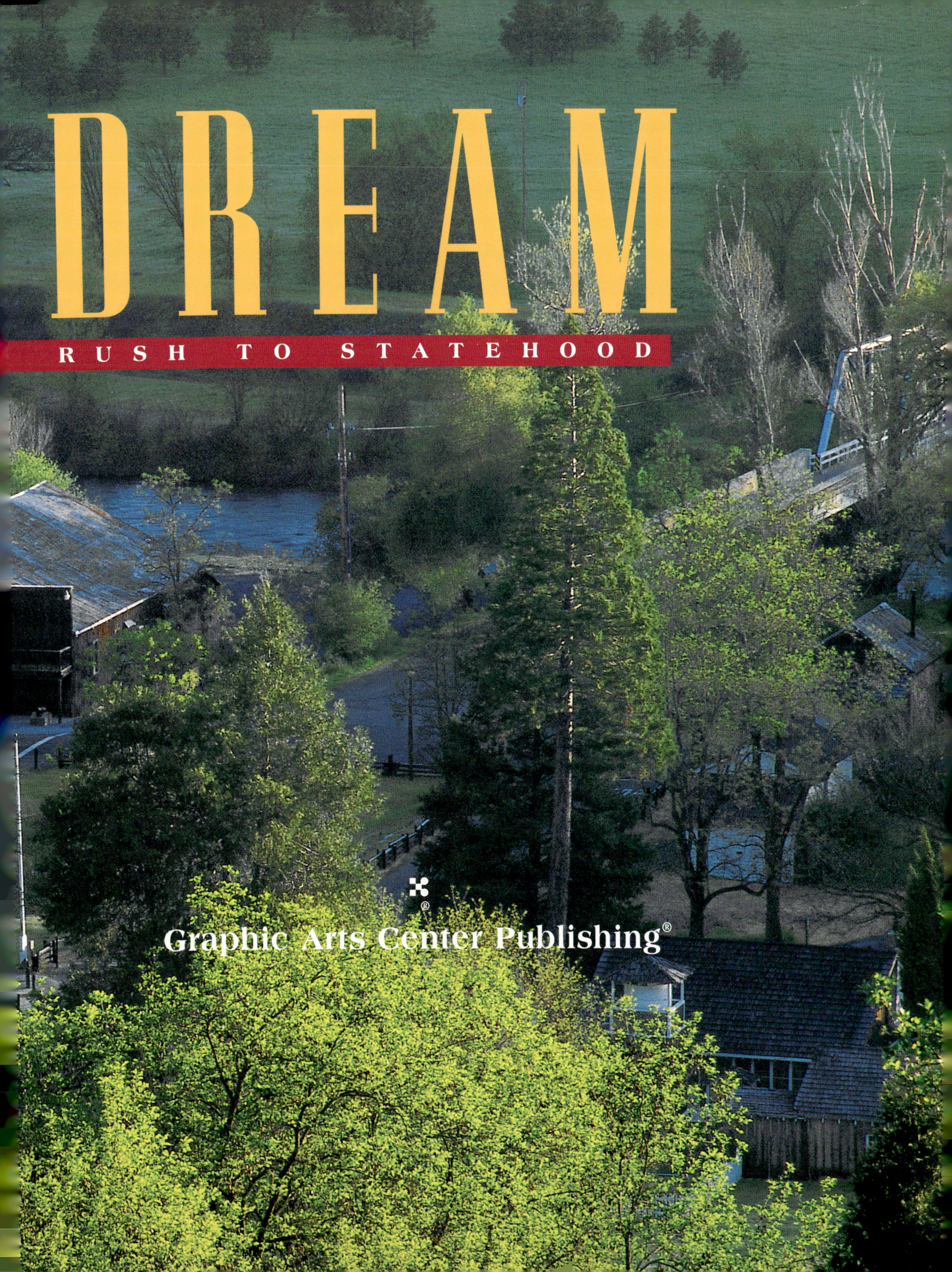

DREAM
RUSH TO STATEHOOD
Graphic Arts Center Publishing®

International Standard Book Number 1-55868-312-7
Library of Congress Catalog Number 97-70197
Photographs © MCMXCVII by Kerry Drager
Text © MCMXCVII by Charles Fracchia
Compilation of photographs © MCMXCVII by
Graphic Arts Center Publishing Company
P.O. Box 10306 ▪ Portland, Oregon 97296-0306 ▪ 503/226-2402

President ▪ Charles M. Hopkins
Editor-in-Chief ▪ Douglas A. Pfeiffer
Managing Editor ▪ Jean Andrews
Photo Editor ▪ Diana S. Eilers
Designer ▪ Constance Bollen
Production Manager ▪ Richard L. Owsiany
Book Manufacturing ▪ Lincoln & Allen Company
Printed in the United States of America

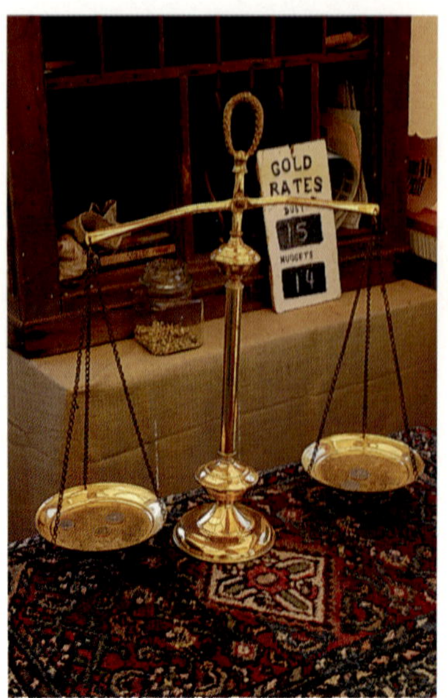

▲ *Columbia Diggins, a living history event at Columbia State Historic Park in the southern Gold Country, includes a re-created miners' bank.*
➤ *Named Fiddletown by Missouri settlers in 1849, the town, once home for a large Chinese population, served as a Gold Country trading center.*

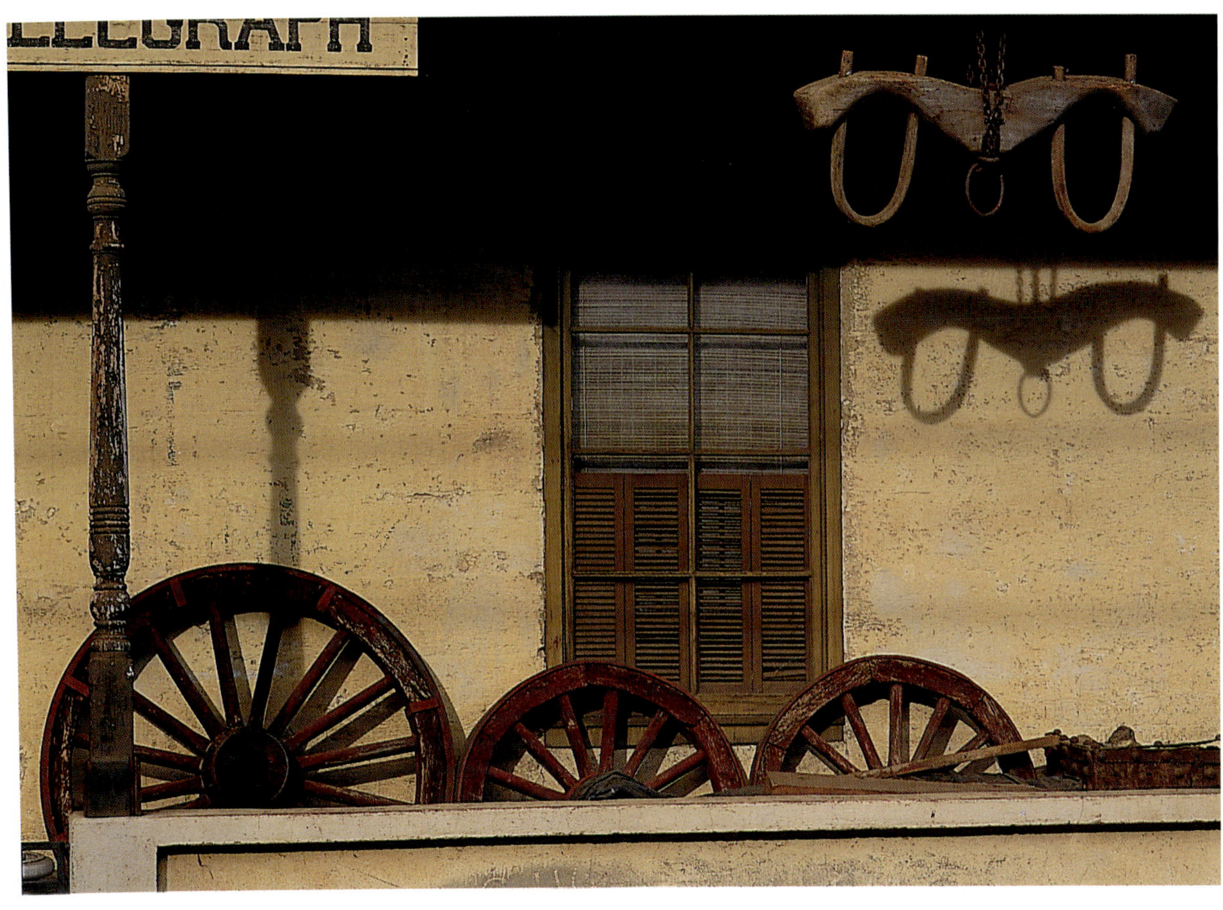

To our wives,

Mary Summers and Elizabeth Feaster Fracchia.

—Kerry Drager and Charles Fracchia

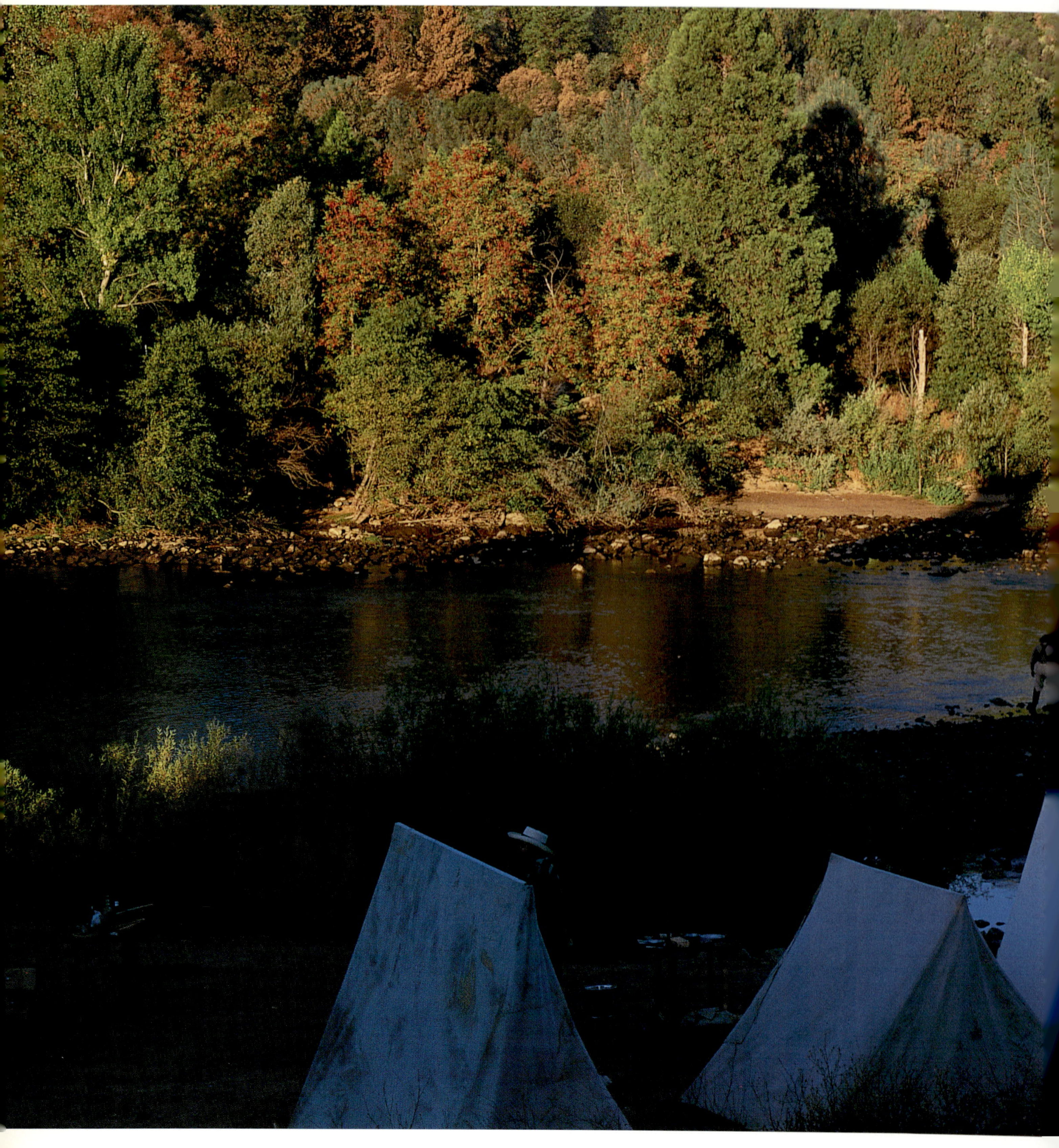

CONTENTS

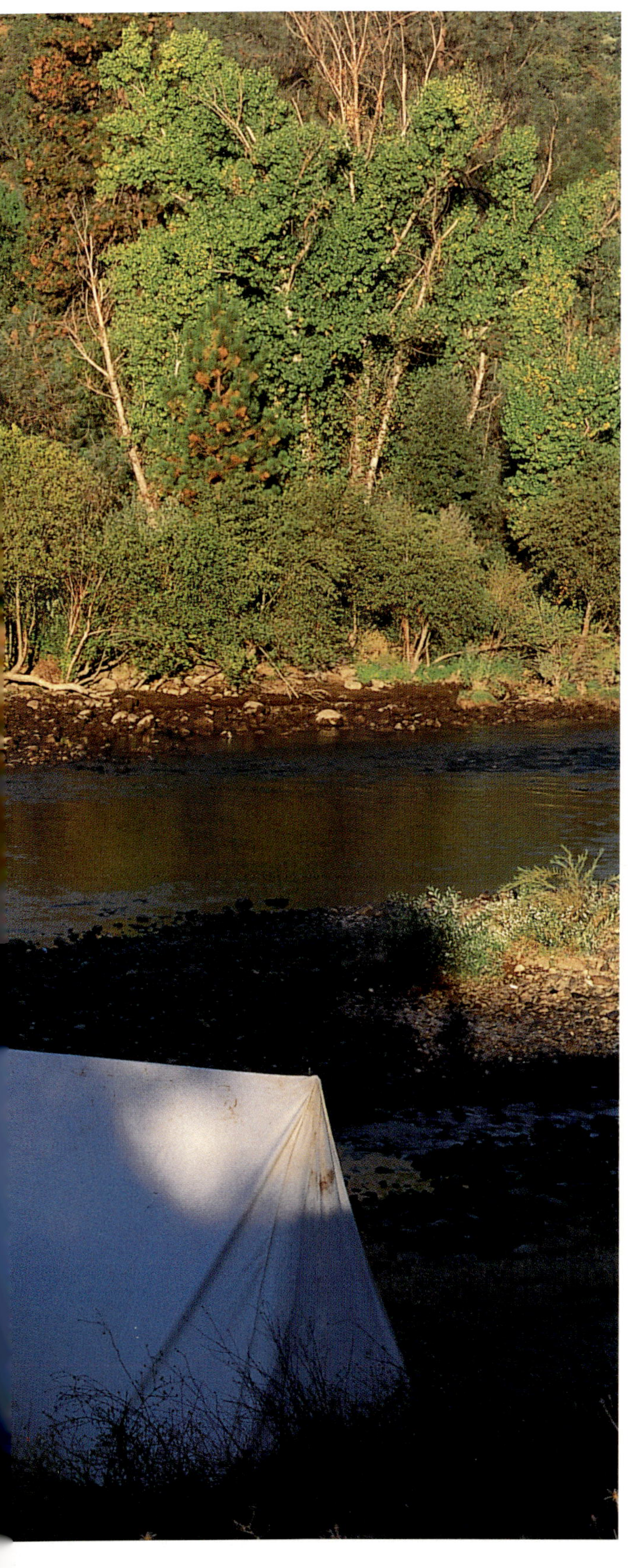

◄ *A re-created prospectors' camp is beside the South Fork American River, Marshall Gold Discovery State Historic Park.*
► *The Marin Headlands, part of the Golden Gate National Recreation Area, provides a view of the Gold Rush gateway.*
► ► *(top left) The advent of brick buildings and firehouses such as this one in Nevada City helped combat fires.*
(top right) An Auburn statue, backdropped by the Placer County Courthouse, honors Claude Chana's 1848 strike.
(bottom) Stamp mills such as these processed ore. In the background, Coloma's restored Chinese store is visible on the left; Sutter's Sawmill replica, on the right.

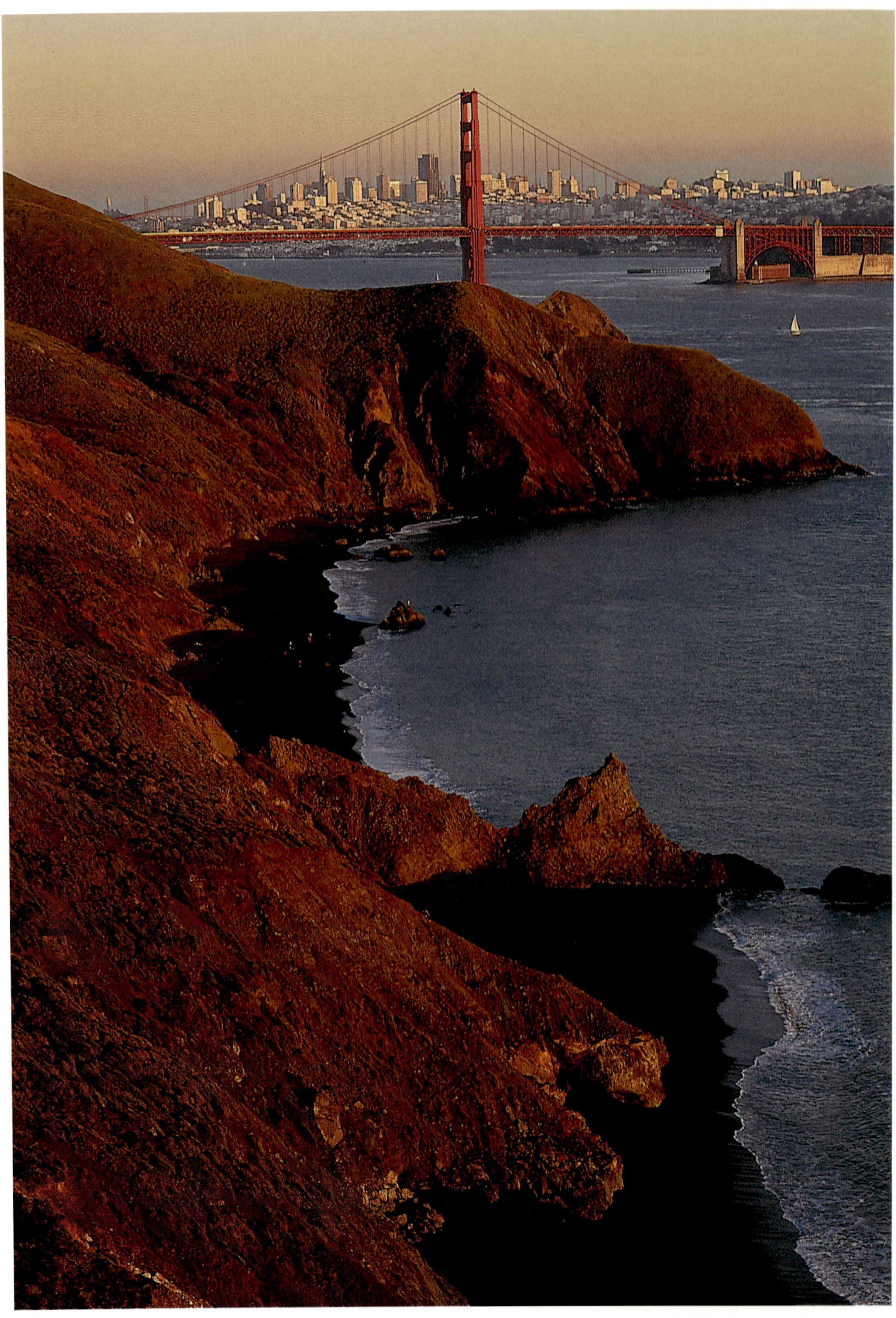

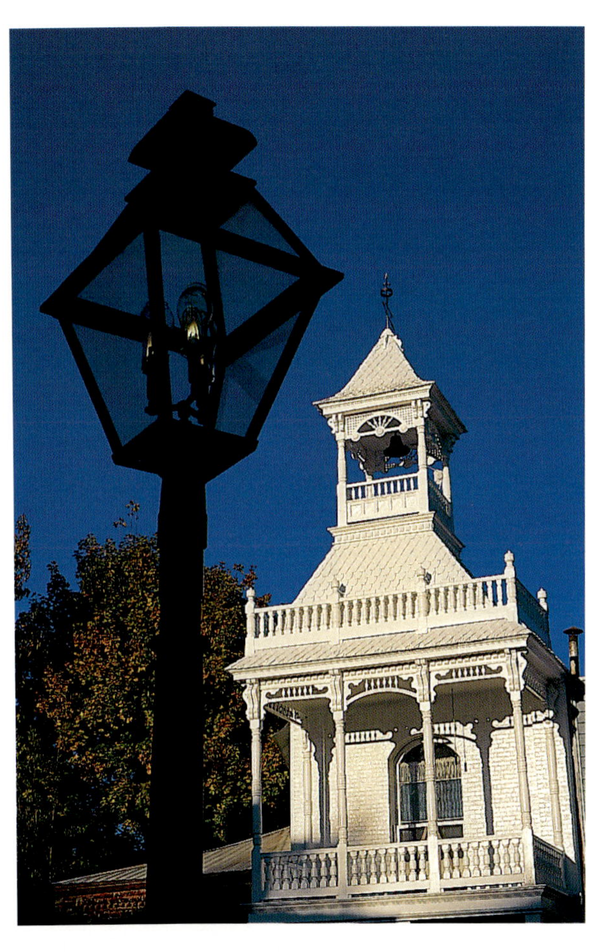
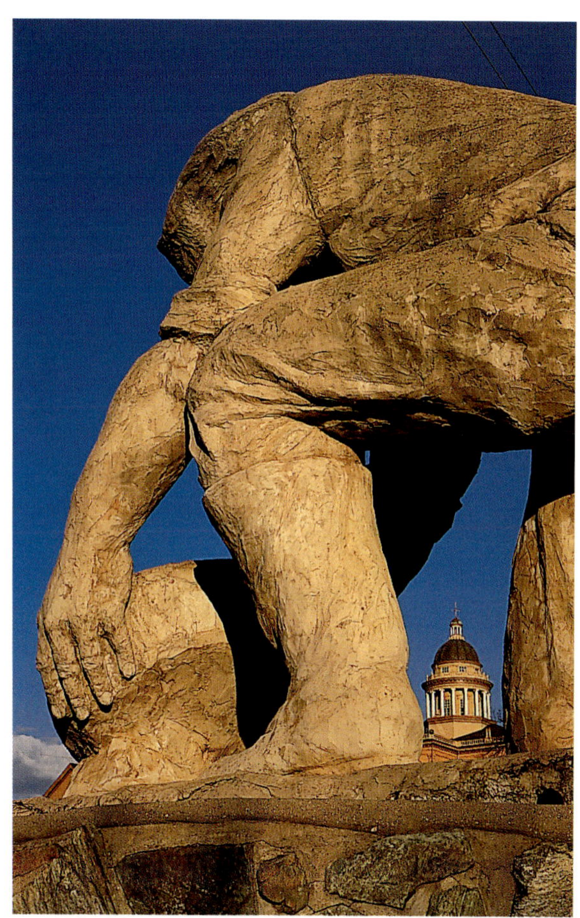
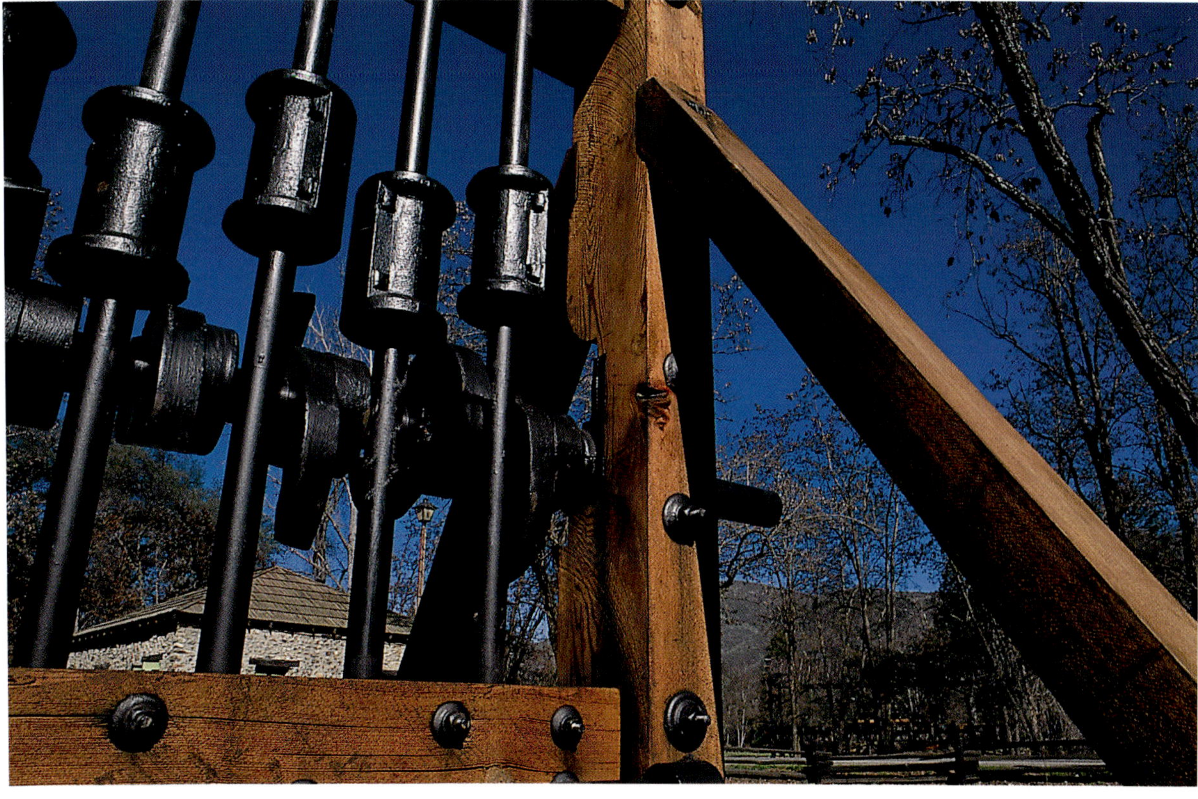

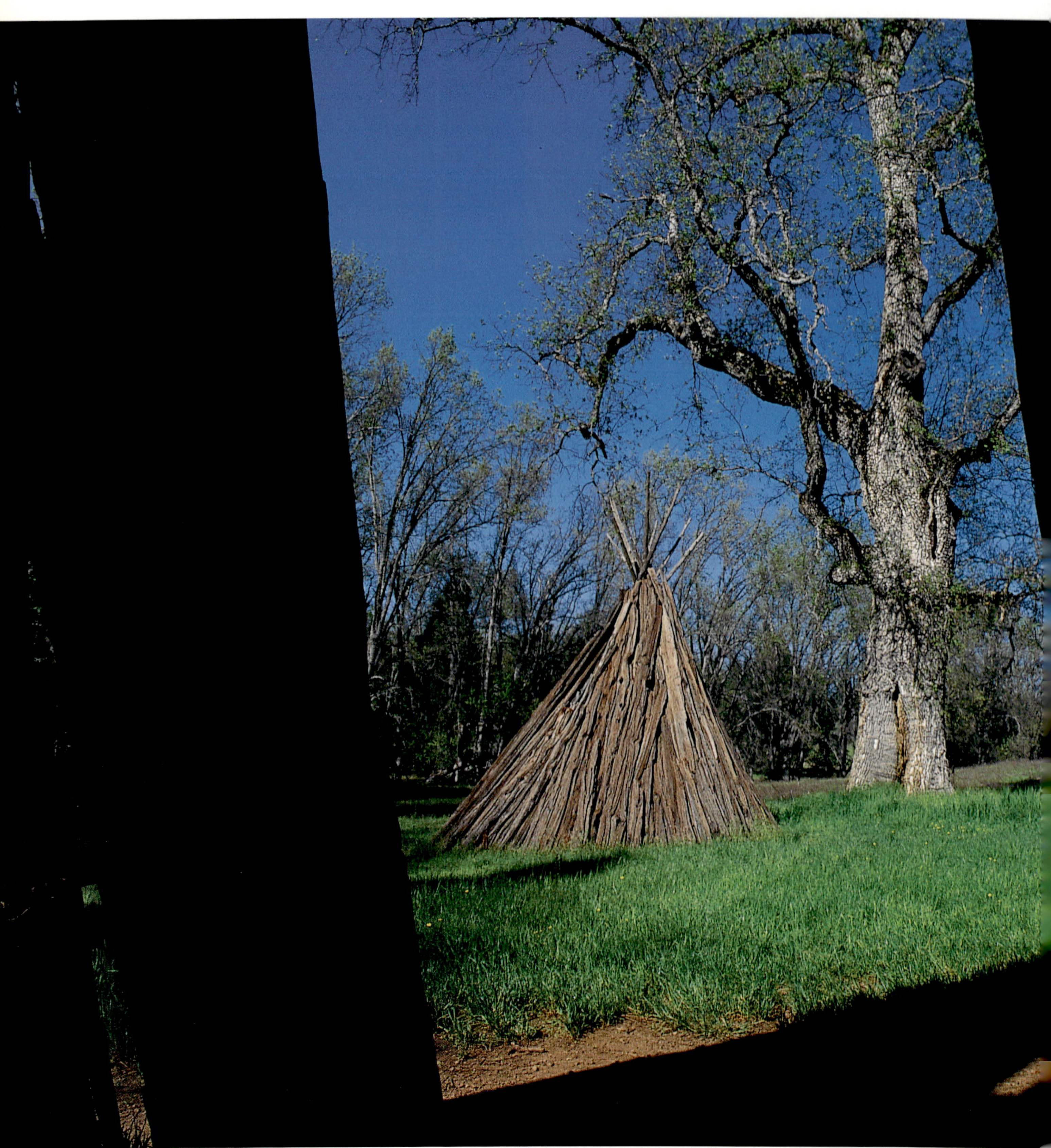

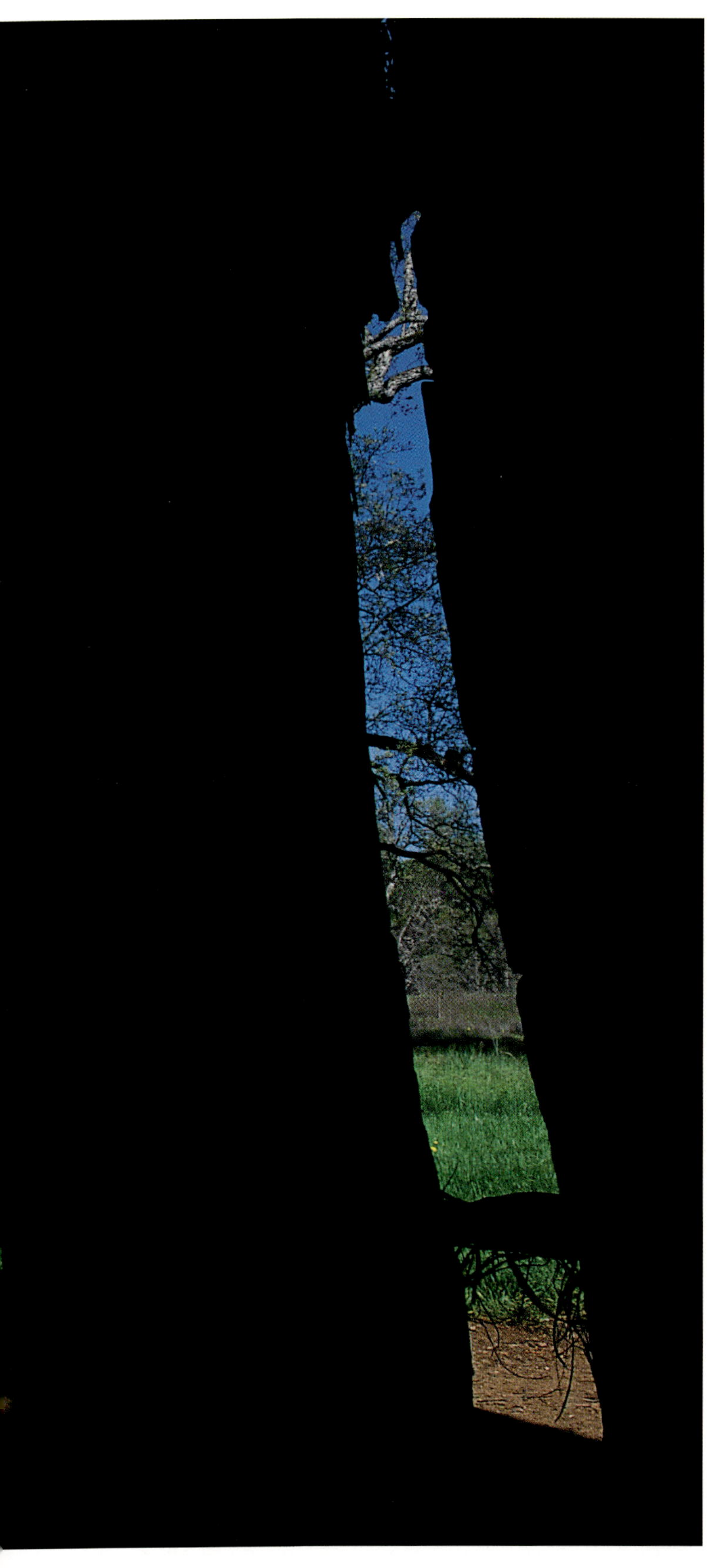

ECHOES OF BEGINNINGS

1. THE GOLDEN LAND FORMS

California, it is thought, was one of the last places on our fiery, molten planet to form from the cooling crust, contorted and heaved by nature's violence beneath it. That shifting and upheaval formed mountains infused with gold, broad plains, valleys ribboned with rivers, and a magnificent seacoast.

What nature wrought was one of the world's most unusual and diverse areas, one that contains nearly every type of landscape on earth: from the wide, white sand beaches in the south to the wild, craggy seacoast to the north; from the towering Sierra Nevada to the vast, fertile Central Valley; from the hot Mojave Desert to the lush rain forests along the northern coast.

2. HUMAN MIGRATIONS

The first human Californians began arriving some seven to nine thousand years ago from the north, having trekked from Asia, across a then-existing land bridge connecting present-day Russia and Alaska. The region became the

◄ *Indian Grinding Rock State Historic Park features a reconstructed Miwok village.*

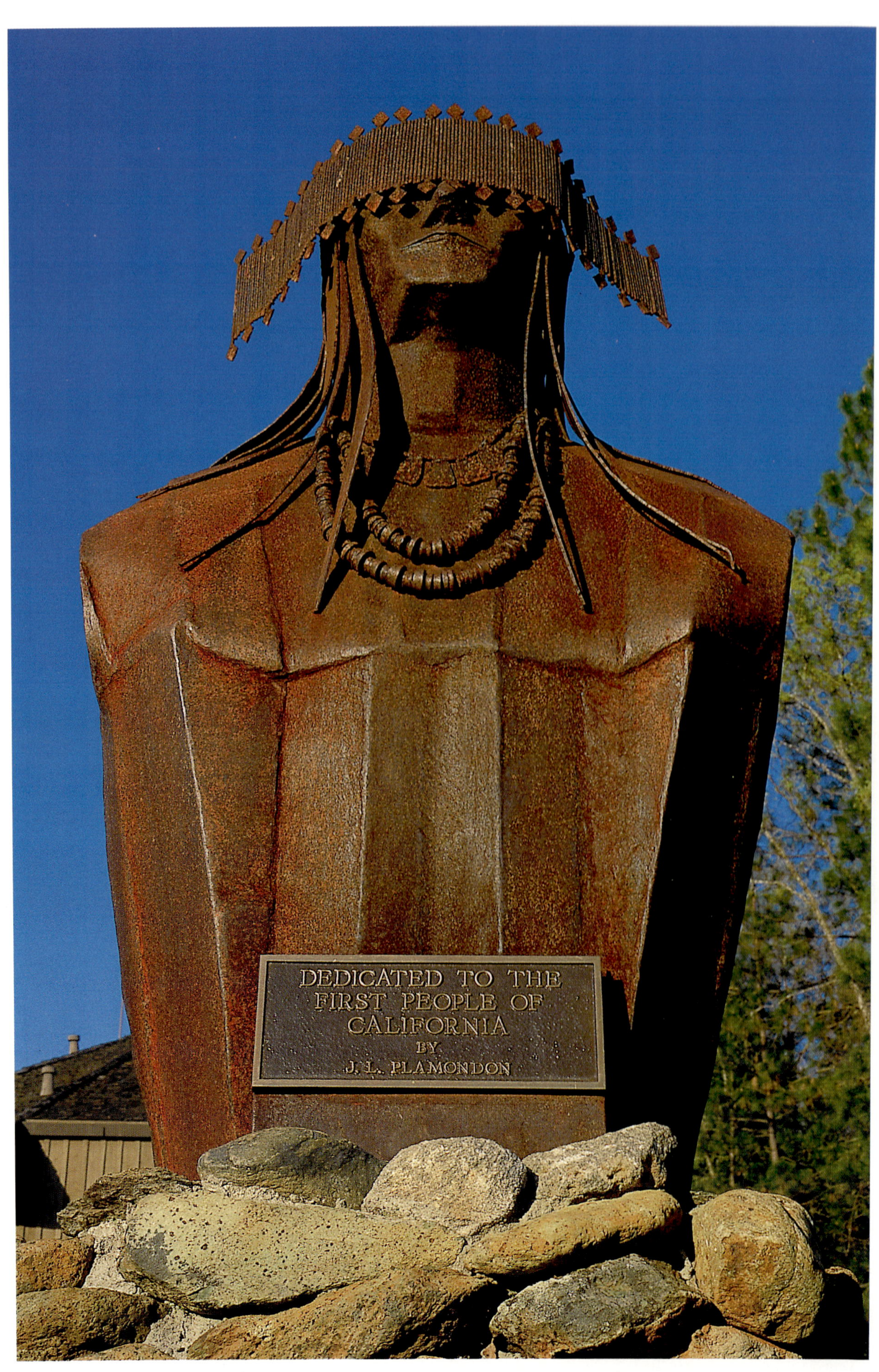

DEDICATED TO THE
FIRST PEOPLE OF
CALIFORNIA
BY
J. L. PLAMONDON

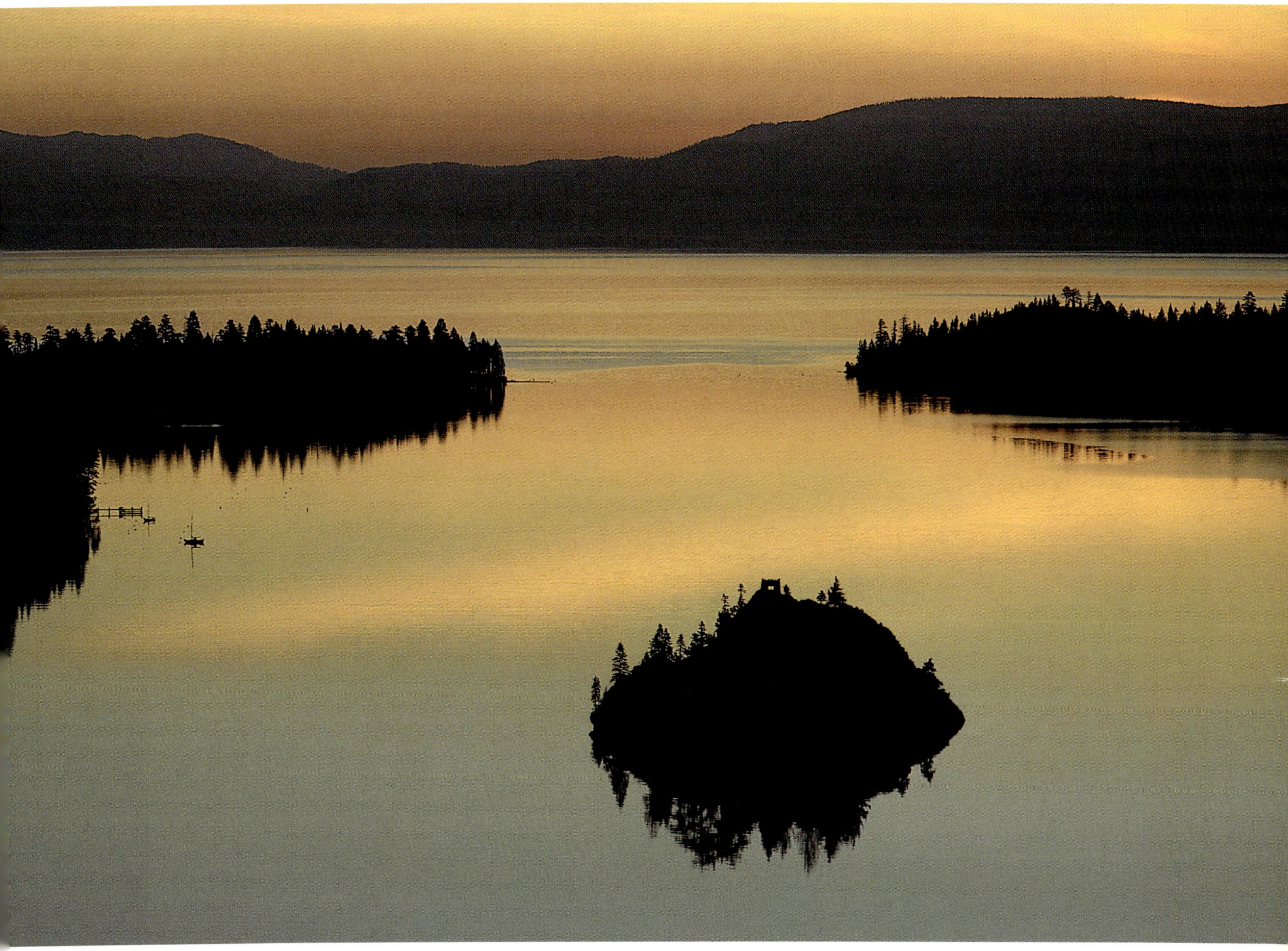

◄ *An Indian Grinding Rock sculpture pays tribute to the pre-Gold Rush indigenous culture of the Sierra Nevada.*
▲ *Lake Tahoe, once the heart of Washoe Indian territory, was "discovered" by John C. Frémont in 1844.*

most densely populated in North America, due, no doubt, to the abundance of food available in the fertile fields, plentiful streams, and coastal waters. Although other early immigrants to the Americas created technologically advanced societies, Californians continued to live in the same simple way they had employed since their migration. They were hunter-gatherers, and so they remained for thousands of years, dwelling in small villages, fishing, hunting game, gathering plants, spending hours in gambling games and in the sweat house.

This is the society first encountered by Europeans in 1542, only fifty years after Columbus's first voyage opened up the continent of the Americas to European exploration. Portuguese explorer Juan Rodriquez Cabrillo, under the Spanish flag, sailed up the west coast of what had come to be known as California, looking for the gold and other treasures he had claimed in the conquests of Mexico and Guatemala. The name California was bestowed by an early

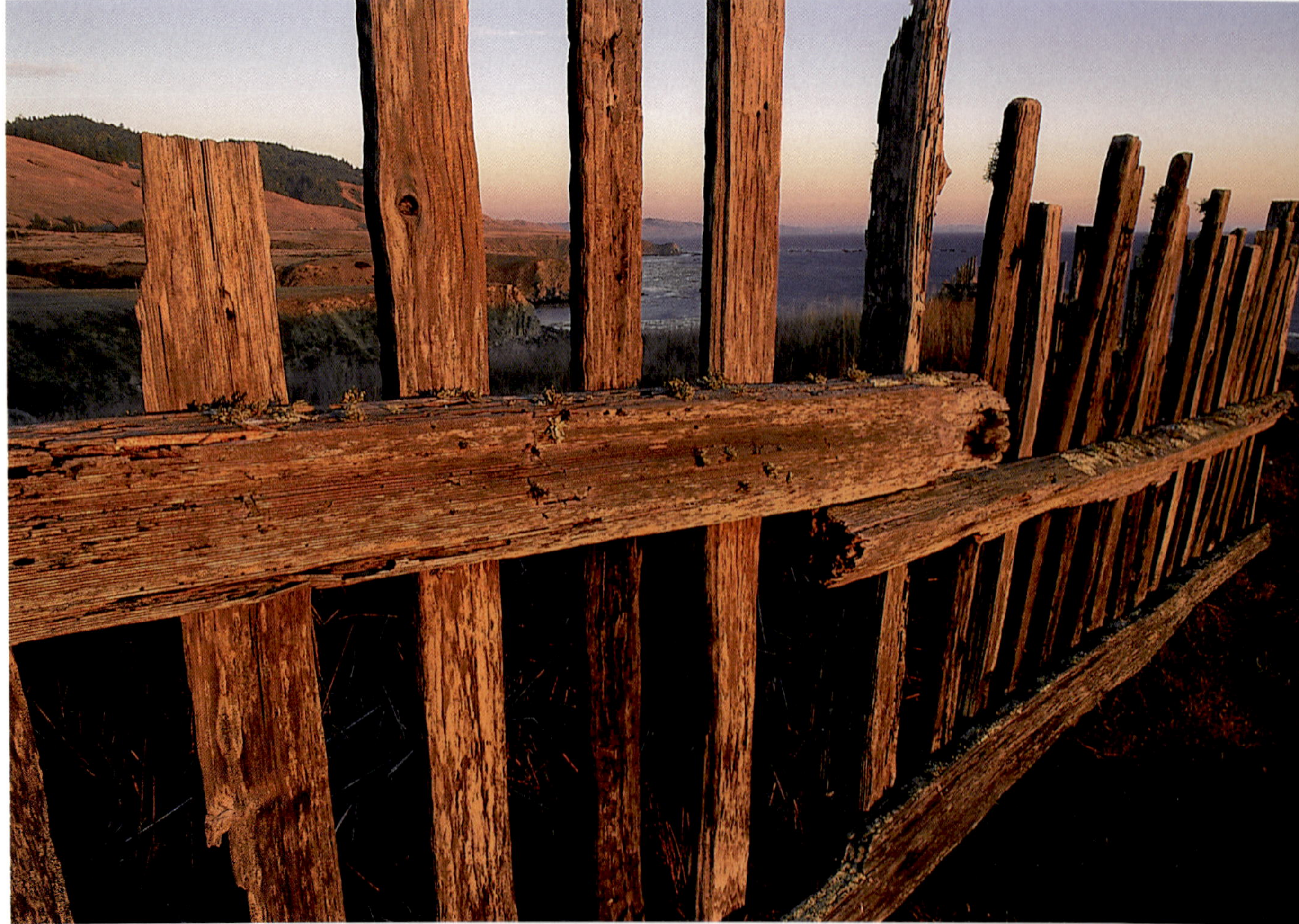

▲ Along Sonoma County's coast stands a one-time Russian outpost, Fort Ross, now a state historic park.
➤ The reconstructed Fort Ross tells the story of the Russian era, as well as the area's original Indian village.

explorer inspired by a popular Spanish novel of the day, *Las Sergas de Esplandian,* by Ordoñez de Montalvo. In this novel, a tribe of comely black Amazons, led by their Queen Calafia, inhabited the island California, said to be located "at the right hand of the Indies" and close to the "Terrestrial Paradise." These warriors wore gold armor and carried golden weapons, and the sands of their island home were gold. Cabrillo died of gangrene without having discovered California's wealth and was buried on the Channel Islands off the coast of Santa Barbara. More than a half century went by before Spain took any further interest in California.

In the interim, another European set foot on the coast of California. In 1577, the English pirate Francis Drake landed his ship, *The Golden Hind,* north of San Francisco at the harbor now known as Drake's Bay, to overhaul her and to take on fresh supplies. Although Drake claimed the land for his sovereign, Queen Elizabeth I, the English government was much more interested in the booty he brought home from Spanish treasure ships.

Spain turned its attention again to the coast of California when it needed a good harbor for trading ships returning from the Philippines. In 1602, Sebastian Vizcaino set out from Acapulco with three ships and sailed into San Diego Bay on November 10. A month later, he entered Monterey Bay, which he recommended as an anchorage. Vizcaino

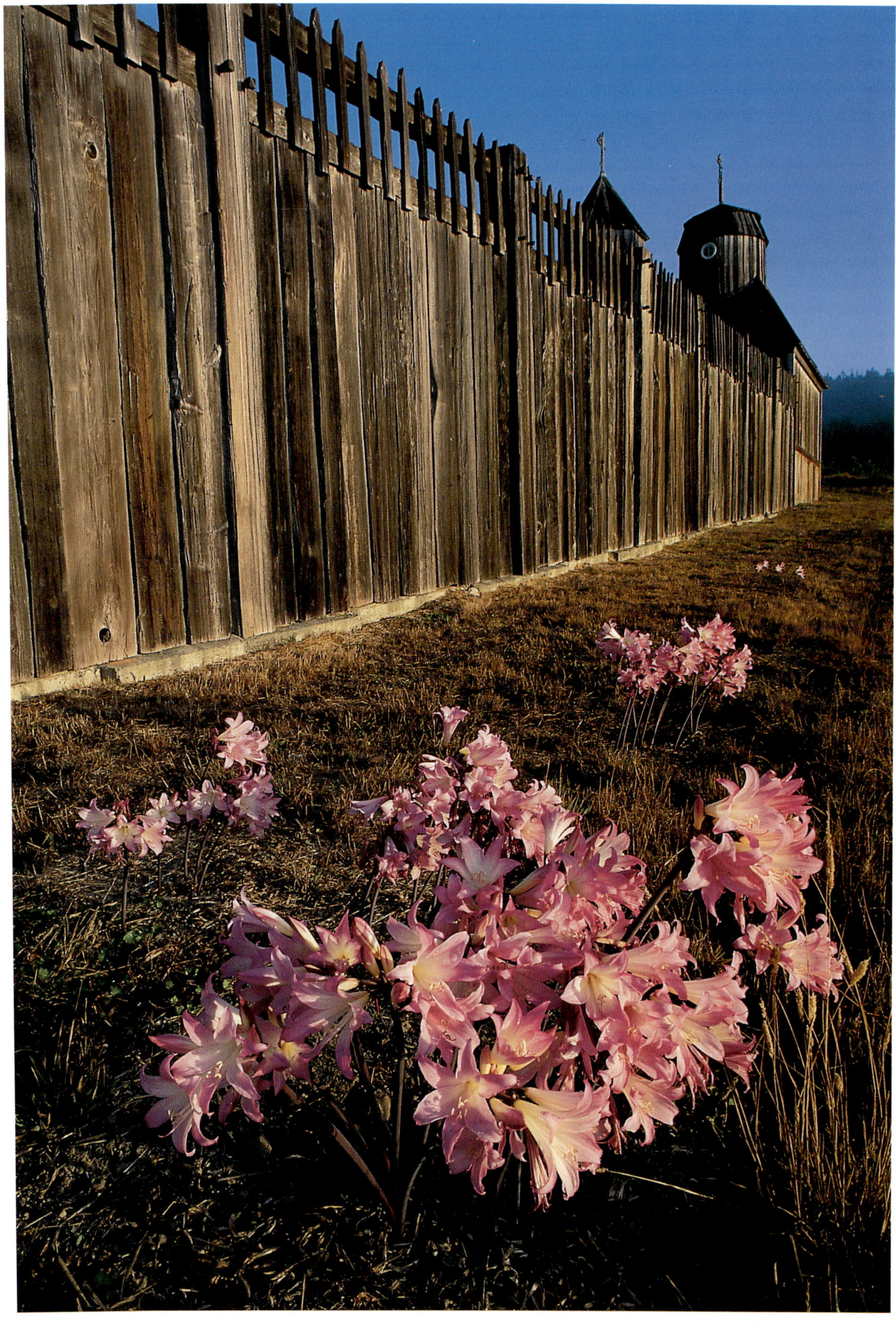

sailed as far north as Cape Mendocino before storms drove him back south. Upon his return, Vizcaino urged Spain to colonize this promising territory, but it would be another 166 years before Spain acted on this recommendation.

Spain had entered a period of political and economic decline. Following disastrous defeats in the Seven Years' War, its new king, Charles III, determined to reorganize his domains. A visitor-general, Jose de Galvez, was sent to Mexico to accomplish this task. Galvez argued to the crown that Alta California needed to be colonized and thus secured for Spain. He warned that the Russians were coming; and indeed they were. The Russians, in their expansion, had crossed the Bering Straits and had begun colonization of North America in the area of Alaska.

The Spanish crown agreed, and in 1769, Don Gaspar de Portola left Baja California with a group of soldiers and their families and missionaries under the command of the passionate and energetic Franciscan friar, Father Junípero Serra, to rendezvous at the bay of San Diego. While waiting for their supply ships to arrive, Portola led a few men

▼ *Sonoma State Historic Park, including Sonoma Mission, documents the end of California's Mexican era.*

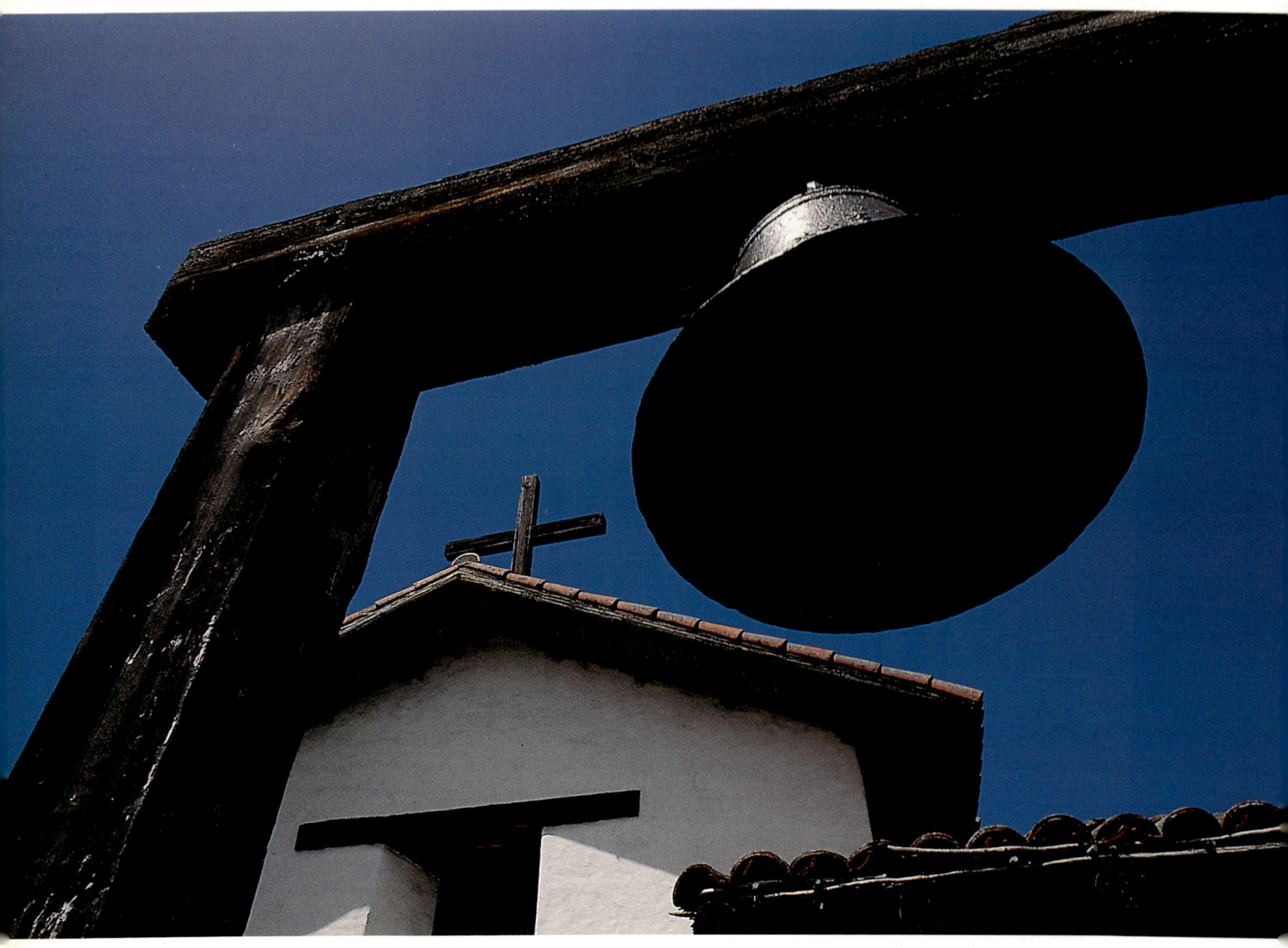

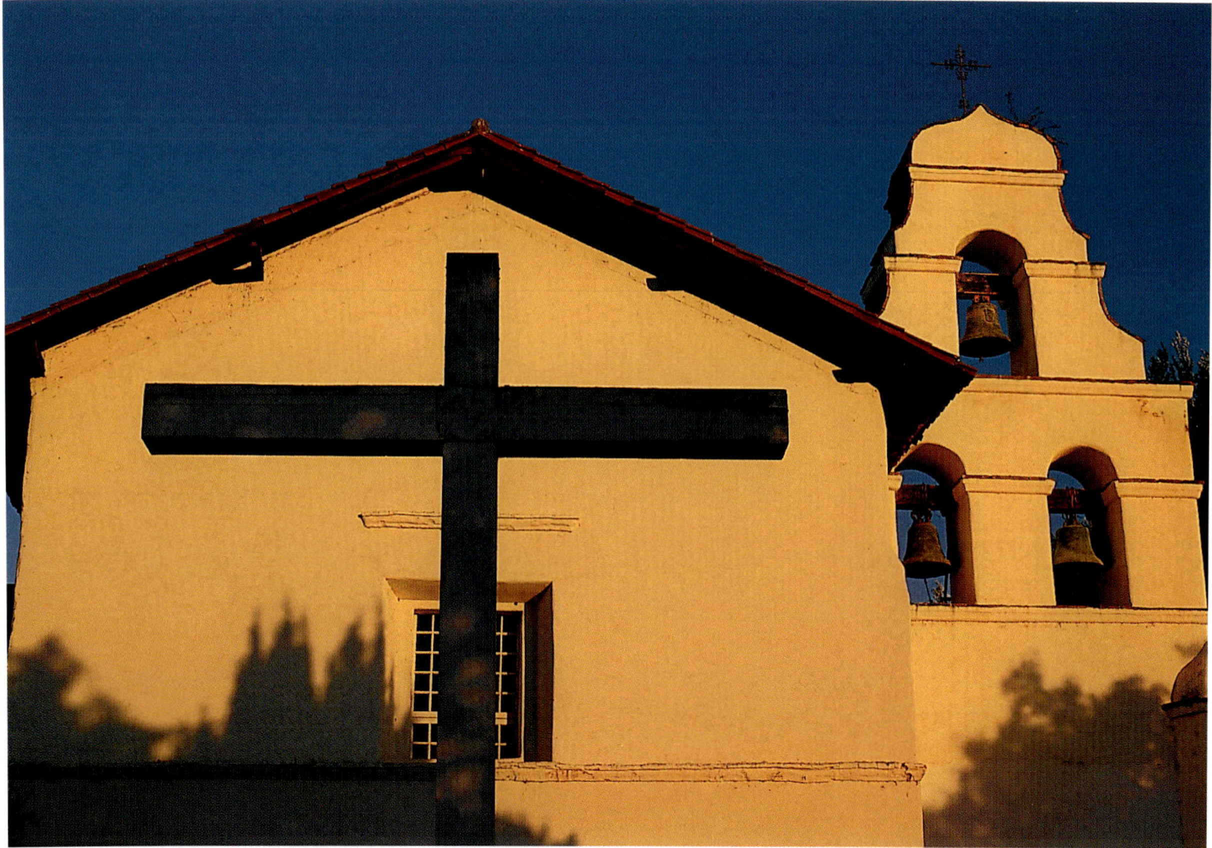

▲ *Mission San Juan Bautista has survived some shaky times due to its proximity to the San Andreas Fault.*

northward to locate the bay of Monterey, where he had been instructed to establish a *presidio* (military fort) and a mission. Portola and his handful of men did not recognize the bay from Vizcaino's overstated description. But as they searched northward they were impeded by a channel and large body of water that three years later would be recognized as one of the world's major harbors—San Francisco Bay. Portola's expedition soon established military and religious outposts at both San Diego Bay and Monterey Bay. With these, European colonization of California began.

Spain ruled California for just over fifty years. This half century saw Spain increasingly embroiled in European clashes and in revolts by the country's New World colonies. Thus taxed, Spain had few resources to expend on development. Nevertheless, twenty missions, four presidios, and three *pueblos*, or towns, were founded in California. (A twenty-first mission, Sonoma, was established in 1823 during the Mexican era.)

Spain ruled with heavy-handed laws and regulations, keeping its colonies dependent and backward. The under-fortified presidios were never actually capable of protecting the vast territory from invasion; the pueblos, formed as they were from the dregs of Mexican society (including criminals paroled from Mexican jails), never coalesced into workable communities. It was the missions of California that proved to be the most successful and practical aspect of Spain's half century of colonization.

The missions created self-contained economies centered around agriculture and ranching. They oversaw the construction of very effective irrigation systems, and, during the years when no supply ships came from Mexico and the presidio soldiers were not paid, the missionaries fed the soldiers and their families and provided other necessities.

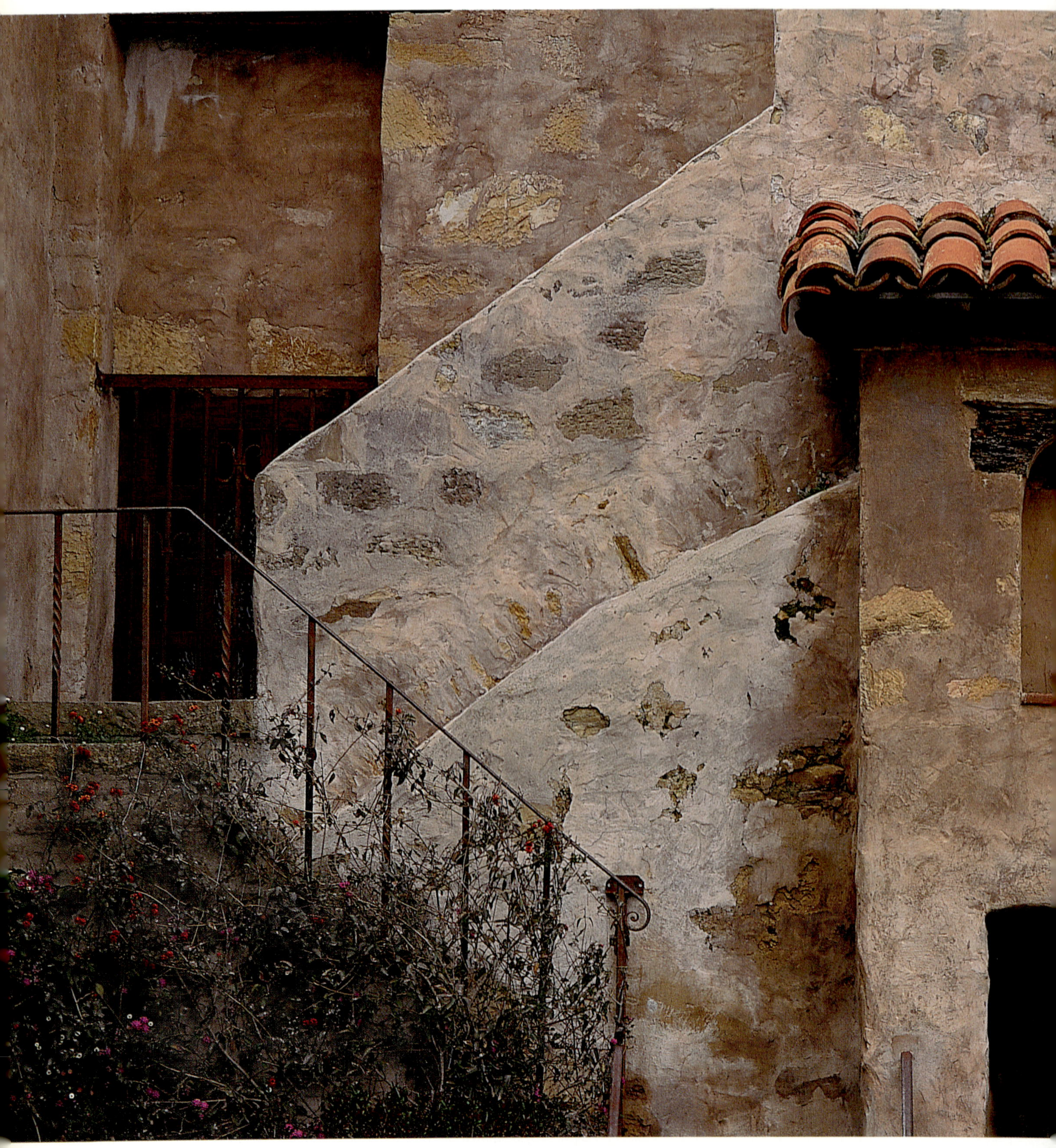

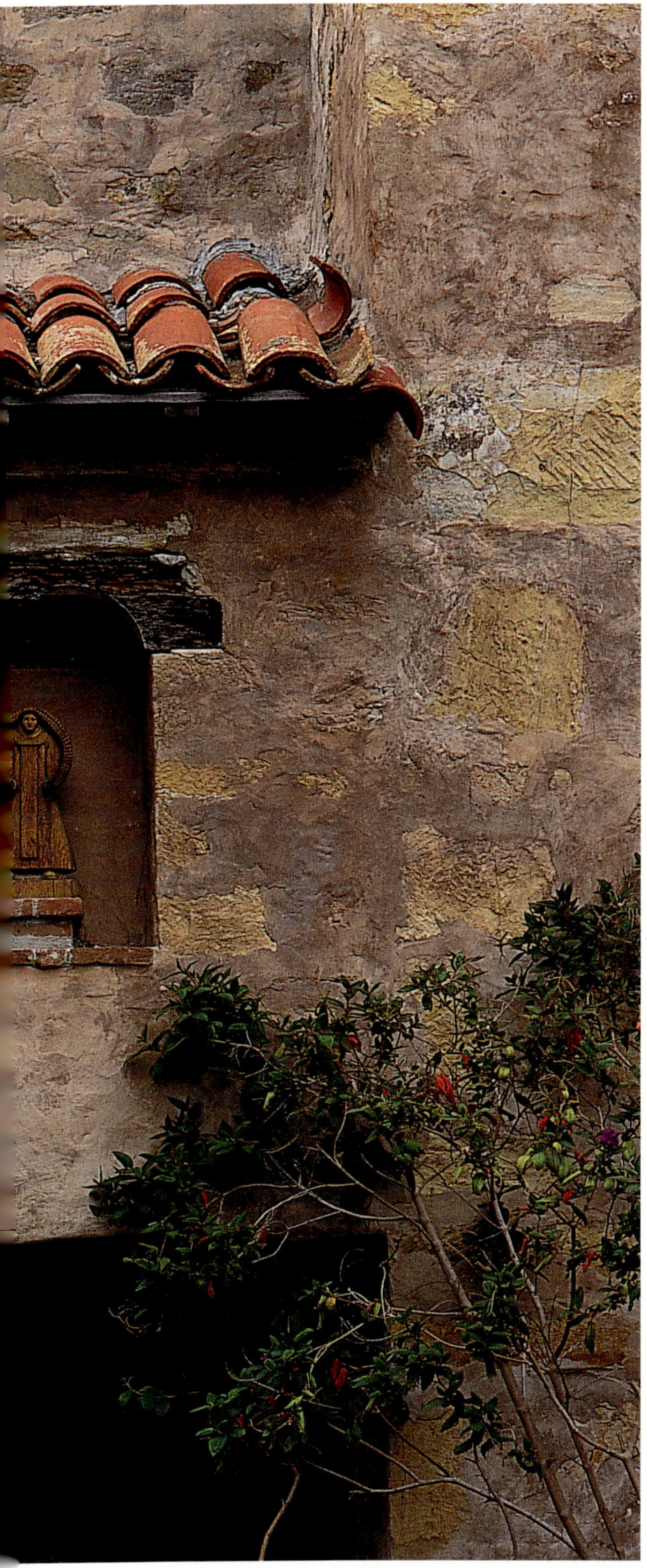

The mission buildings, although buffeted by earthquakes and the elements, were generally in good repair.

The Franciscan missionaries were charged with the responsibility to Christianize and civilize the Native population, and they set about this task with zeal. The converts were made to conform to the rigidly structured life of the mission. They were required to work long hours in the mission's fields and ranches and were segregated at puberty into closely guarded dormitories. Under these conditions, diseases for which the Natives had no immunities spread to epi-

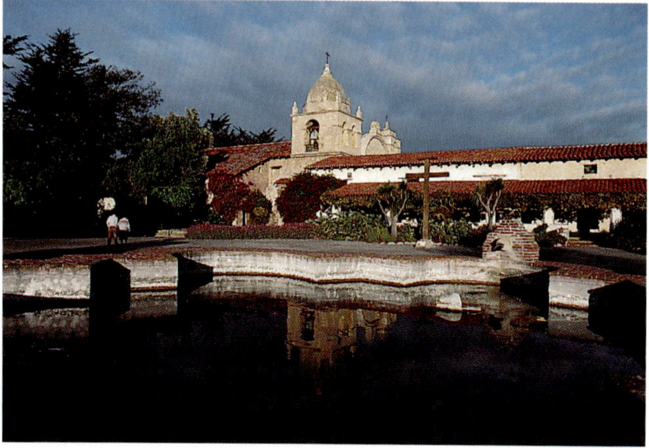

demic proportions. In spite of the abuses and drawbacks, these missions did provide a system of integrating the Natives into the European-style society in California. The Natives' traditional lifestyle was replaced by farming, ranching, and other skills and arts useful in European society.

The end of Spain's rule came in early 1821, when Mexico won independence from Spain through revolution. California was now part of Mexico, and with its liberalized rule, trade with Euro-Latin America and the United States expanded. The hides and tallow from the vast cattle herds of California were much in demand; and in trade for them, foreign ships brought manufactured goods to the territory for the first time.

◄ Carmel Mission, called the quintessential California mission, holds the burial site of Father Junipero Serra, who established many of California's Spanish missions.
▲ Indigenous Californians played a key role in the life of Carmel and other missions.

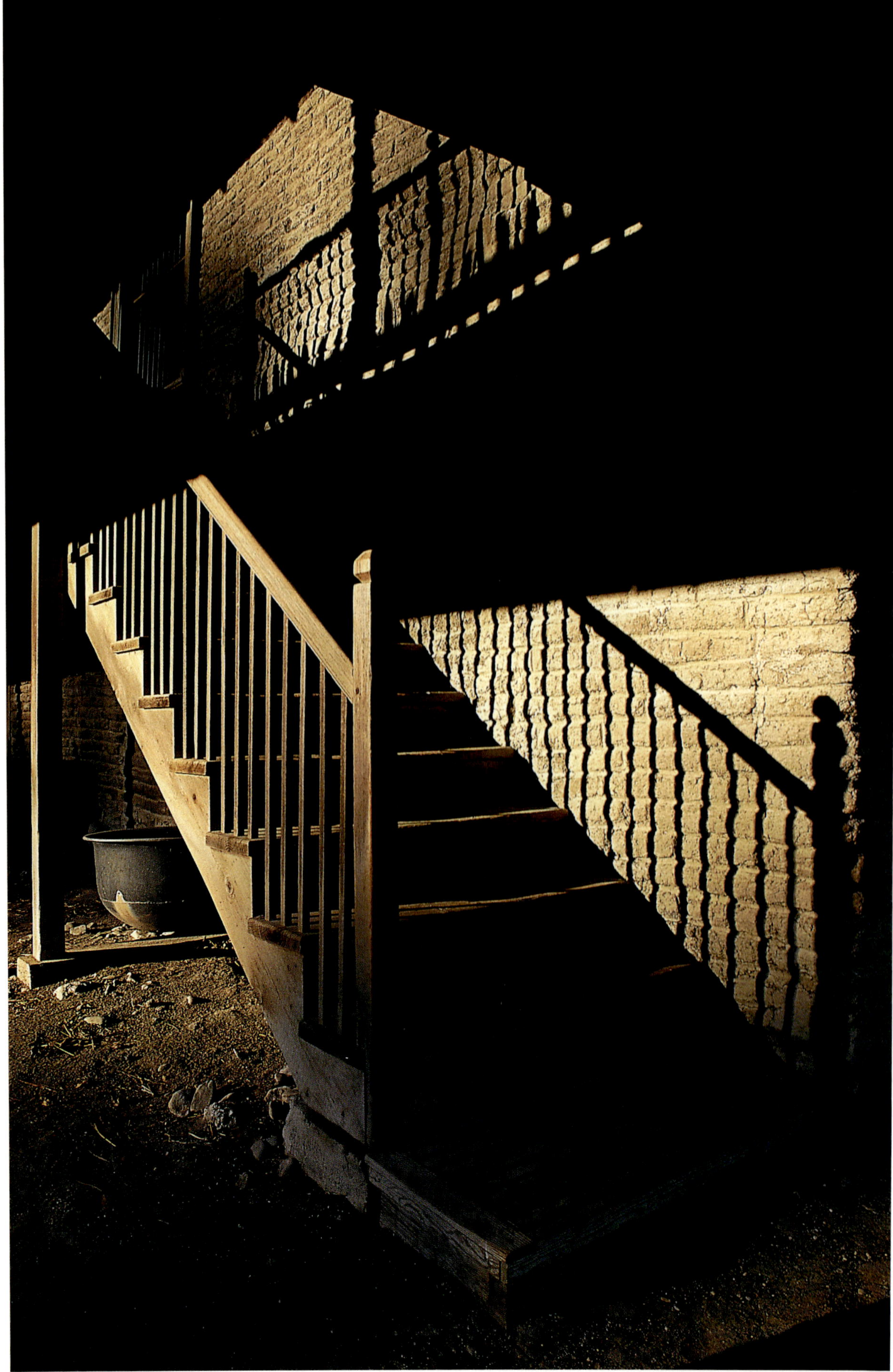

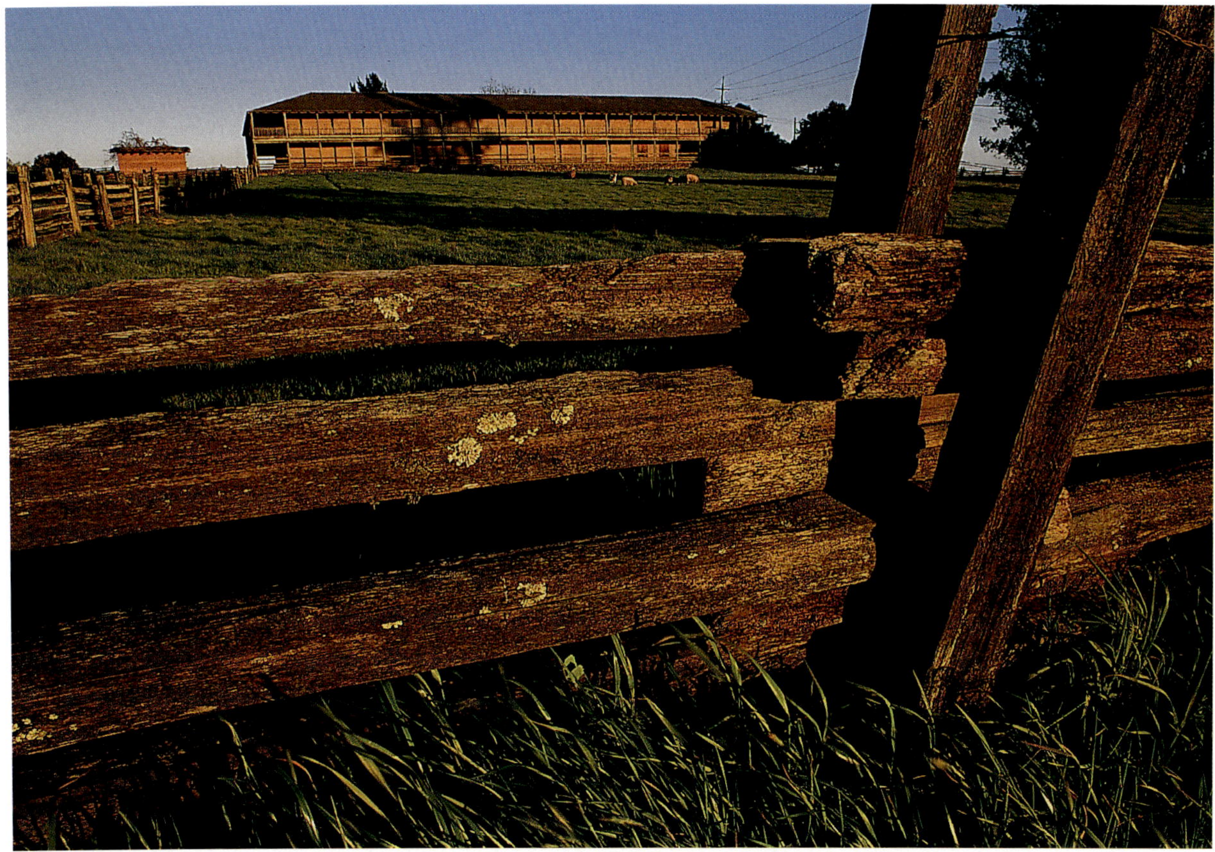

◄ *The gracious home of General Mariano Vallejo, the Mexican administrator of Northern California at the time of the Bear Flag Revolt of 1846, is preserved as part of the Petaluma Adobe State Historic Park, near Sonoma.*
▲ *Vallejo's vast ranch supported much livestock, which was seized when he was taken prisoner during the revolt.*

The immense land holdings that had been held in trust by the missions for their Native charges were confiscated and parceled into almost one thousand large *ranchos*. These were granted to Hispanic Californians and to some of the increasing numbers of immigrants from Europe and the United States who had become naturalized citizens of Mexico. The former Native charges of the Franciscan missionaries provided the labor for these ranchos, and the rancheros presided over a simple, almost-feudal world.

This idyllic, indolent world of California began to dissolve in the mid-1840s. For some years, the United States had set its sights on territorial expansion. The annexation of Texas—after that territory successfully rebelled from Mexico and set itself up as an independent republic—had exacerbated the already strained relations between the two countries. It was onto this stage that Captain John C. Frémont, an energetic and ambitious young U.S. army officer, rode in 1845, leading a survey party of the U.S. Topographical Engineers.

The expedition wandered to the settlement surrounding Mission San Juan Bautista, not far from Monterey, the capital of California. Frémont was asked to withdraw by the California Mexican authorities, who mistrusted the nature of his mission. Frémont responded by barricading himself on Gavilan Peak and defied any attempt to dislodge him.

Eventually, Frémont left his fortified position and headed north. After crossing into Oregon, Frémont was overtaken by a United States naval officer in disguise and presumably traveling through Mexico and California.

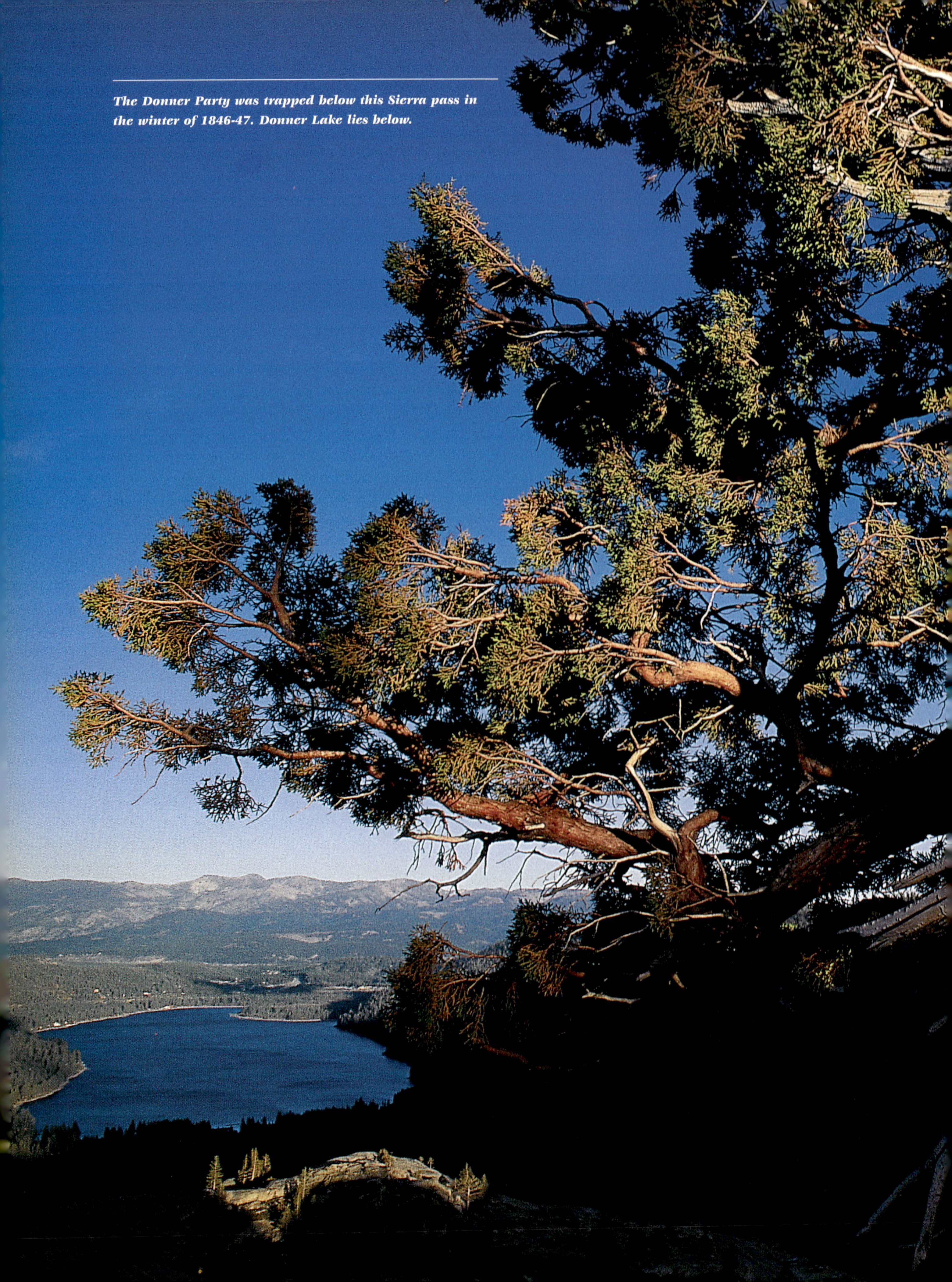

The Donner Party was trapped below this Sierra pass in the winter of 1846-47. Donner Lake lies below.

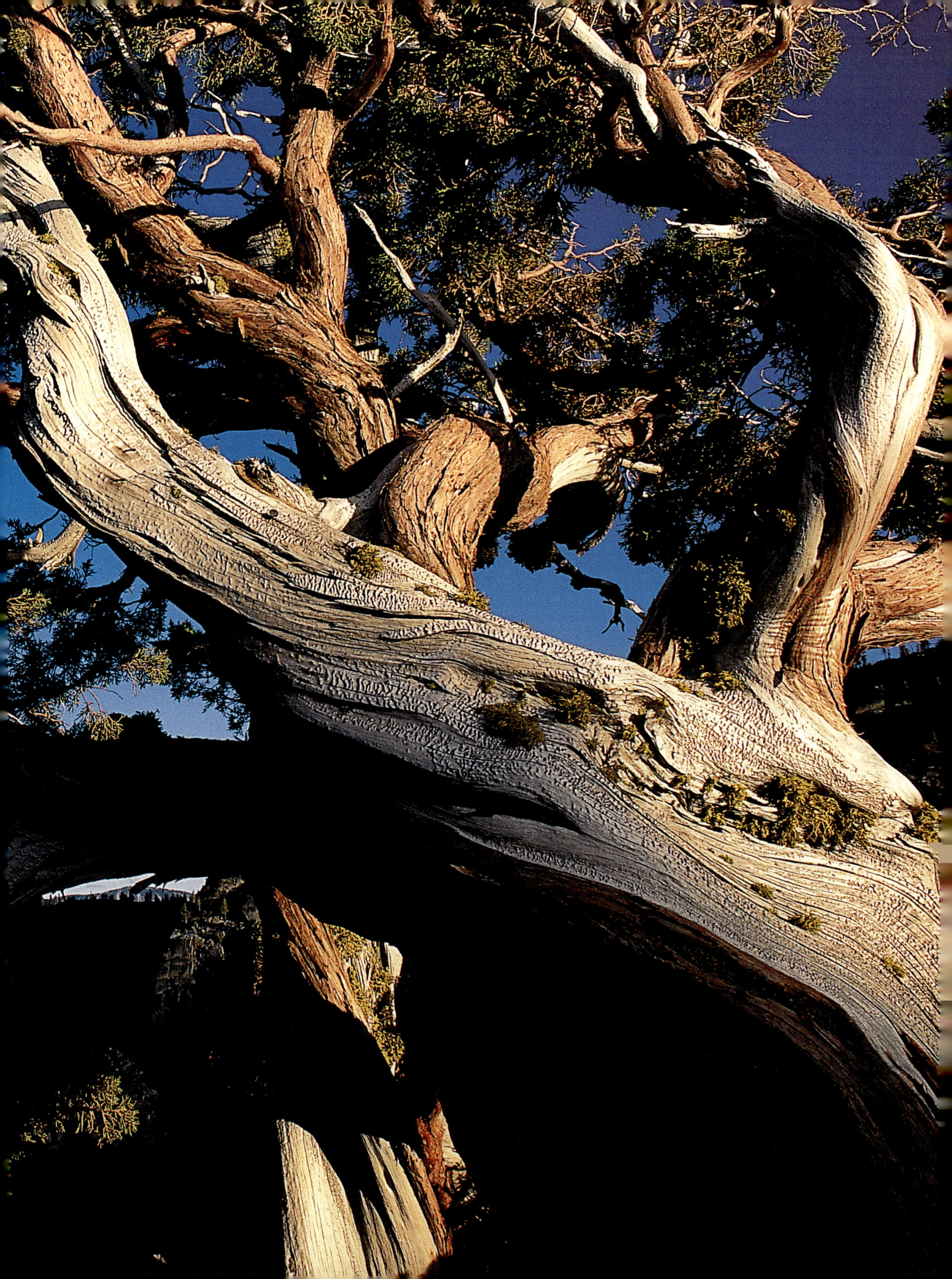

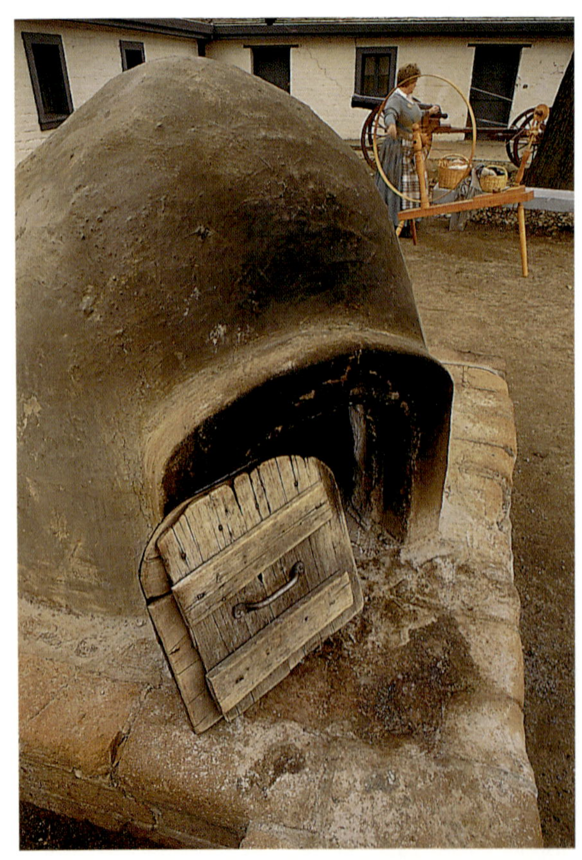
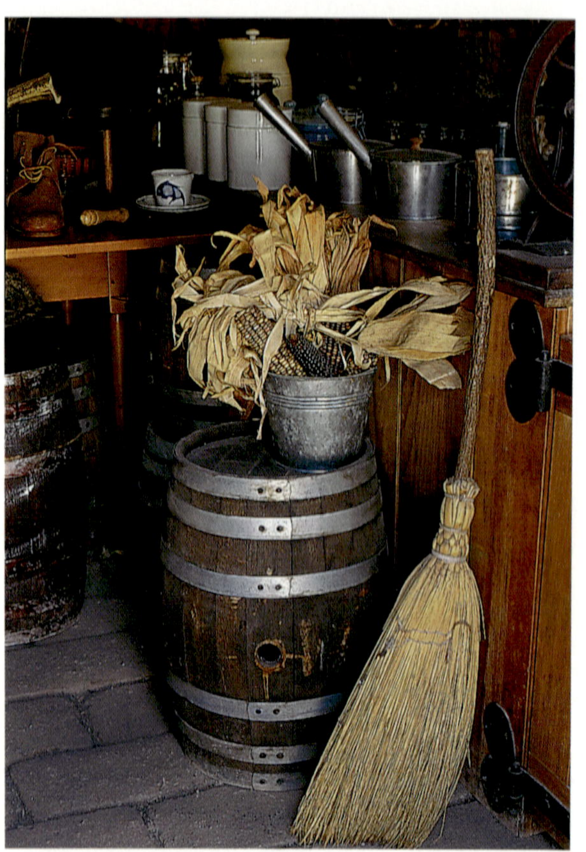
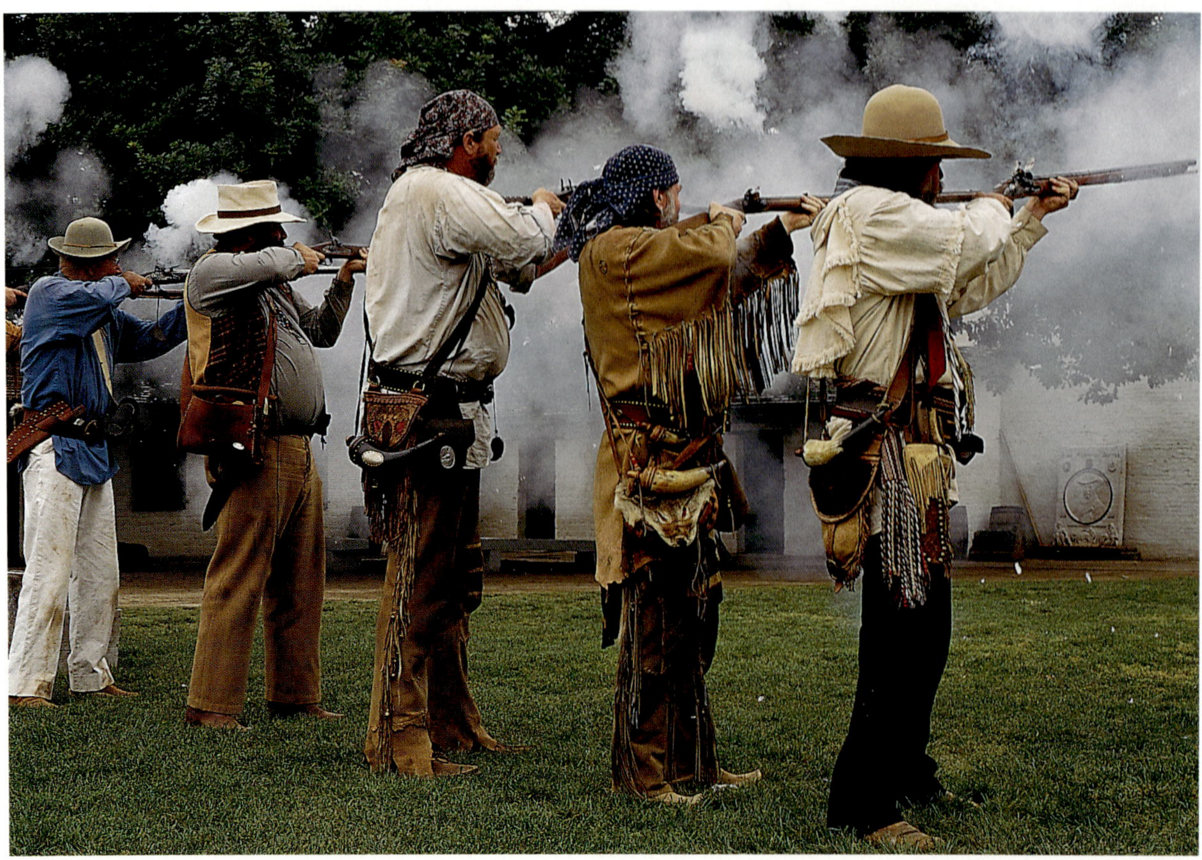

The officer carried with him written and verbal instructions, reportedly from the president of the United States, the secretary of state, and Frémont's father-in-law, a senator from Missouri. Though it is not known what these communications contained, the result was that Frémont headed back into California, fomenting rebellion against Mexican rule among the settlers in the Sacramento Valley as he went.

In response to this agitation, a group of ruffians seized the town of Sonoma and from its captured fort flew a home-made flag emblazoned with a grizzly bear, a star, and the words, "Republic of California." This event was dubbed the "Bear Flag Revolt." Frémont then consolidated his forces with this group of disaffected, drunken louts, marched south to Marin County, and crossed the straits (which he named *Chrysopolae*—a term the ancient Greeks gave to the opening of splendid harbors and which he translated as the "Golden Gate").

Frémont captured the abandoned presidio of San Francisco and was then saved from the consequences of his folly when the news arrived in California on July 8, 1846, that war had been declared the previous May between the United States and Mexico.

Commodore John Sloat, commanding officer of the Pacific Squadron of the U.S. Navy, took possession of Monterey on July 8; his subordinate, Captain John B. Montgomery, took possession of Yerba Buena the following day. Yerba Buena was the settlement on the northern end of the peninsula that forms the southern entrance to the bay; it was the beginning of today's San Francisco.

Within a few months, the combined U.S. forces overcame the Mexican loyalist *Californios,* and on January 12, 1847, the opposition capitulated. Sleepy California—with its presidios and its crumbling missions, its ranchos dotting coastal areas from the Mexican border to what is now called Lassen Peak, and its handful of small settlements—was now firmly under the military control of the United States. With the signing more than a year later of the Treaty of Guadalupe Hidalgo, the Mexican American War ended, and California was ceded to the United States.

But before that event, there occurred a discovery in the foothills of the mountain chain called the Sierra Nevada that would dramatically alter the destiny of California.

◄ (top left) At Sutter's Fort State Historic Park in Sacramento, costumed docents portray 1846 frontier skills.
(top right) This period store illustrates the role of Sutter's Fort as a destination for pioneers and a supply center for the '49ers.
(bottom) During the heyday of Sutter's Fort, John Sutter maintained power over the lives within his empire with a private army.
▼ Living history programs bring the 1840s to life at Sutter's Fort.
▼▼ Sutter's Fort offers a variety of authentic rooms.

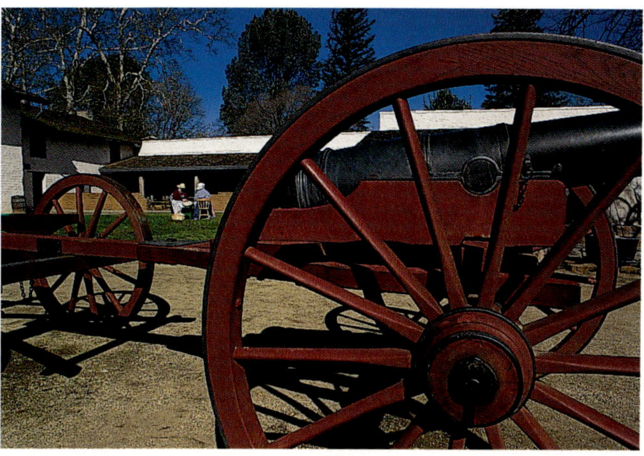

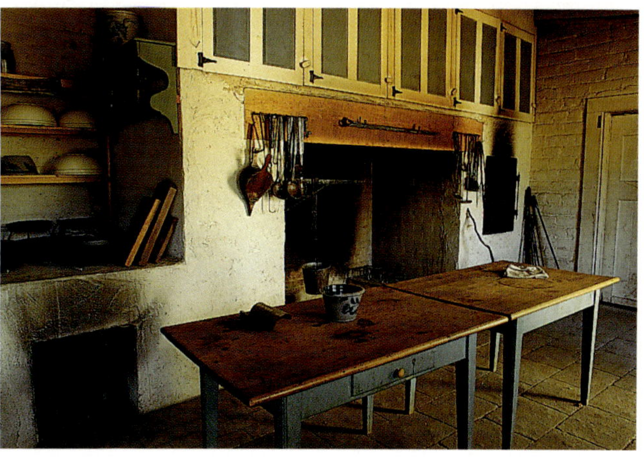

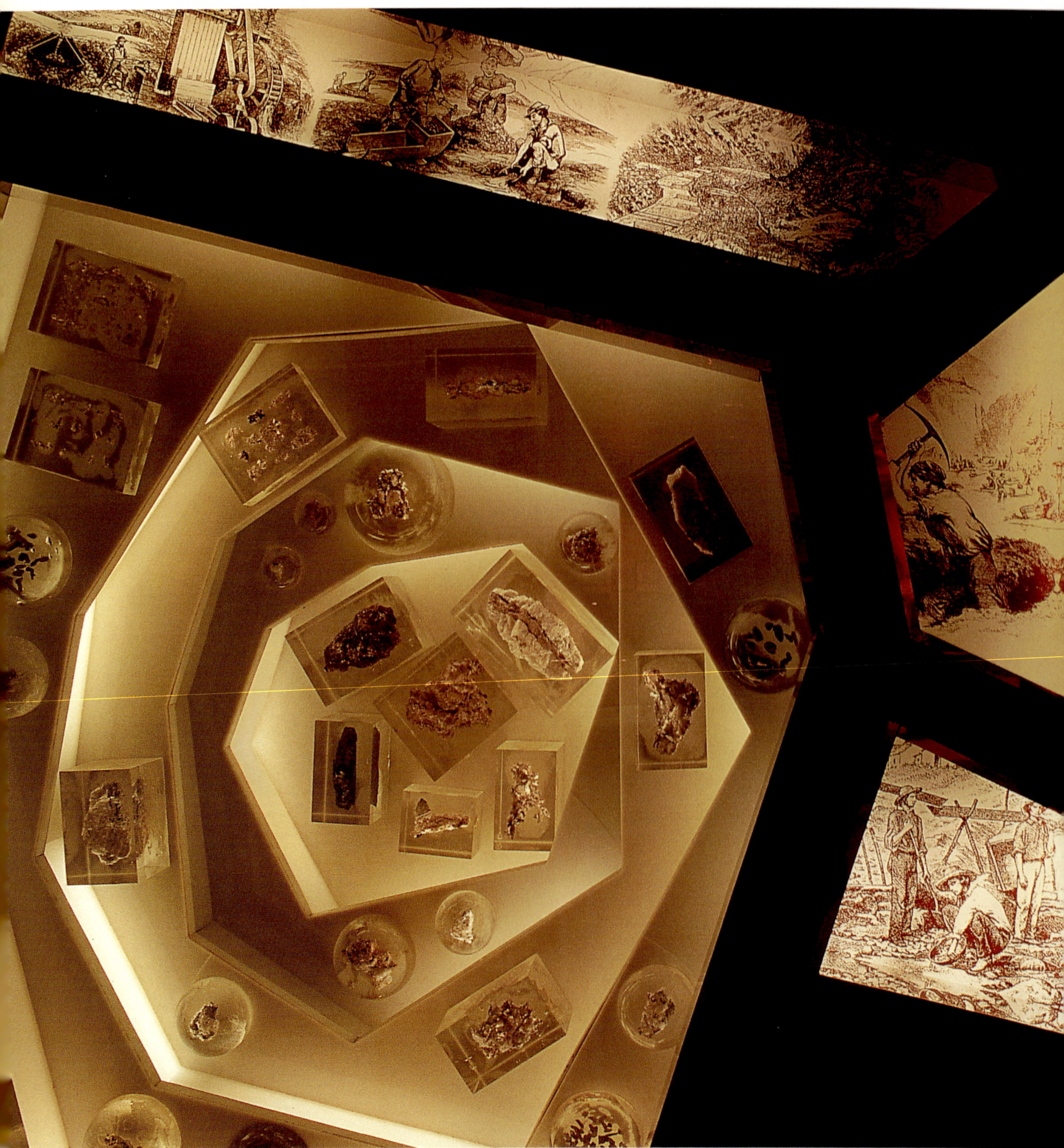

GOLD IS DISCOVERED

1. GOLD IS FOUND

California's legendary Mother Lode was first uncovered on January 24, 1848, on the American River by James Marshall, a carpenter from New Jersey, who was more interested in having a sufficiently strong current to turn the wheel of his sawmill. Neither he nor John Sutter could guess that they had happened upon a vein of gold exceeding one hundred twenty miles in length along the foothills of the Sierra Nevada. Or that by the end of 1857 some $370,000,000 of gold would be taken from California's streams and hills.

Immigrants from the United States began to pour into California even before the conquest of the area in 1846. For example, in 1841, John Bidwell and John Bartleson led an overland wagon train into Northern California; at about the same time, William Workman and John Rowland led another into Southern California. And within the next few years, increasing numbers came overland into California.

This immigration was viewed with interest by the enterprising John Sutter, who had a land grant in the Sacramento Valley. With California's annexation by the United States, Sutter reasoned,

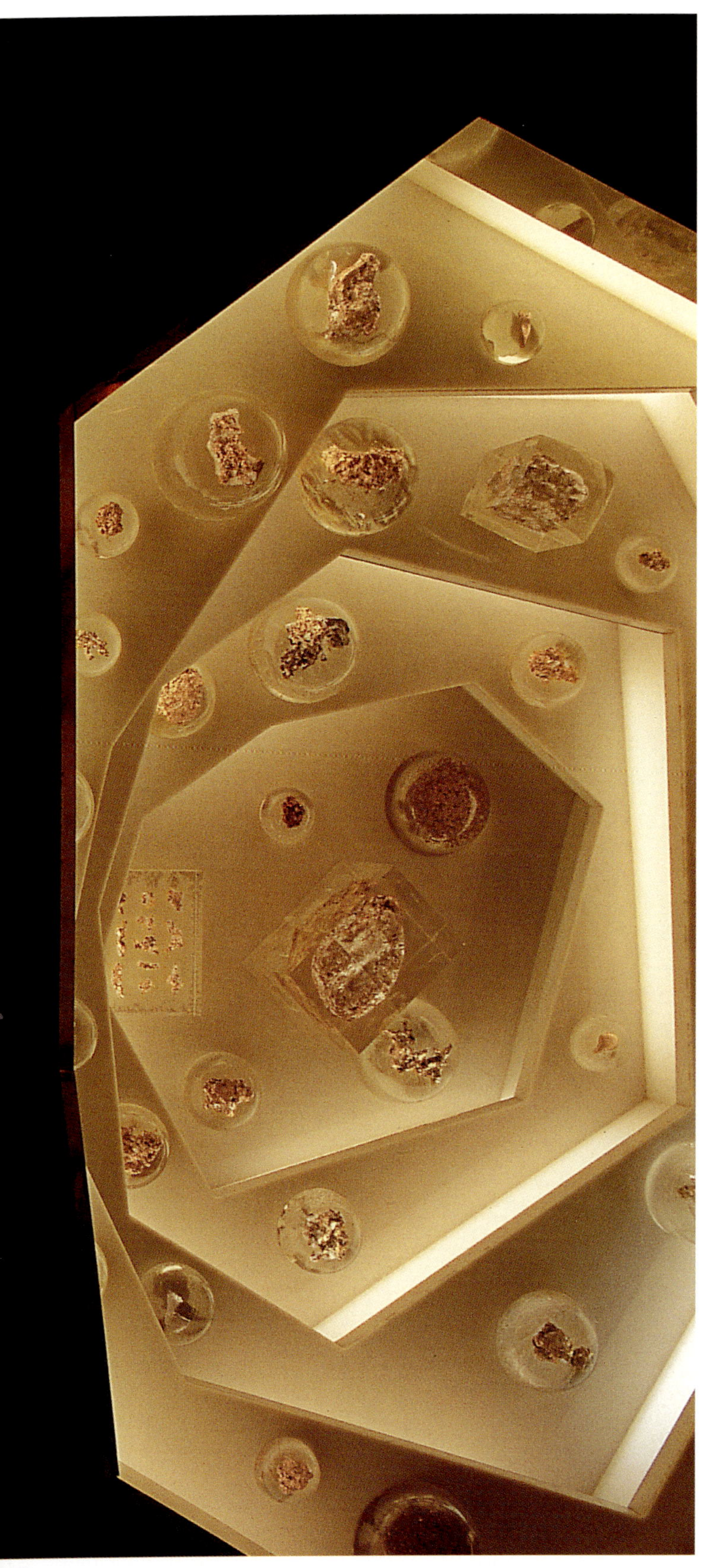

◄ *At Old Sacramento, the Discovery Museum displays the Bank of America gold collection.*

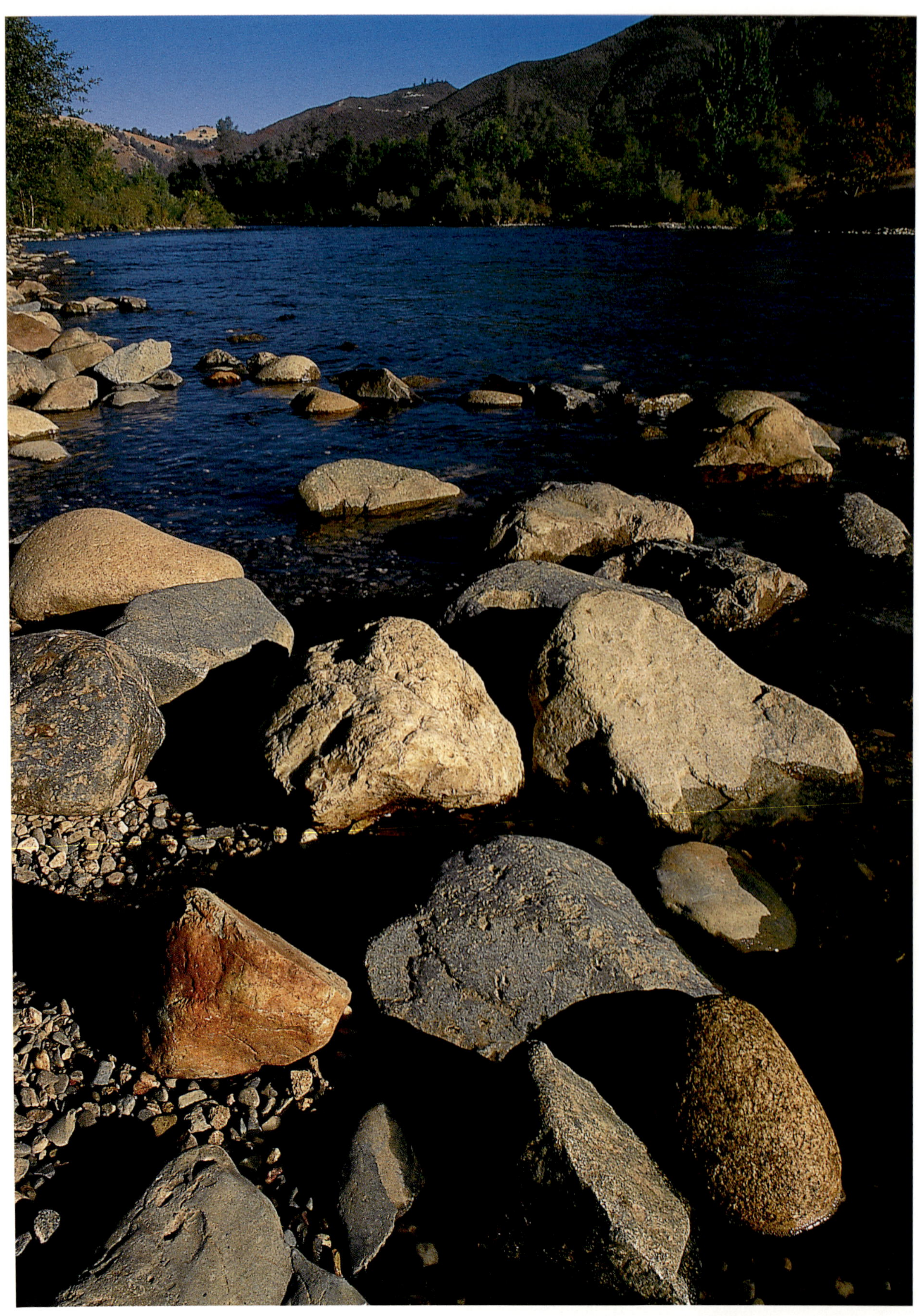

▲ **James Marshall set the Gold Rush in motion near this spot along the South Fork of the American River. Ironically, both Marshall and John Sutter died in relative poverty.**

immigration could only increase. This growing population would need the foodstuffs he grew and the manufactured goods his workmen turned out.

Thus, in mid-1847, Sutter signed a partnership agreement with James Marshall to build a sawmill at a place called by the Indian name of Coloma, on the South Fork of the American River, about forty-five miles east of Sutter's hacienda, called Sutter's Fort, in present-day Sacramento.

The sawmill was almost finished in early 1848 when Marshall discovered that the current was not strong enough to turn the wheel. Blasting was done to deepen the channel and increase the strength of the current. On the evening of January 23, 1848, water began to flow through the deepened channel. The next morning, Marshall waded into the stream to test the effectiveness of the blasting and noticed some yellow streaks in the riverbed. He stooped to pick them up: they were yellow flakes of a soft metal.

Though Marshall suspected they were gold, he and his workers remained incredulous. For the next four days, Marshall picked up more and more of the metallic flakes in the American River, until finally he mounted his horse and

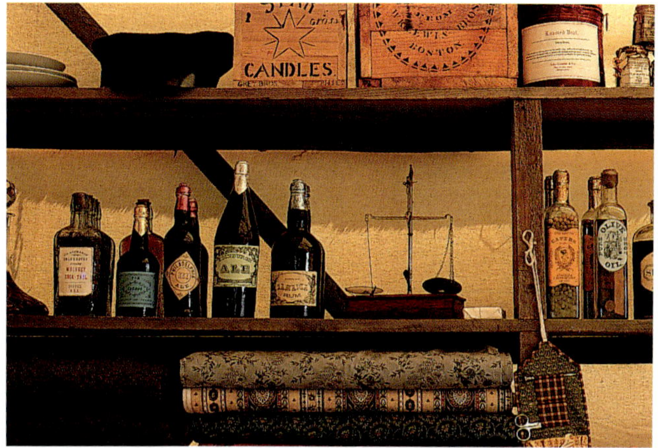

▲ *Columbia Diggins—the "Gem of the Southern Mines"— is re-created in shops, saloons, banks, mines, and homes.*

▼ *(left) Mining equipment awaits use at the annual Gold Rush Days, Marshall Gold Discovery State Historic Park. (center) A Long Tom, a trough for sifting particles, dominates this exhibit at Old Sacramento's Discovery Museum. (right) The annual Columbia Diggins relives the Gold Rush era with period scenes, including this miner's camp.*

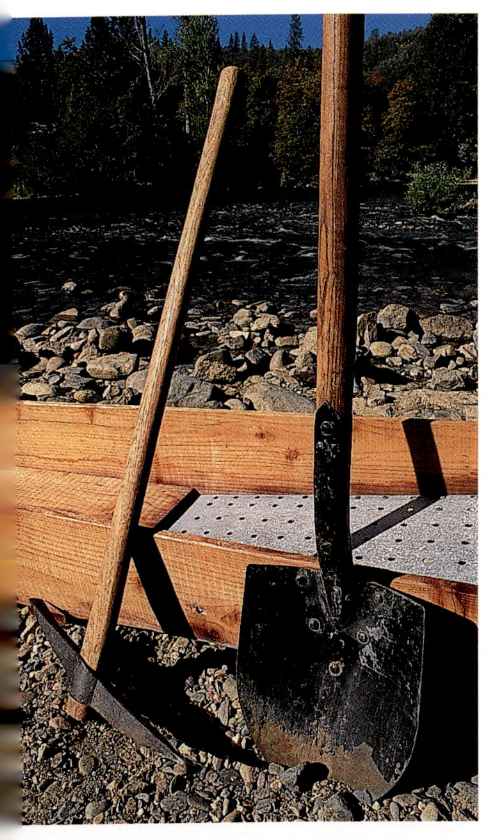

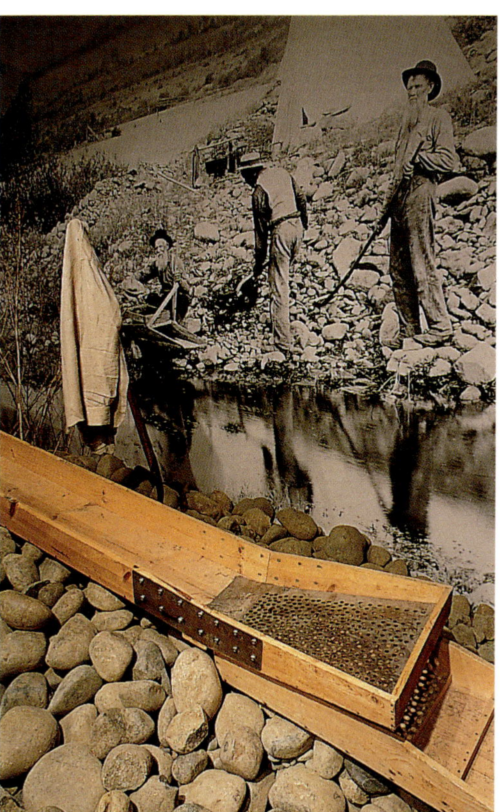

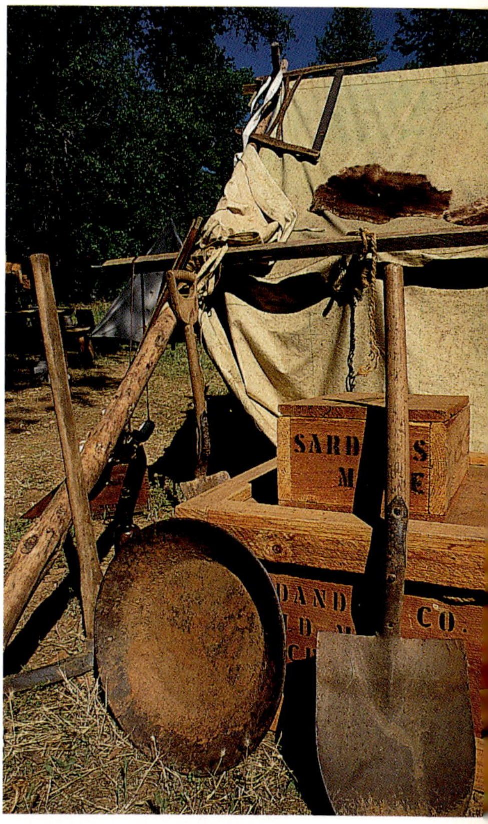

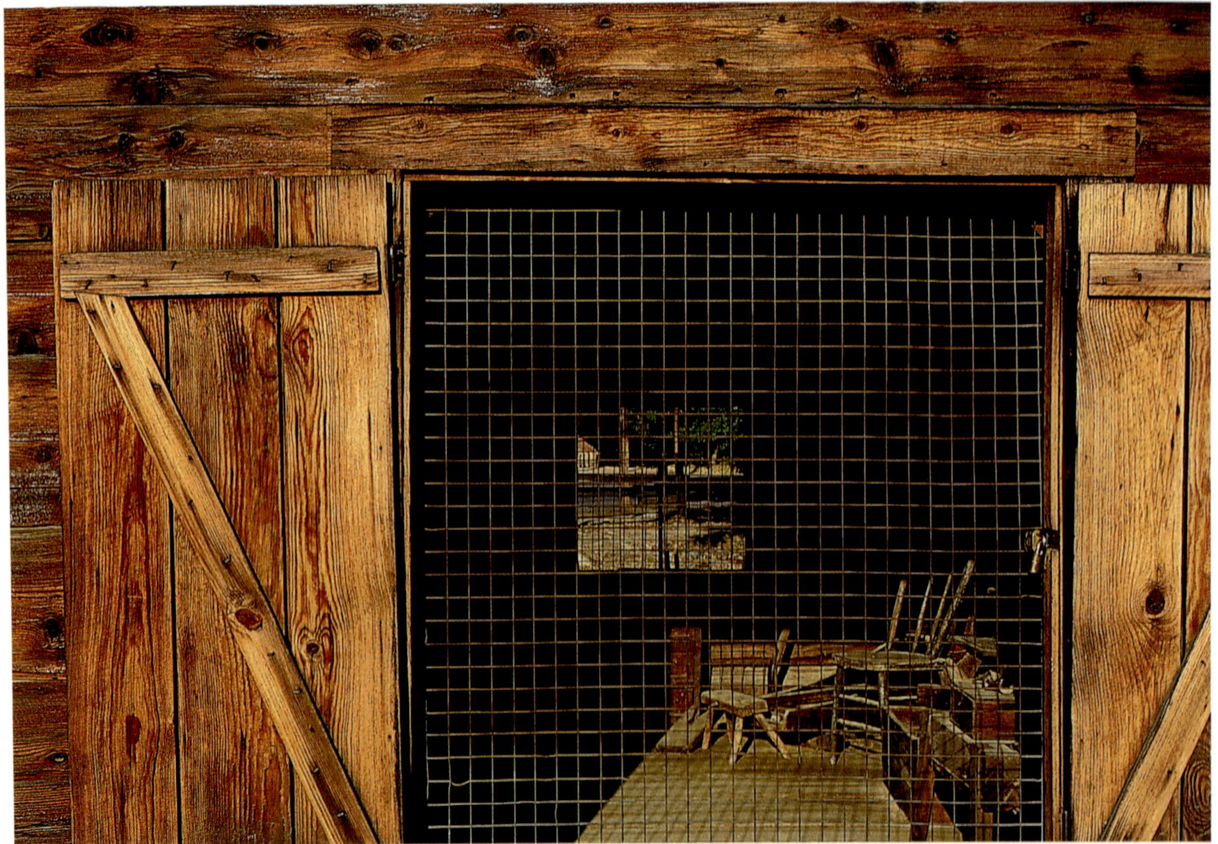

▲ *This Coloma cabin is an example of a Gold Rush miner's quarters. The earliest structures were made from sailcloth from ships abandoned in San Francisco's harbor.*

galloped off to Sutter's Fort. There he and Sutter, using as a guide an old encyclopedia that was at the hacienda, tested the shiny flakes to determine if they were gold. The tests confirmed Marshall's suspicions.

The two men rode back to the sawmill, where Sutter asked the workmen not to talk about the discovery, lest the area be inundated with gold seekers. And he ordered them not to stop working on the sawmill. Sutter's injunctions were not followed for long. Soon Marshall's crew set down their tools and began to prospect for gold full-time. One prospector wrote to a friend about the discovery. Others chattered to the few travelers through the area about it. A workman of Sutter's, sent to Monterey to see if the military governor would allow Sutter to acquire the land on which he had been building the sawmill, advertised the discovery of gold all along his journey.

2. THE GOLD RUSH BEGINS

"Gold! Gold on the American River," shouted Sam Brannan, running down the main beach street of the trading village of San Francisco (which just a short time ago had been called Yerba Buena) on a day in April of 1848. People stared in astonishment as the robust, black-bearded Mormon immigrant held aloft two quinine bottles filled with gold nuggets and then deposited them in a storefront window.

Within a few days, San Francisco became a deserted town.

Sutter's Mill was remote from the towns that had sprung up in California, so despite the lax secrecy surrounding the discovery, news about the gold find traveled slowly. It was not until March 15 that a small notice about the discovery appeared on the back page of one of San Francisco's two newspapers, the *Californian*.

A few days later, the rival *California Star's* editor, Edward Kemble, traveled to Sutter's Fort and lumbermill. Accompanied by Sutter, Kemble was told that very little gold had been found, and he returned to San Francisco to warn his readers to stay home, that the gold discovery was "a sham." This did not dissuade the owner of that newspaper, Sam Brannan, who packed up and traveled to Coloma to see for himself.

Everyone in this town of several hundred people knew Brannan as an ambitious, canny, and successful Mormon leader. He had arrived in San Francisco on July 31, 1846, less than two years before, on the ship *Brooklyn* out of New York, leading a group of two hundred Mormons. This relatively new sect had met with a great deal of bigotry and hostility, and Brannan's journey was part of a larger migration of Mormons, seeking a "new Zion," a land where the members of the religious community could gather and control their own destiny.

Brannan had been in trouble with church authorities in the Midwest in the past, and there were recent rumors that he had been using the tithes he collected from his flock for his own business ventures, which included ownership of the *California Star*. According to one story, when Brigham Young requested the tithing funds, Brannan responded that he would deliver them

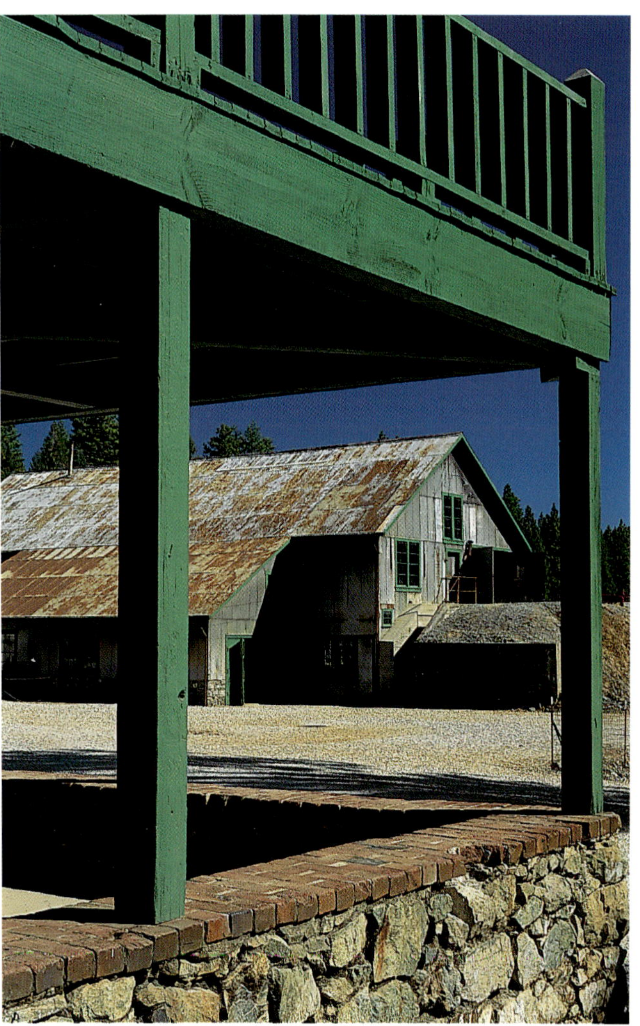

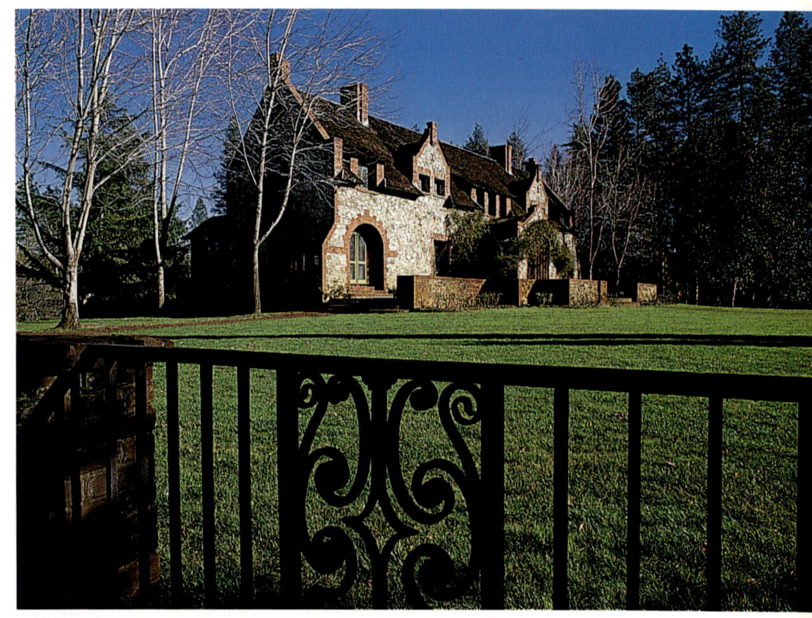

➤ *(top) Empire Mine in Grass Valley yielded six million ounces in gold from 1850 to 1956.*
(bottom) This estate, now in Empire Mine State Historic Park, was built by William Bourn Jr.

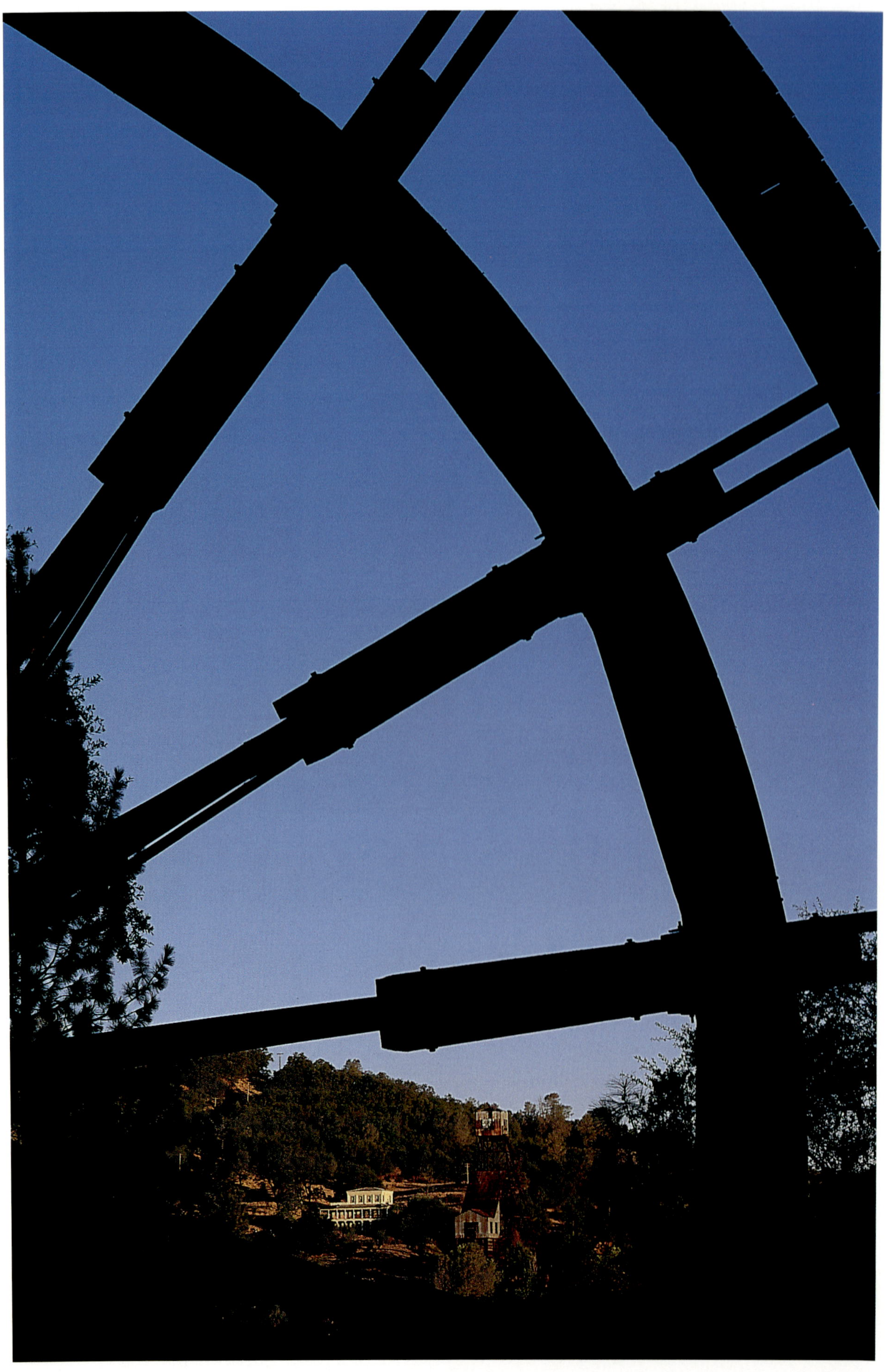

personally to the Lord when the Lord asked him for them.

By the time rumors about the discovery of gold had been circulating for several weeks, the wily Brannan decided to travel to the site on the American River. Brannan avoided Sutter, who had talked down the news, and saw for himself that a growing number of men were finding considerable quantities of gold.

Brannan opened a store in Coloma, where the sawmill was situated, and another mercantile operation on the Sacramento River, near Sutter's home and center of operations. Within a few weeks, Brannan had filled two bottles with gold nuggets and returned to San Francisco.

The dramatic announcement by one of the town's most prominent citizens virtually emptied San Francisco of most of its residents. The newly appointed schoolteacher, a minister, the editors of both newspapers, merchants, laborers, seamen whose ships had arrived in the harbor, soldiers who happened to be in town—all left for where gold had been found. Businesses fell into disrepair. No one could be found to perform various labors. Property prices plummeted, and the cost of some goods skyrocketed.

Soon the Northern Californians were followed by those from Southern California, from Oregon, the Hawaiian Islands, Mexico, Peru, and Chile. By the summer of 1848, newspaper accounts began to

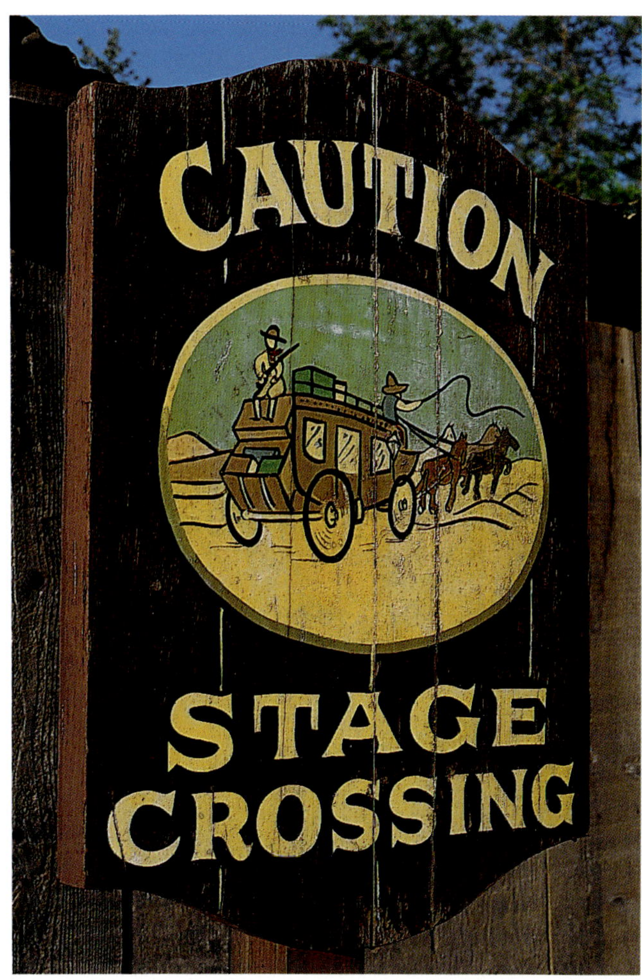

◄ *Framing the old Kennedy Mine is this giant wheel, built to transport mill waste near the gold city of Jackson.*
▲ *Relics like this, plus authentic street scenes, transform Columbia State Historic Park into a living museum.*

appear in the Midwest, and rumors had made their way East. Then, on December 8, U.S. President James K. Polk announced that gold had been discovered in sizable quantities in California and that Colonel Richard Barnes Mason, the military governor, had sent him an official report, as well as a tea caddie filled with gold dust.

The reaction to Polk's announcement was as if an electric spark had gone around the world: suddenly, tens of thousands headed to California with the intention of making their fortune and returning home rich. Those who had poured into the gold-producing area in 1848 from the west coast of the United States and Latin America were now joined by fortune seekers from every part of the United States, from Europe, even as far away as China, Australia, and Malaysia.

Those who set off on their long journey to this wild and little-known region came from every possible socioeconomic strata: a former governor of Missouri, the son of a governor of Connecticut, scions of two of Virginia's most prominent families, a congressman from Mississippi, an unsuccessful aspirant to the U.S. Congress from New York, yeoman farmers, unskilled laborers, lawyers, doctors, merchants. Any who had or could borrow the funds for a journey to California flocked to fulfill their fantasy of instant wealth.

It is estimated that 95 percent of those who came to California during the Gold Rush were men, and by far the majority were in their late teens and twenties. Their motives, other than the fundamental ones of instant wealth and ambition, were diverse.

Many young men from the United States had fought in the Mexican-American War, and after leaving the narrow

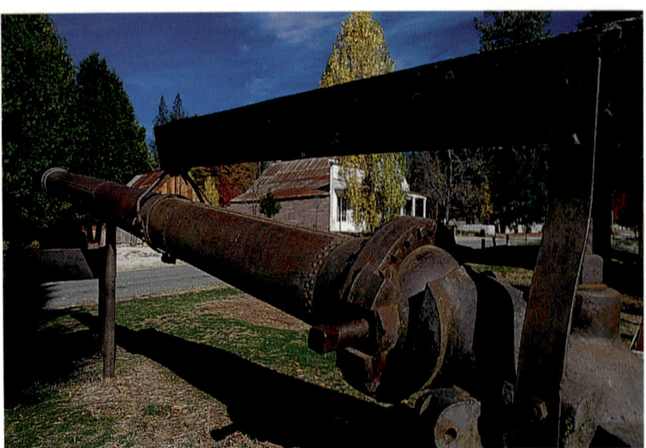

▲ *Giant water monitors, like this one in Malakoff Diggins' restored mining town, blasted hillsides to get the gold.*
▶ *Hydraulic mining, a practice ended in 1884, produced these cliffs at Malakoff Diggins State Historic Park.*

confines of the farm, village, and town for battle in an exotic country, had no desire to return to the dull rhythms of life at home. Looking for gold in California provided another great adventure.

In Australia, then a British penal colony, the governor decided that the least violent of his prisoners could be allowed to leave and go to California, thus saving the crown the cost of their incarceration.

Canton, traditionally China's most entrepreneurial district, had suffered through a civil war, leaving in its wake poverty, banditry, and suffering. Many merchants who could afford the trip sought greater stability and opportunity in California. Poorer citizens of the province obtained loans from Cantonese merchants to make the journey to "Gold Mountain," where they mined or found employment.

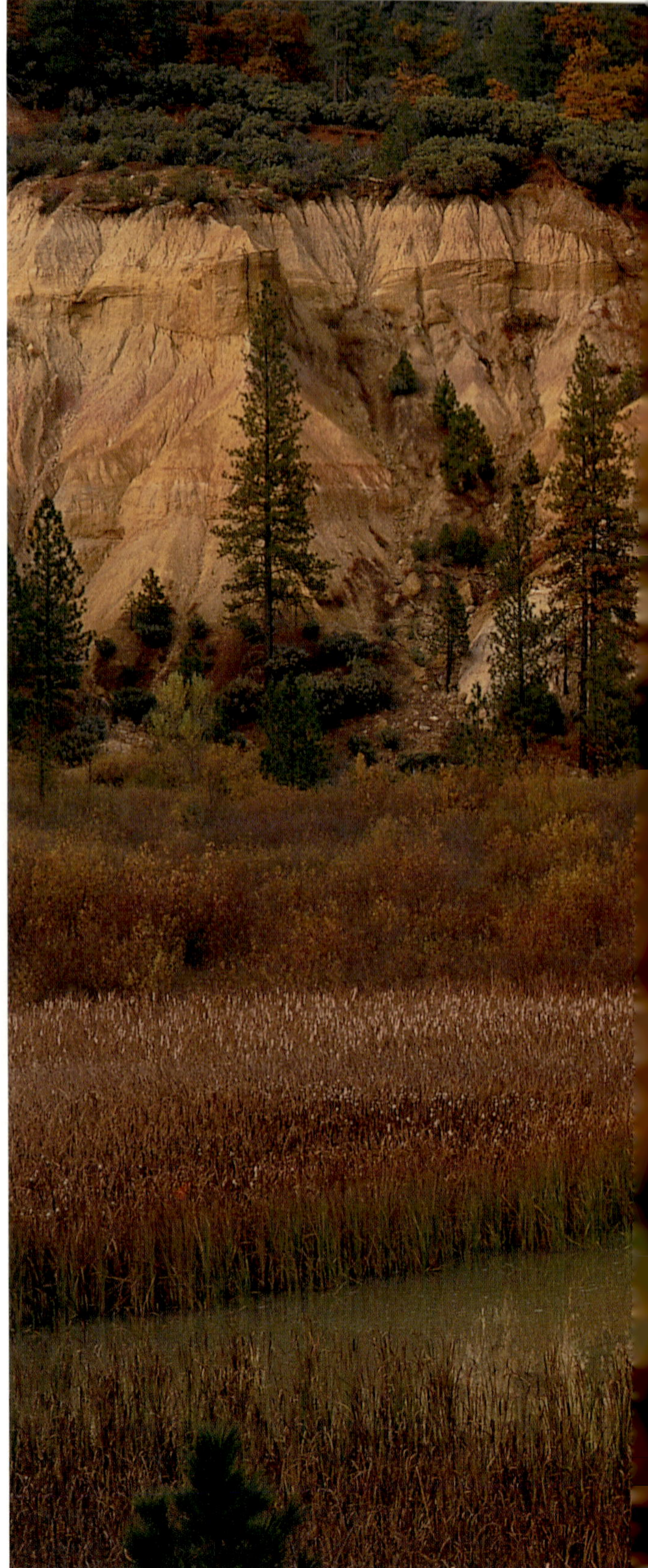

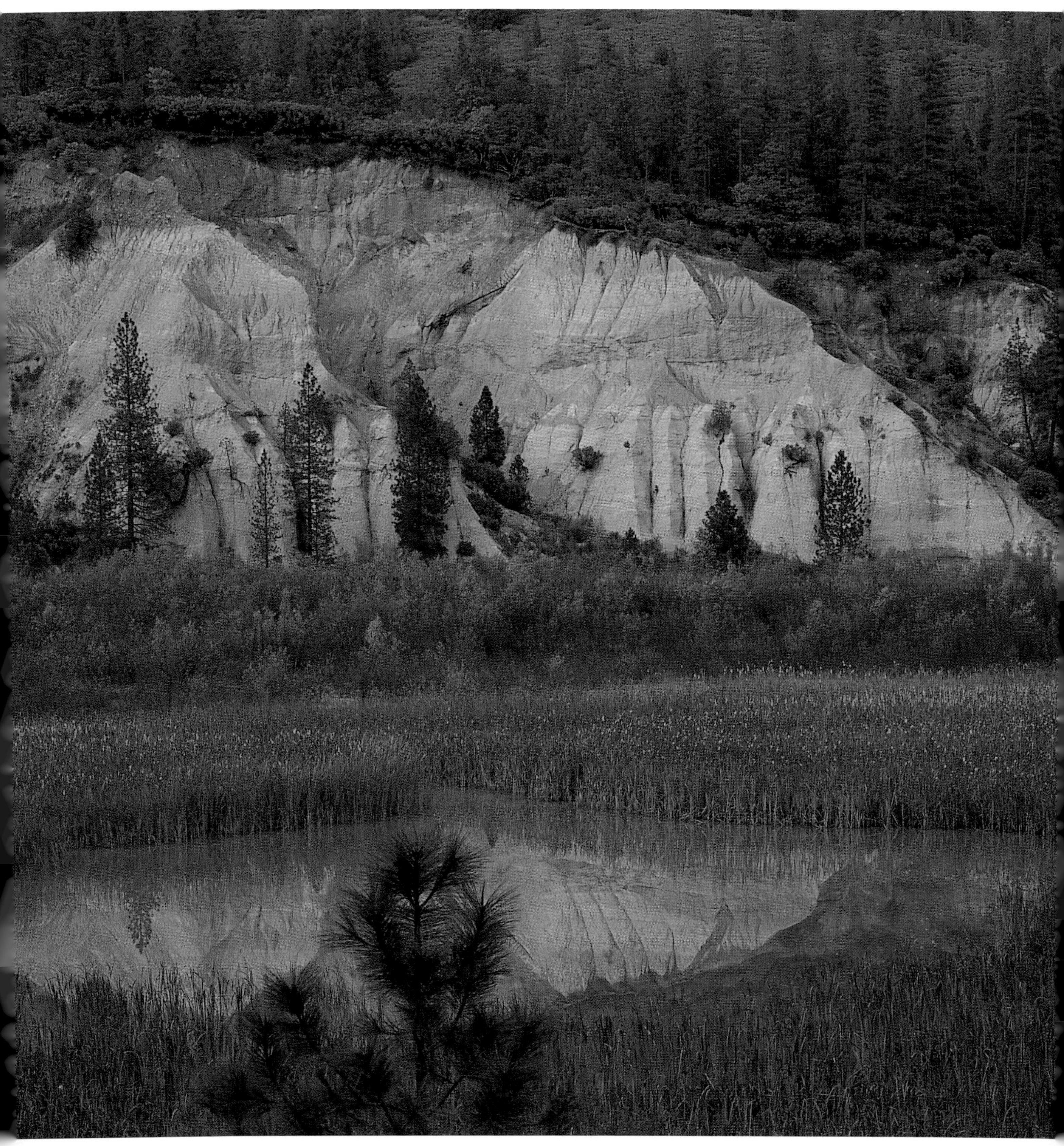

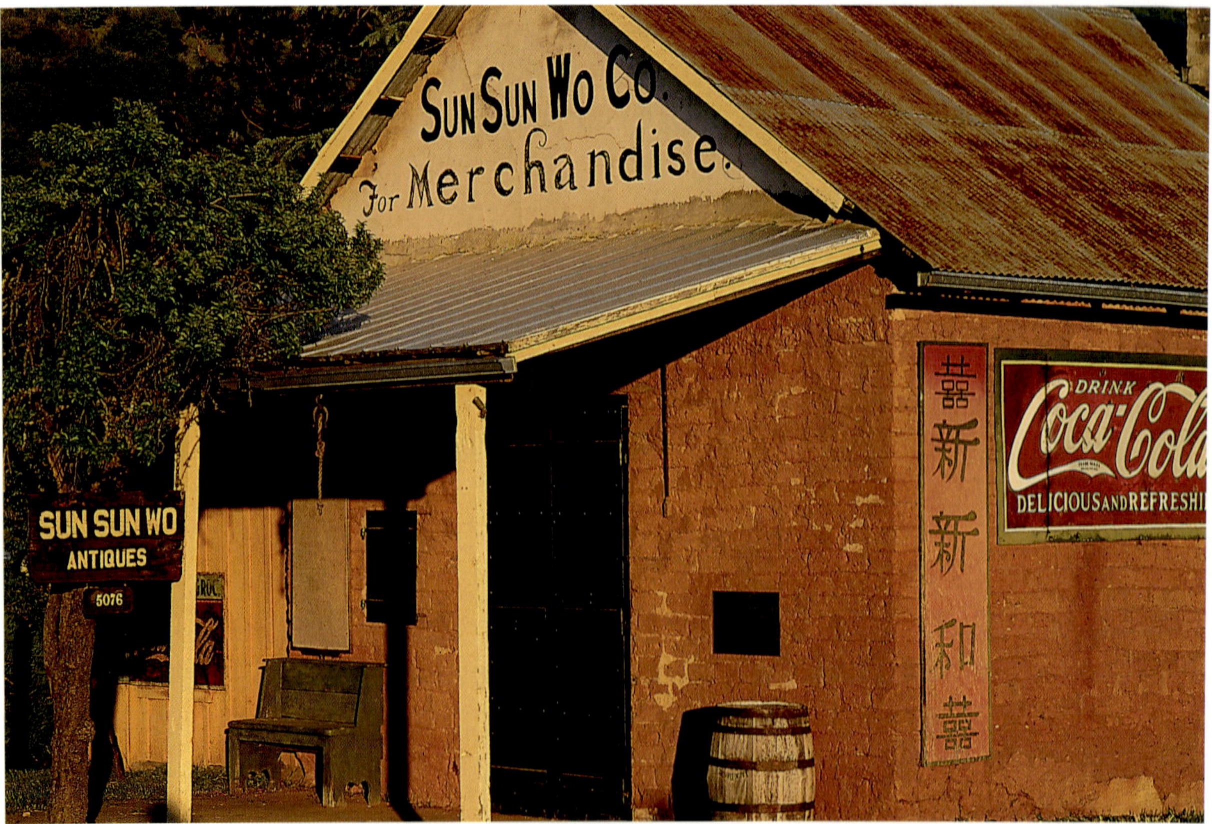

▲ *The Sun Sun Wo Company store in Coulterville, along Highway 49 between Mariposa and Sonora, is an 1851 adobe remnant of a Chinese settlement.*

The year 1848 had been a time of revolution in Europe; the resulting chaos and the repressive regimes installed there sent people looking for greater freedom and opportunity in California. English, French, Irish, Italians, and Germans journeyed to the gold fields for adventure, economic opportunity, and political freedom.

Many Latin Americans who had experience in mining saw the chance of a lifetime—the opportunity to seek their fortunes where individual effort could bring them great rewards.

And so, from every corner of the world, came thousands upon thousands to the land where it seemed that the fantasies could be fulfilled, a land where instantaneous wealth was possible merely by picking up gold nuggets from the streams and hills.

The reality for most would be quite different.

3. PATHS TO THE GOLD FIELDS

Ignorance, incompetence, and hardship characterized the rush toward gold. In all, perhaps one hundred thousand gold seekers attempted the pilgrimage to California, very few with any knowledge or experience in the difficulties of the journey. Thousands of copies of hastily published guidebooks, pieced together from Frémont's reports or excerpts from published letters of those who made the trip, were sold to these greenhorns. Virtually all of these guidebooks were imaginative constructs of their greedy authors—varying from the totally useless to the dangerous. These guidebooks advised the gold seeker to purchase "essential" goods for his journey: India-rubber boots, alcohol, sheet-iron stoves, fly traps, wading boots, air mattresses, and massive gold-extraction machines—all paraphernalia as useless as it was difficult to haul.

Another useless endeavor was the formation of gold mining companies, societies, associations, and brotherhoods—often organized and financed by groups in the towns and cities of the East. They bankrolled communal gold-seeking expeditions (buying the equipment described above) with the idea of sharing the rewards between the gold diggers and financial backers. Virtually none of these associations lasted the voyage to California.

It has been estimated that some 60 percent of those who came to California during the Gold Rush came by land. These would include many of those who came from Mexico. But the great majority came by one of the overland trails across the United States. This meant congregating in St. Joseph, Missouri, by April of the year of embarkation and joining one of the covered wagon trains that made its slow progress across mountain ranges, prairies, and deserts, arriving in California before winter snows closed the passes across the Sierra Nevada.

This was a tedious and dangerous journey of six or seven months, fraught with hunger and thirst, death in many forms, and back-breaking efforts to cross mountains, rivers, and deserts. Horses and oxen often had to be killed because of lack of grass and water or for food. Cholera struck whole wagon trains. Travelers lived in terror of Indian attacks and of river crossings, where many drowned. Wagons sometimes actually had to be lifted over mountaintops,

▼ Columbia State Historic Park maintains its Gold Country character with period shops and re-created businesses, including this Wells Fargo office.

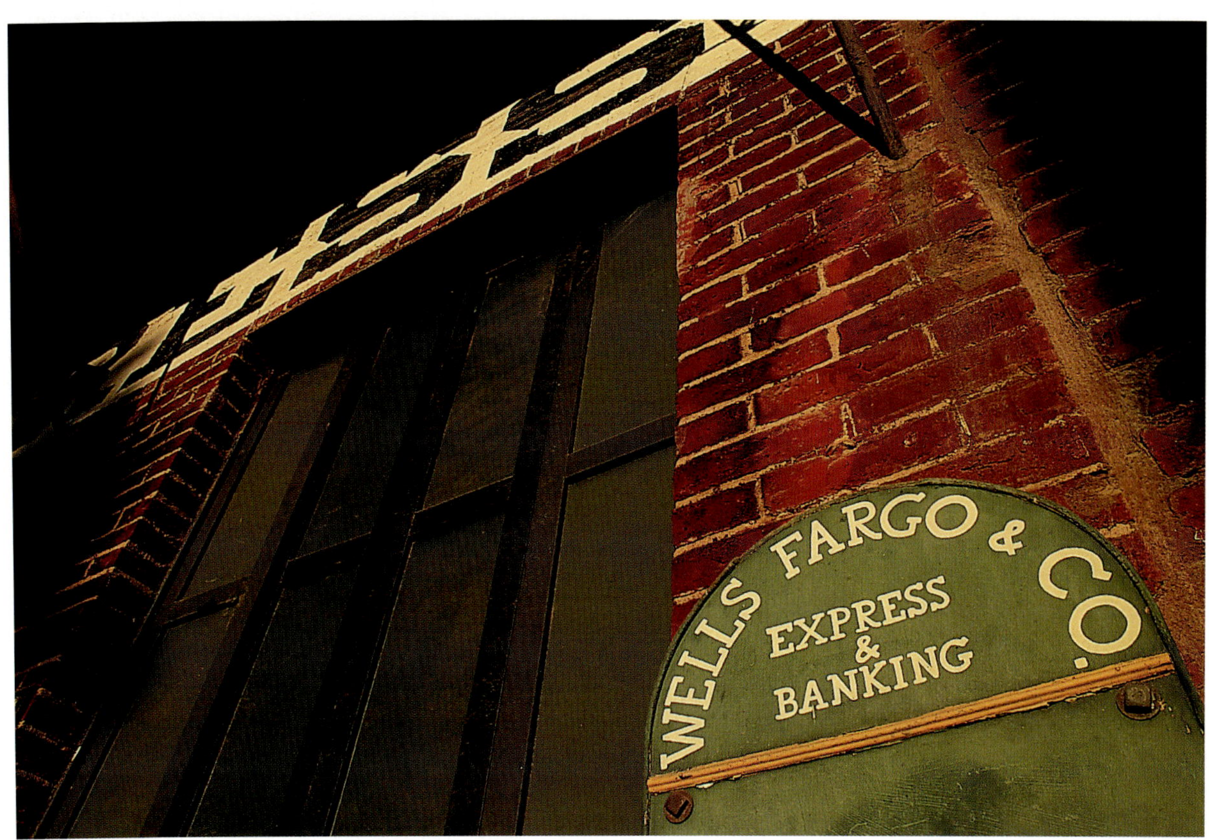

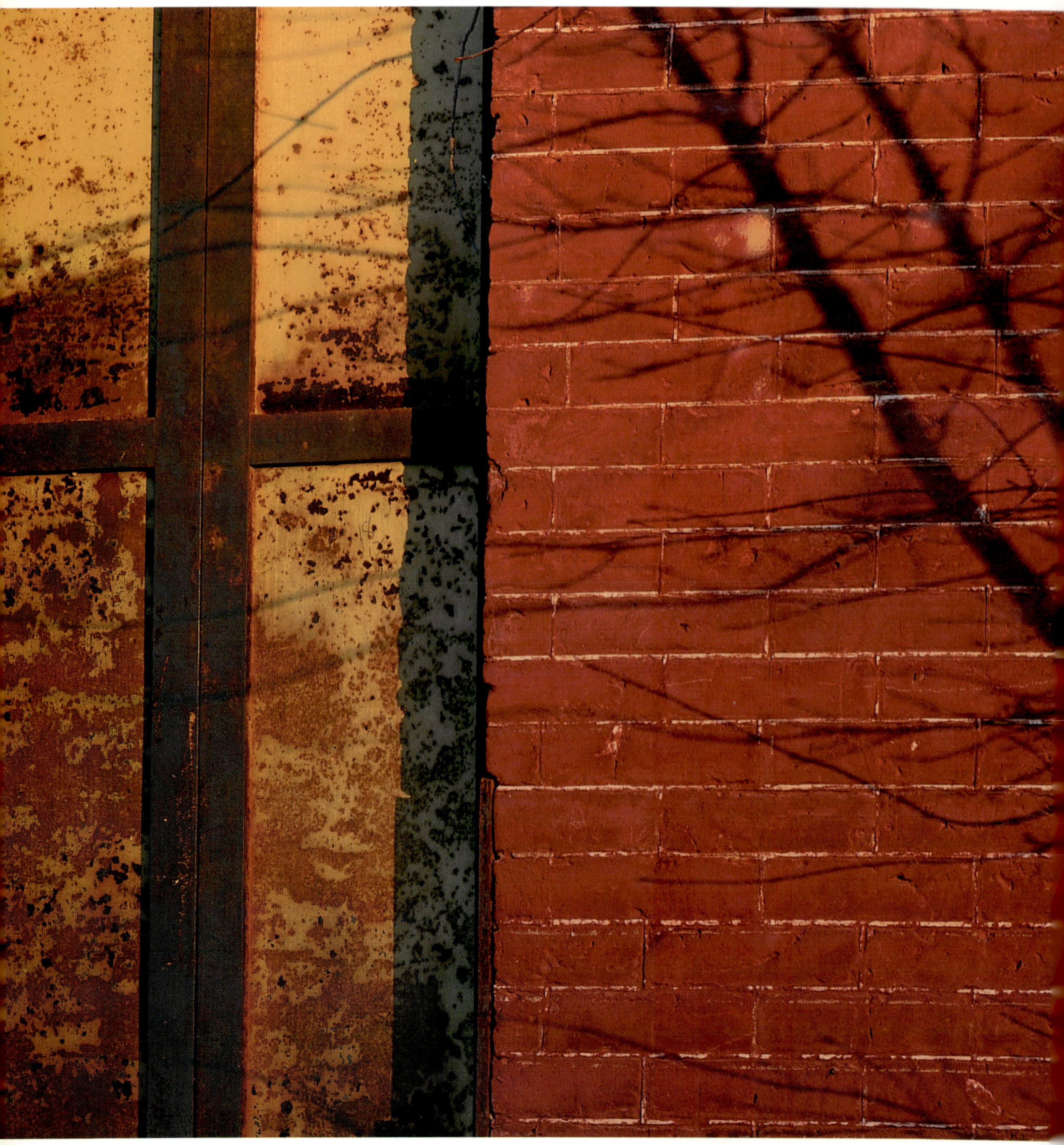

and the unimaginably hot deserts of Utah and the Southwest took their toll.

Those who came by sea from the United States had the choice of sailing south around the tip of South America and then northward, hugging the coast along two continents to San Francisco (a voyage that could take up to nine months), or a much quicker trip to Central America, then across either the Isthmus of Panama or Nicaragua. These latter two routes, although much quicker ways of reaching the gold fields than either the overland trails or around the tip of South America, were quite dangerous. Crossing Nicaragua was extremely difficult with the threat of robbery and the difficulty of finding needed provisions and accommodations; but even more dangerous was crossing the fifty-mile Isthmus of Panama.

A ship to Panama would disembark the gold seekers on the Atlantic side. These adventurers would then travel the difficult terrain of the Isthmus by dug-out canoe, on foot, and on mule-back through overgrown jungle and humid swamps as they made their way to the Pacific side of the Isthmus. There they often suffered interminable delays waiting for a ship to take them to San Francisco in the sweltering, fever-ridden Spanish colonial town turned boomtown.

Many went to their graves in Panama, and many others would find their lives considerably shortened and plagued with illness as a result of some disease acquired in Panama.

4. MINING CAMPS AND BOOMTOWNS IN THE GOLD RUSH

The experience of leaving home for an adventuresome and dangerous voyage to California—at a time when very few ever traveled more than fifty miles from their abodes—left an indelible impression on the gold seekers. The

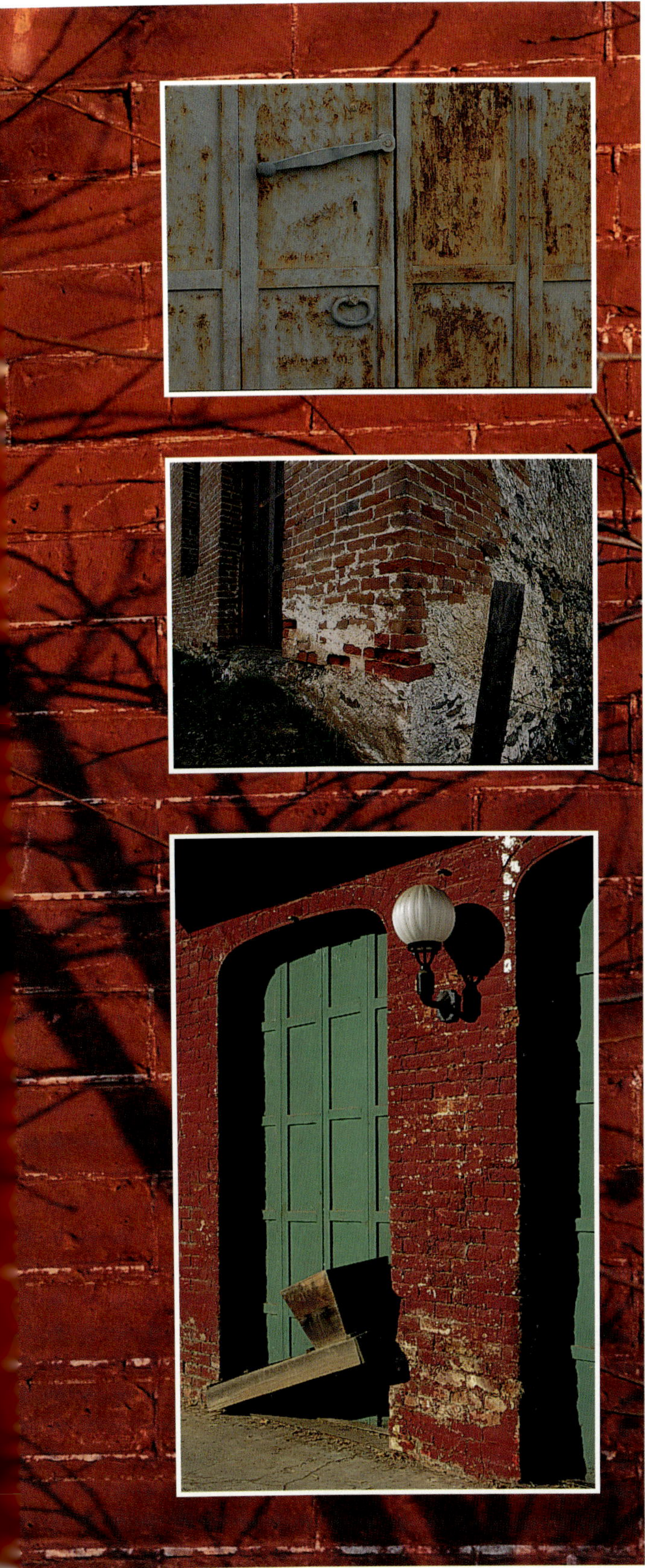

◄ (background) Brick buildings, such as this 1855 Lawyers Row in Auburn, replaced fire-susceptible wooden ones.
(top) Heavy iron fire doors, including these at Hornitos, are familiar Gold Country architectural features.
(center) This antique Chinese store, in the Gold Country town of Plymouth, is made of brick and fieldstone.
(bottom) Drytown, a gold community in Amador County, began as an 1848 mining camp on Dry Creek.

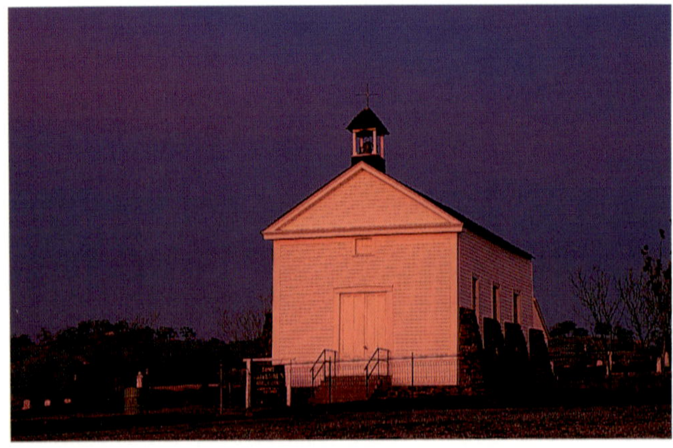

▲ *Quaint churches, such as this one in Hornitos, are familiar sights throughout the Gold Country.*

Gold Rush is one of the most documented events in the history of the United States: thousands of letters and diaries have been preserved and many retrospective accounts of the voyage to the gold fields and the experiences there survive. Each account reflects the sense that the author had participated in an epic adventure.

The great question in the mind of a gold seeker upon reaching California was: where do I find gold? If he had come by sea, he would inquire in San Francisco as to where gold was being dug and then head for such a place. This was not a foolproof tactic, since the success of the find might have been exaggerated, or even based entirely on a false rumor. The prospector would then have to scramble to find a more productive location.

Once a promising site was found, the prospector would stake a claim, usually along one of the many streams which crisscross the Mother Lode country, build a log cabin or set up a tent or lean-to, and begin the back-breaking

▼ *In 1849, a group of African-American miners staked their claim, known as Negro Bar. It is now included in Folsom Lake State Recreation Area near Sacramento.*

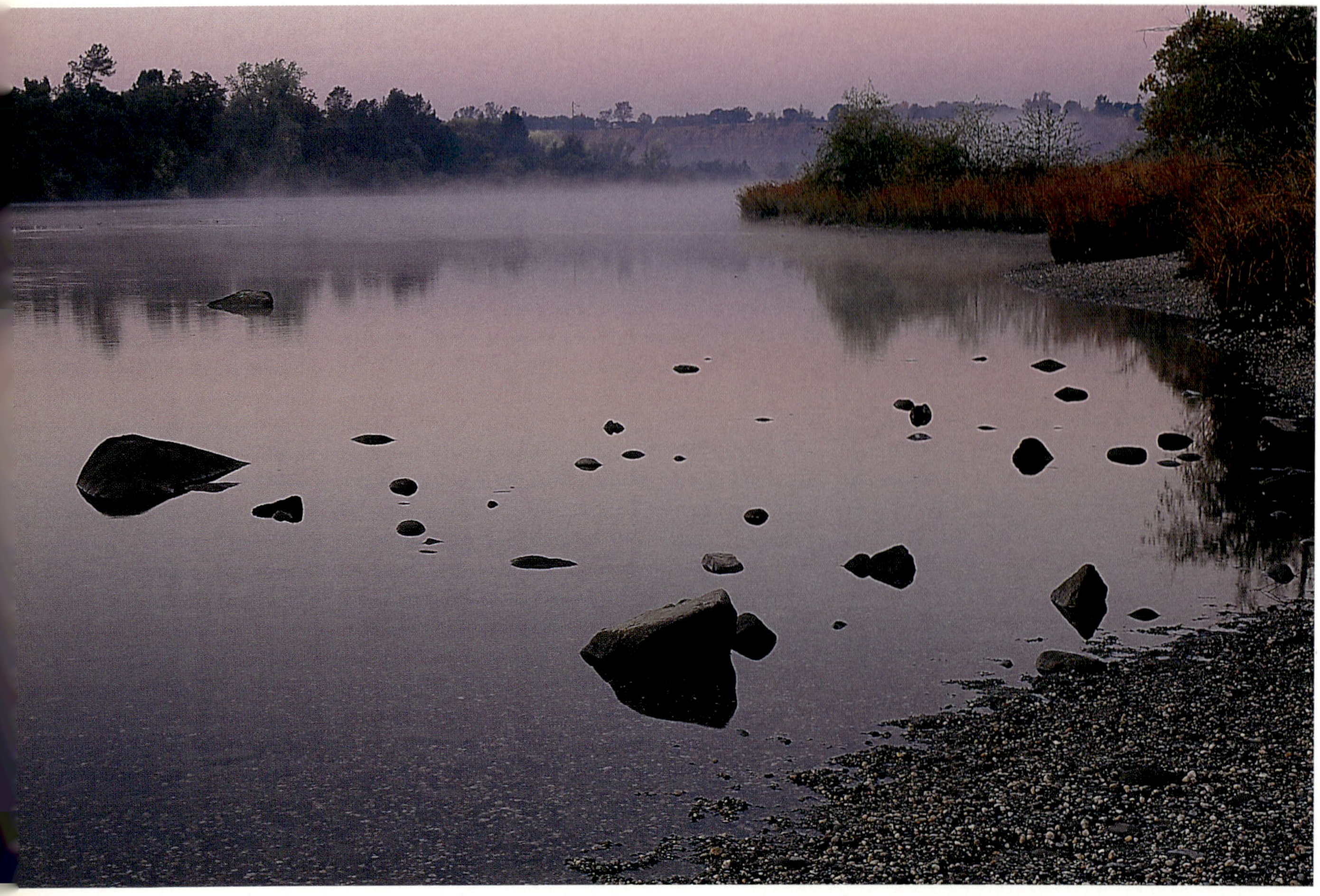

work of looking for gold. Picks, shovels, Long Toms, rockers, and other equipment were used to separate the dust and nuggets of gold from the sand and gravel in which it was hidden.

Although lone prospectors roamed every isolated bit of California—hidden ravines and desolate mountain peaks, quiet forests and rocky wilderness—whenever someone found gold, he was certain to have company. Soon, hundreds of other prospectors staked their claims, and a mining camp was established.

For six days each week, the camps and waterways hummed with industrious gold seeking. Hour after hour, the eager prospectors plied the streams and rivers to uncover the gold. With broad-brimmed hats under the hot sun, their limbs aching, up to their hips in the cold mountain streams, the gold prospectors sought to bring to fruition the visions that had brought them to California. In one passage from a book of reminiscences published in 1851, *Sixteen Months in the Gold Diggings*, Daniel Woods writes:

> This morning, notwithstanding the rain, we were again at our work. We must work. In sunshine and rain, in warm and cold, in sickness and health, successful or not successful, early and late, it is work, work, WORK! Work or perish! All around us, above and below, on mountain side and stream, the rain falling fast upon them, are the miners at work—not for gold, but for bread. Lawyers, doctors, clergymen, farmers, soldiers, deserters, good and bad, from England, from America, from China, from Islands [Hawaiian], from every country but Russia and Japan—all, all at work at their cradles. From morning to night is heard the incessant rock, rock, rock! Over the whole mines, in streamlet, in creek, and

COLOMA

Coloma, an Anglicized spelling of an Indian word, became the name for a spot on the South Fork of the American River. This was where John Sutter and James Marshall decided to build a sawmill in late 1847. The meaning of the original Indian word is unknown, but Bancroft's statement that it means "beautiful vale" is just a romantic myth.

The gentle, rolling hills with ample timber that constitute the landscape of Coloma is typical of

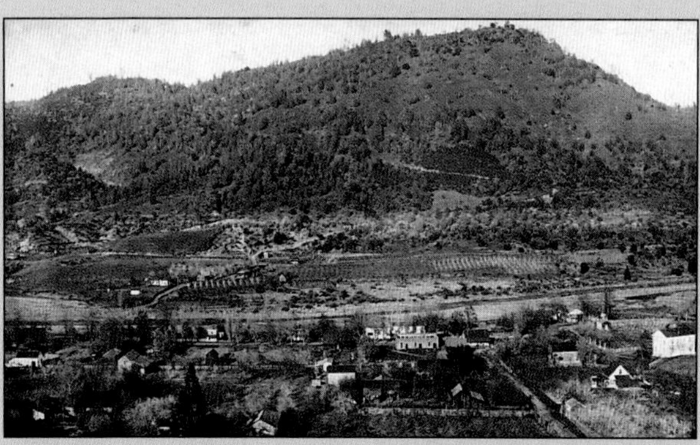

the terrain of the Sierra foothills where the Mother Lode was situated. It was here that the first gold seekers joined forces in the search for gold with the Mormon workmen who had been engaged in building the sawmill.

Soon, a sprawling town, the first of California's mining camps and towns, grew up on the spot. San Francisco newspaper owner Sam Brannan started a grocery store there in the spring of 1848. Sometime later, a gold seeker from the Midwest by the name of John Studebaker built wheelbarrows there for the miners. He later returned to the Midwest, where he became a pioneer in the automotive industry.

*in river, down torrent and through the valley, ever
rushes on the muddy sediment from ten thousand busy
rockers. Cheerful words are seldom heard, more seldom
the boisterous shout and laugh which indicate success,
and which, when heard, sink to a lower ebb the spirits
of the unsuccessful. We have made 50 cents each.*

Few saw their fantasies become reality. Ever greater
numbers of prospectors sought the metal, and it took increasing effort to extract the gold. Inflation and scarcity made the
necessities of life expensive. Instead of instant wealth, the
adventurers found a constant diet of hard bread and beans
baked in grease, loneliness and homesickness, along with
unceasing back-breaking work in every kind of weather,
plagued by insects of all kinds. For all this, the miners were
rewarded with barely enough compensation to sustain life.

Most camps were ephemeral: they were set up when
gold was found, and then dismantled when the claims proved
disappointing or were exhausted.

The camps were supplied with necessities, either by
peddlers who came from the major market towns of
Sacramento, Stockton, Marysville, and ultimately from San
Francisco, or by the prospectors themselves who traveled
miles over difficult terrain to the nearest towns.

If an area produced a great deal of gold and was also
conveniently situated for transportation, the tents and log
cabins eventually gave way to brick buildings and wooden
structures. Instead of makeshift shelters strewn over the
terrain in no coherent fashion, these newly constructed
mining towns followed the grid patterns of streets that had
come to dominate urban development in the United States.

And so it was that a chain of towns grew during the Gold
Rush from the Trinity Alps to the mouth of the Yosemite
Valley. Some of these towns survived the collapse of gold
mining—survived as county seats, as stops along the wagon
roads, as centers of the ranching and agricultural communities that replaced mining. Today, at the end of the twentieth
century, many of these towns have disappeared, marked
only by shards of brick walls, or a brick facade decorated

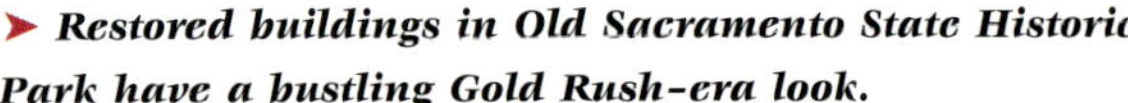

➤ *Restored buildings in Old Sacramento State Historic
Park have a bustling Gold Rush-era look.*

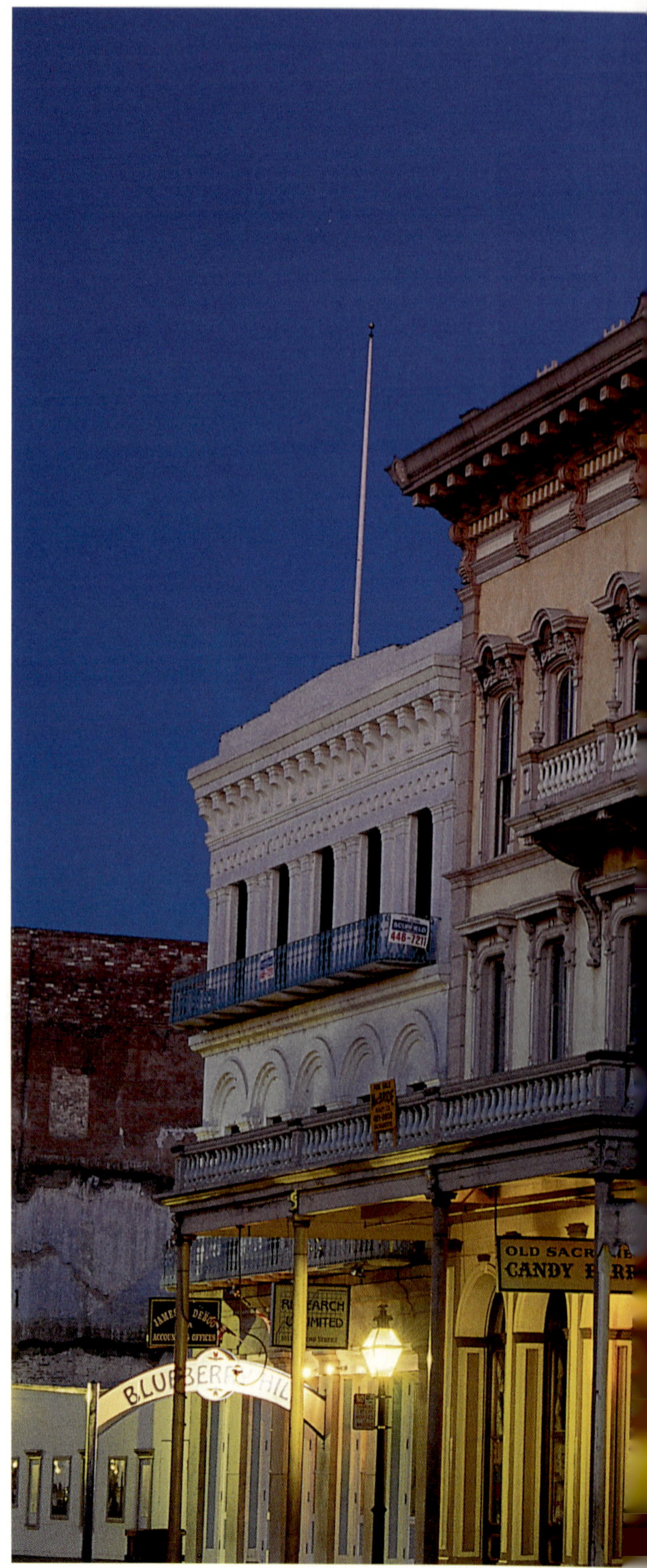

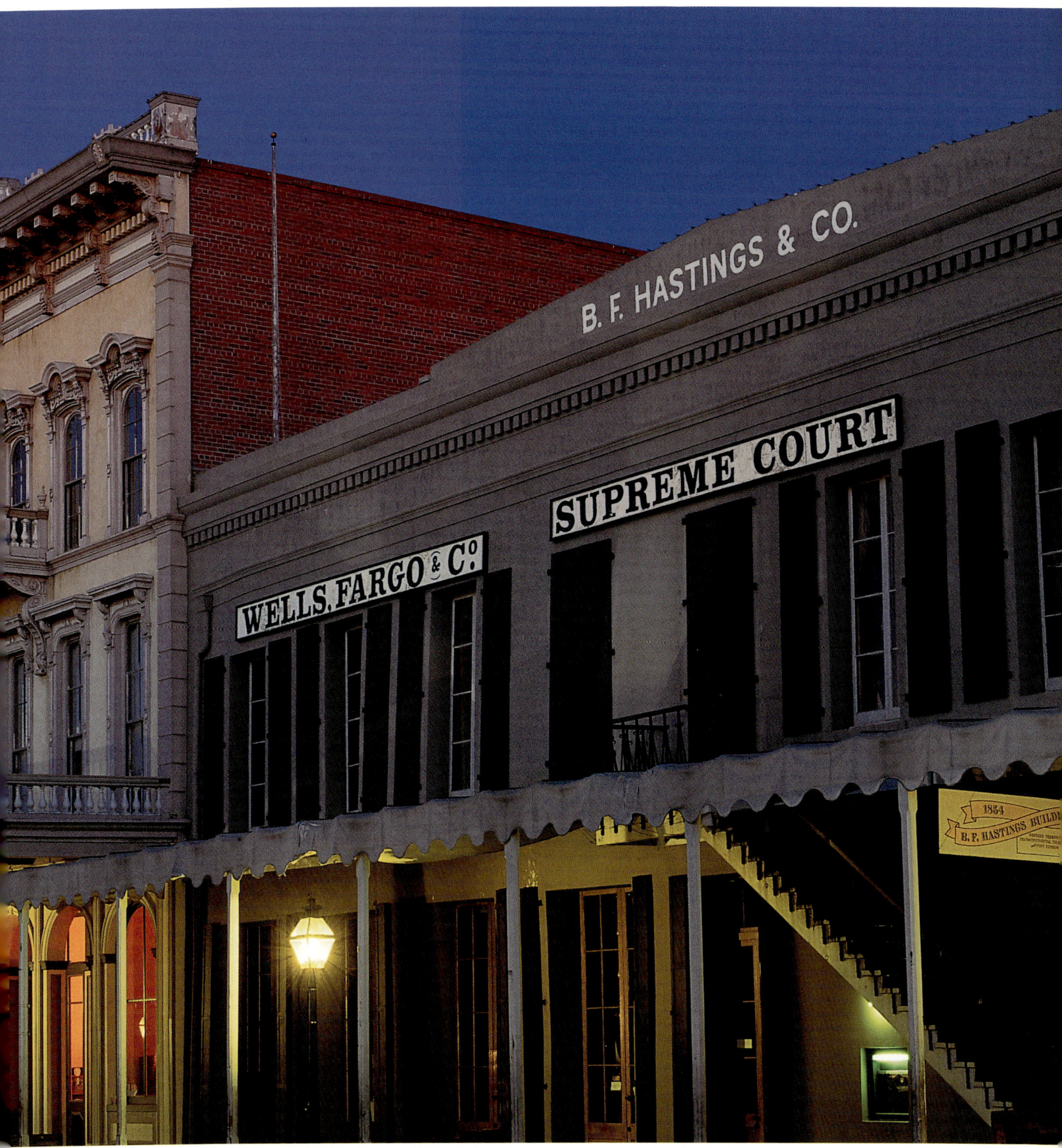

B. F. HASTINGS & CO.
SUPREME COURT
WELLS. FARGO & Cº.
1854
B. F. HASTINGS BUILD

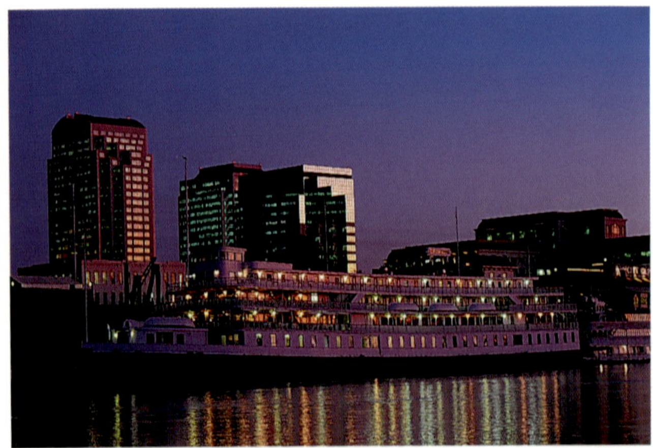

▲ *With the Gold Rush, the new town of Sacramento boomed along the Sacramento River.*
➤ *Old Sacramento boasts this restored former hotel.*

with green iron shutters, or, perhaps, only by a historical marker.

The towns, today so quiet, small, and sleepy, were once boisterous, roiling centers of economic and social activity. Entertainers included the gold towns on their tours. Politicians looked for votes there when campaigning for public office.

These were typical frontier towns of the West, where the conventions and traditions of the East did not hold; where the constraints of family and friends in communities back home had no power. Heavy drinking, consorting with prostitutes, gambling away one's substance—these were staples of the Gold Rush towns. So was crime. Murder, robbery, and beatings were common, frequently resulting in summary trials and spontaneous hangings.

The very names of the gold towns give some indication of their exuberant nature: Fiddletown, Volcano, Rough and Ready, You Bet, Timbuctoo. Before it became self-conscious, the town of Placerville was called Hangtown. Hornitos, French Gulch, and Chinese Camp give us a sense of the heritage of the miners who labored there. Michigan Bar tells us the origin of those who first began to prospect there, and Rich Bar indicates the nature of the lode—or its hoped-for wealth.

The architectural remains of these towns hold the story of their history during the Gold Rush. Hostelries such as Nevada City's National Hotel, Mokelumne Hill's Leger Hotel, and Volcano's St. George Hotel dotted the Gold Country. Murphy's Hotel—in whose old register you can read the names of Mark Twain, U. S. Grant, Horatio Alger, and J. Pierpont Morgan—was situated in the town of the same name. These old hotels catered to the many travelers who traversed the foothills of the Sierra Nevada: businessmen, actors and actresses, politicians, and sightseers among them.

A number of Odd Fellows buildings—both intact and in ruins—indicate the popularity of that fraternal organization among the lonely miners.

Gold Rush churches and *joss* houses (Chinese places of worship) offset the rowdy and randy reputation of the Mother Lode, while firehouses and stores speak for the practical needs of the Gold Rush towns.

Columbia, the "Gem of the Southern Mines," has been extensively restored and is now a state park where one can see a Gold Rush town just as it existed almost a century and a half ago. Wells Fargo Bank and Express Company's building still stands, reminding tourists of that business's role in transporting the gold the miners extracted and in financing much of the economic development of the communities it served. Columbia also contains the building that housed a branch of the Bank of D. O. Mills, headquartered in Sacramento.

Today, the Gold Country is a tranquil area, popular with tourists. It features antique stores, wineries, and the charming remains of the brick buildings that, during the Gold Rush, replaced the wooden ones swept away by fire. Fields carpeted with wildflowers during the spring hide any traces of the tent towns that sprang up overnight whenever the rumor of a strike attracted thousands of eager prospectors. Crumbling tombstones in the myriad of old cemeteries tell little of the physical pain and illness which haunted every mining camp and town. The frenzy of the Gold Rush has now become a colorful and romantic memory.

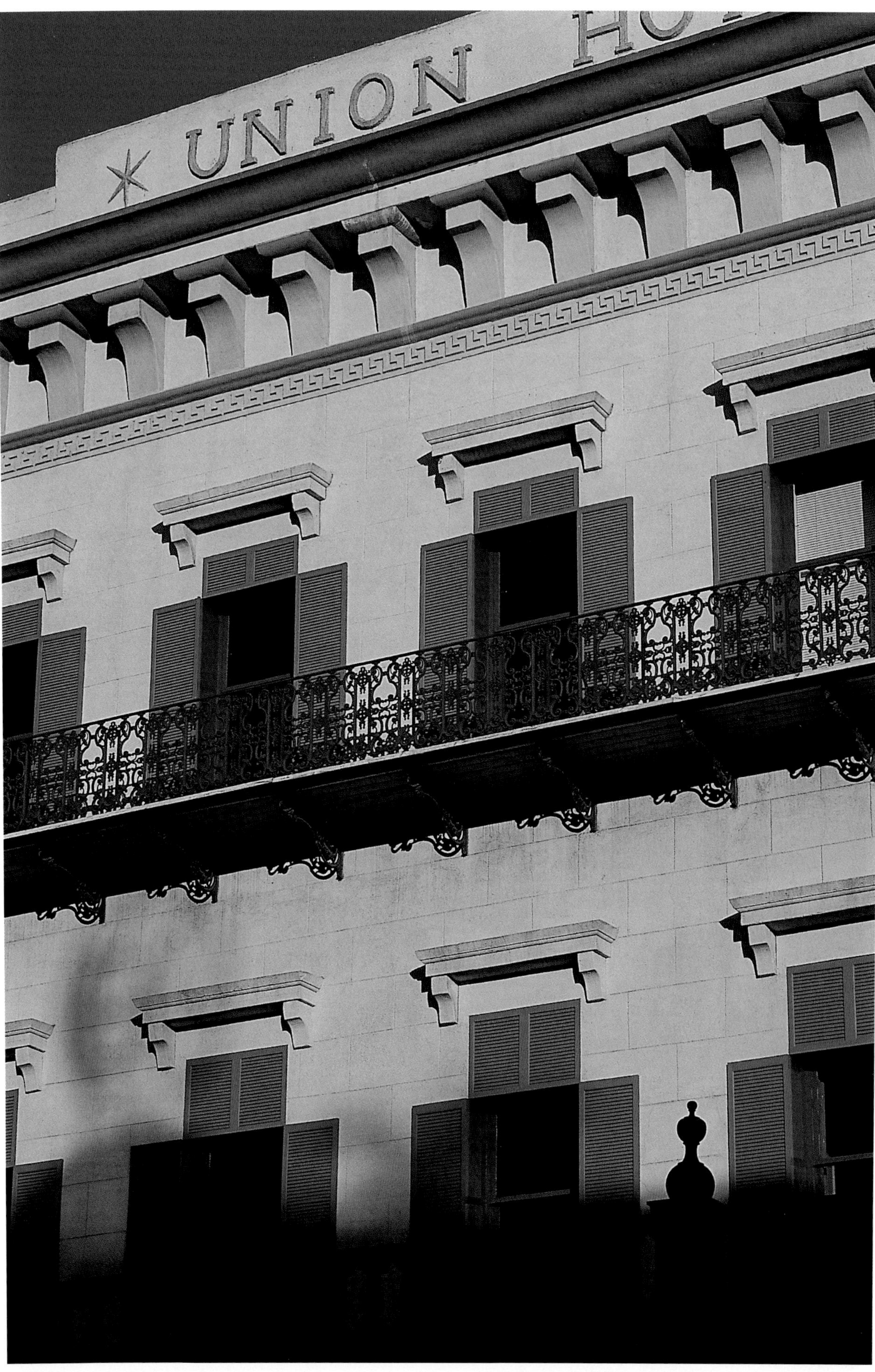

UNION HO

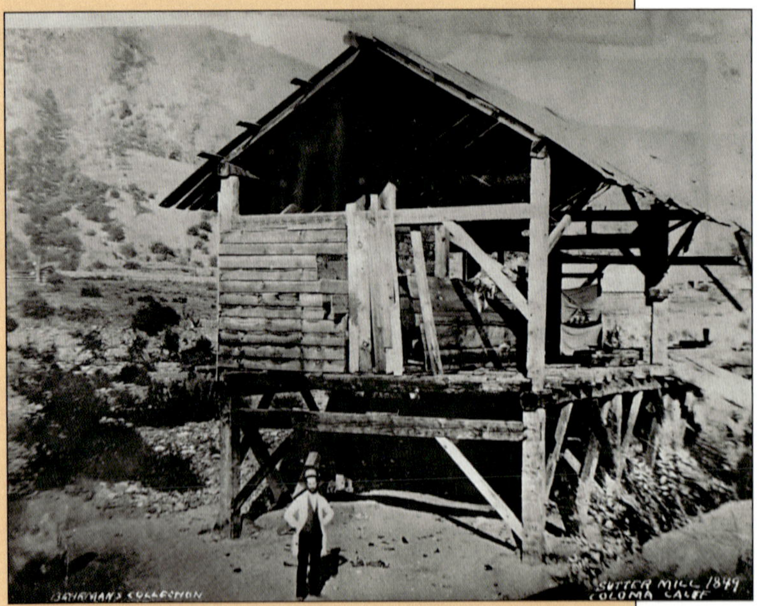

SUTTER'S MILL

John Sutter, a German immigrant to Mexican California, was given a large land grant in the Sacramento Valley. In 1847, he started to build a sawmill on the South Fork of the American River, to take advantage of the increased immigration the U.S. occupation of California would bring.

He chose as his partner James Marshall, a carpenter from New Jersey, who selected a crew, and construction began in late 1847. As the mill neared completion on January 24, 1848, Marshall made his momentous discovery of gold, thereby inaugurating the Gold Rush.

During the 1850s, a flood swept away the original mill, but in 1967, a duplicate mill was established on higher ground. The full-size reproduction—measuring sixty feet long by twenty-five feet wide—is based on Marshall's sketches and description and on the original timbers, which were excavated in 1947.

Before gold was discovered, it would have been impossible to predict that the Sacramento Valley, situated in the northern part of California's Great Central Valley—so remote and unexplored during the Spanish era of California history and so little probed even during the Mexican period—would become the vibrant center of commerce that it did during the Gold Rush.

The saga of what was, during the mid-nineteenth century, California's second-largest city (after San Francisco), began modestly. An immigrant named John Augustus Sutter (an inveterate liar who claimed Swiss ancestry but was actually from Germany), whose entrepreneurial impulses usually outran his business ability, fled his country to escape a large indebtedness. He made his way to California by way of Russian Alaska and the Hawaiian Islands. Once there, he received a land grant in Sacramento Valley from Governor Alvarado.

In 1839, Sutter sailed from San Francisco up the Sacramento River and settled on a rise of land near the confluence of the American and Sacramento Rivers. He built a complex— shops for his various enterprises, dwellings, and other buildings—surrounded by four adobe walls. The complex became known as Sutter's Fort and was a destination for the overland immigrants who began arriving in the early 1840s by wagon train. After the rigors of their arduous journey, these immigrants received rest, food, supplies, and advice at this hub of Sutter's agricultural and business empire.

Although from the beginning he was notoriously slow to pay for his purchases and his creditors began to look askance at his business dealings, Sutter continued to prosper.

Ironically, it was one of Sutter's countless business ventures—that of building a sawmill at Coloma on the American River and the discovery of gold—that turned Sutter's dreams of fortune into a nightmare.

Sutter's Fort became the natural stop for those coming up from San Francisco to the gold fields, and Sutter foresaw that more money could be made from supplying the miners than from digging for gold. He planned to found a commercial town near Sutter's Fort, to be called Sutterville, to take advantage of his fortuitous location; but Sam Brannan (who had started a store at Sutter's Fort) and other entrepreneurs moved their mercantile operations to a place on the Sacramento River called the Embarcadero. Though Sutterville was better situated to escape the floods of the Sacramento River than the rapidly growing settlement on the Embarcadero, the aggressive promoters of the new town had soon captured the river trade between San Francisco and the mines. Sutterville was doomed. The Embarcadero became known as Sacramento City.

Sutter no longer ruled his empire. He was deserted by his employees, his crops were trampled, his fruit trees cut down, and his vast holdings began to slip through his fingers. Sutter's dreams were shattered, and within a couple of years, he plunged into a poverty from which he never recovered.

The new village grew rapidly. Ships crowded alongside its riverbank; trade with mines was brisk; and buildings were rapidly thrown up. Urban amenities sprouted: newspapers, California's first theater (the *Eagle*), and gambling saloons. This boisterous, bustling town was not without its growing pains. Several fires ravaged the rapidly growing town, as they did in San Francisco, but its citizens were quick to rebuild after each one. Cholera raged in 1850. And early that same year, heavy rains caused the river to flood its banks, and Sacramento was inundated.

▼ *Wagons like these at Marshall Gold Discovery State Historic Park supplied gold towns throughout the Sierra.*

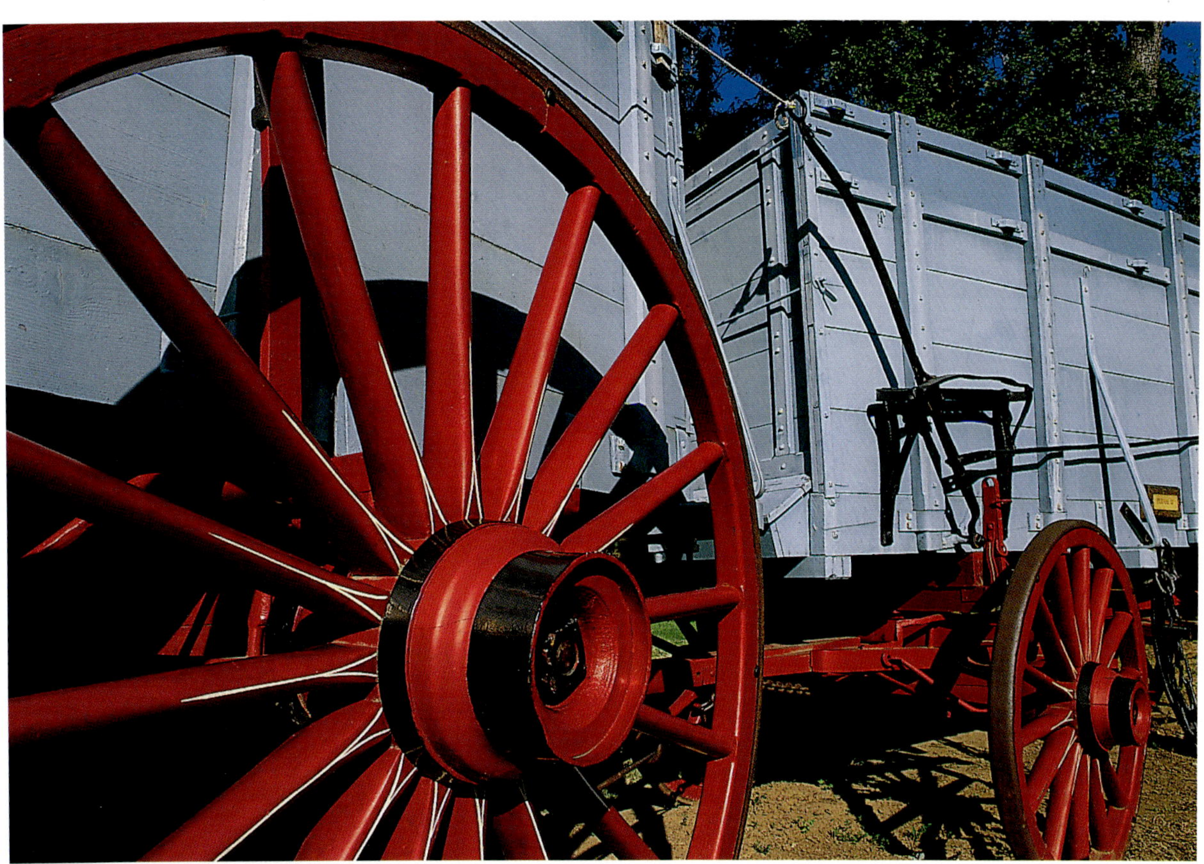

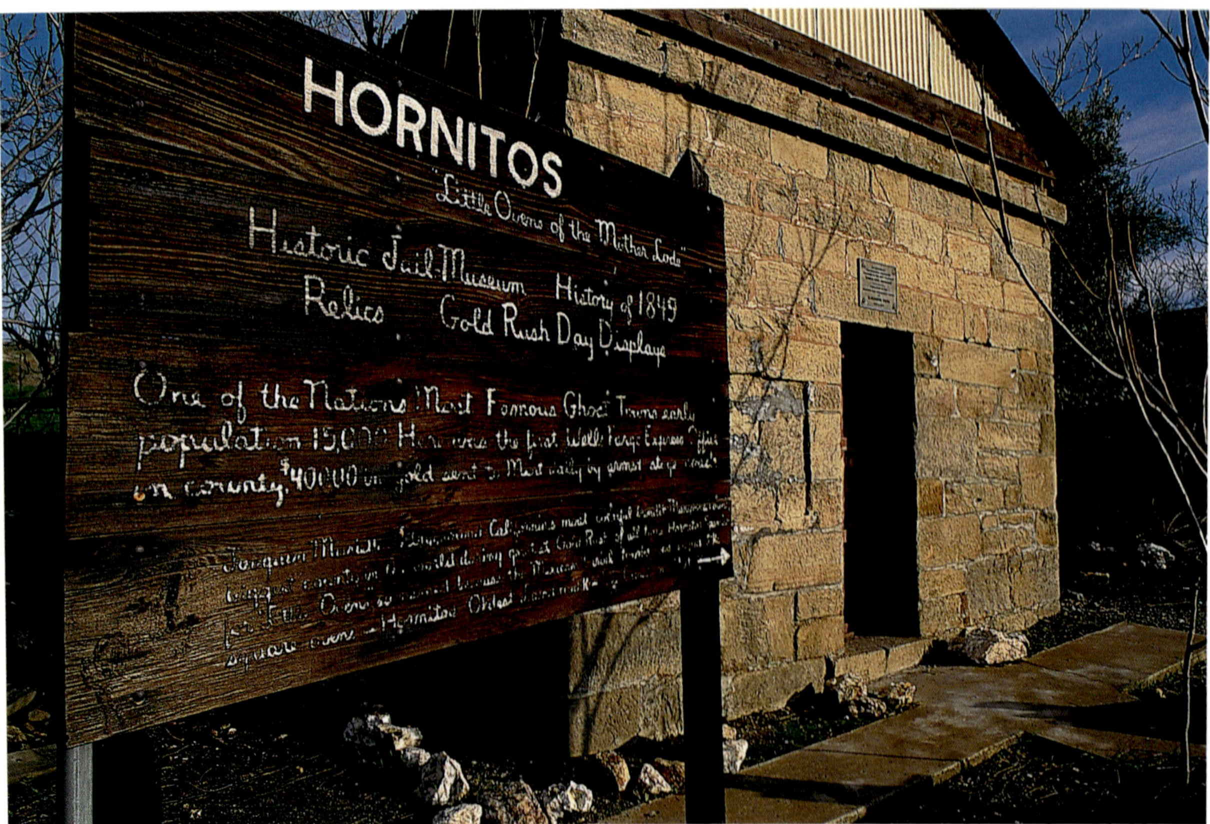

▲ *The rich, rowdy, multicultural mining camp of Hornitos was established in 1850 by outcast Mexican miners.*
► *This vintage jail is one of the remnants of a mining town included in Columbia State Historic Park.*

Almost from the beginning, land grabbing had been part of the frenzied pursuit of wealth in Sacramento. The struggle between the Mexican land grant owners (or those speculators who had bought from the original owners) and the so-called settlers who overran Sutter's and others' claims came to a head in 1850 with the Squatters' Riots.

Tension between the two groups—the owners and the squatters—had been heating up for some months, fueled by the outcome of several legal cases. Both sides armed themselves. Finally, two shoot-outs left several dead, including the city assessor and the sheriff, and others wounded, among them Sacramento's mayor.

Today Sutterville and Sutter's Fort are all incorporated in the sprawling city of Sacramento, which has been California's capital since 1854. Its initial urban baptism in water, fire, disease, and unrest are all but forgotten now. Its prosperity is no longer based on supplying the gold mines, but on being the political center for the richest and most populous state in the nation.

Sutter's dream of an inland empire, a huge feudal operation based upon agriculture and supplying a multiplicity of goods to a rapidly growing area, collapsed in the whirling storms of the Gold Rush. But his dreams were inherited by others: the aggressive merchants of Sacramento, the farmers who began to till the rich valley soil, the dry goods and hardware barons who built the western half of the transcontinental railroad, and the politicians and administrators who engineered California's complex public works, innovative educational system, and splendid highways.

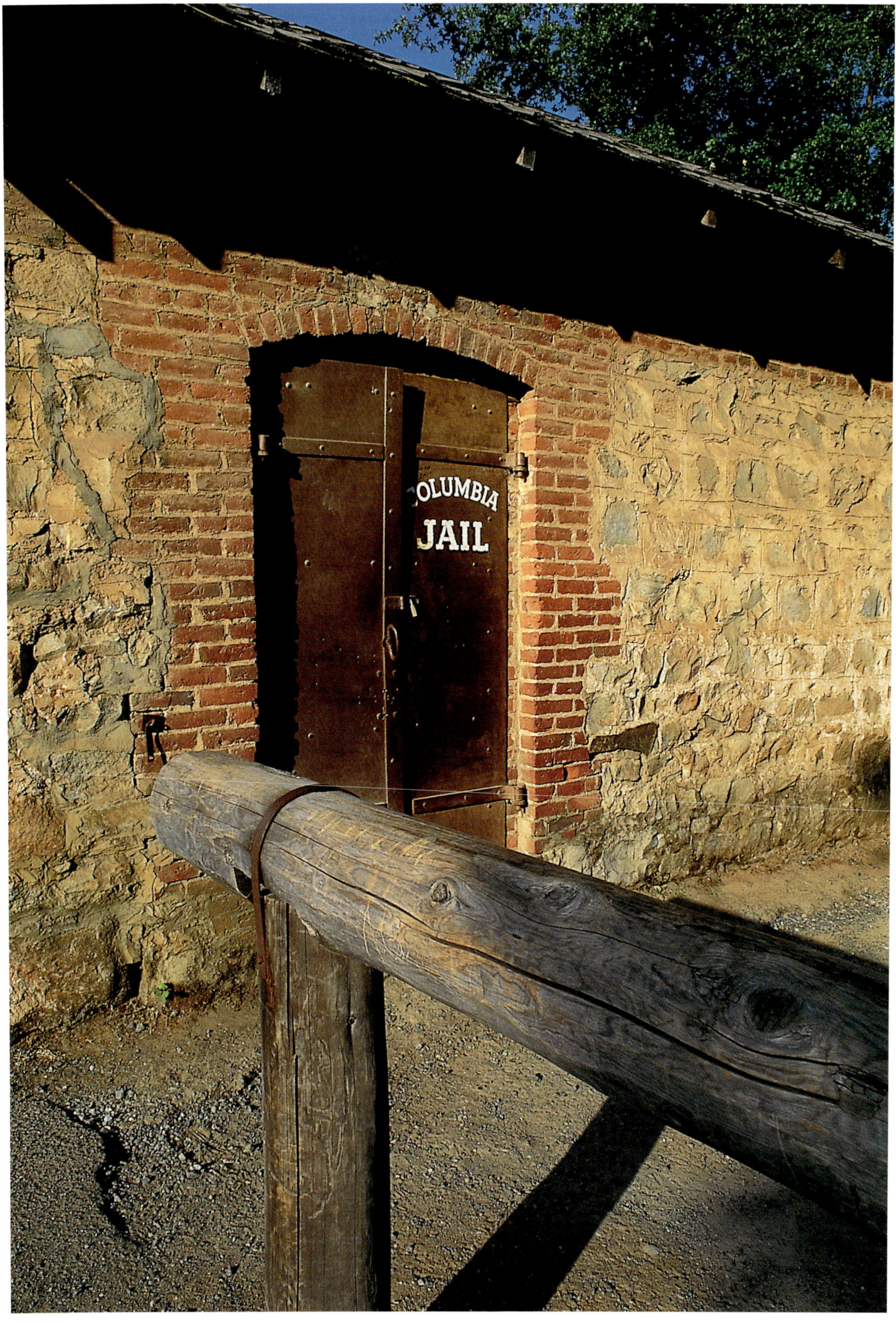
COLUMBIA
JAIL

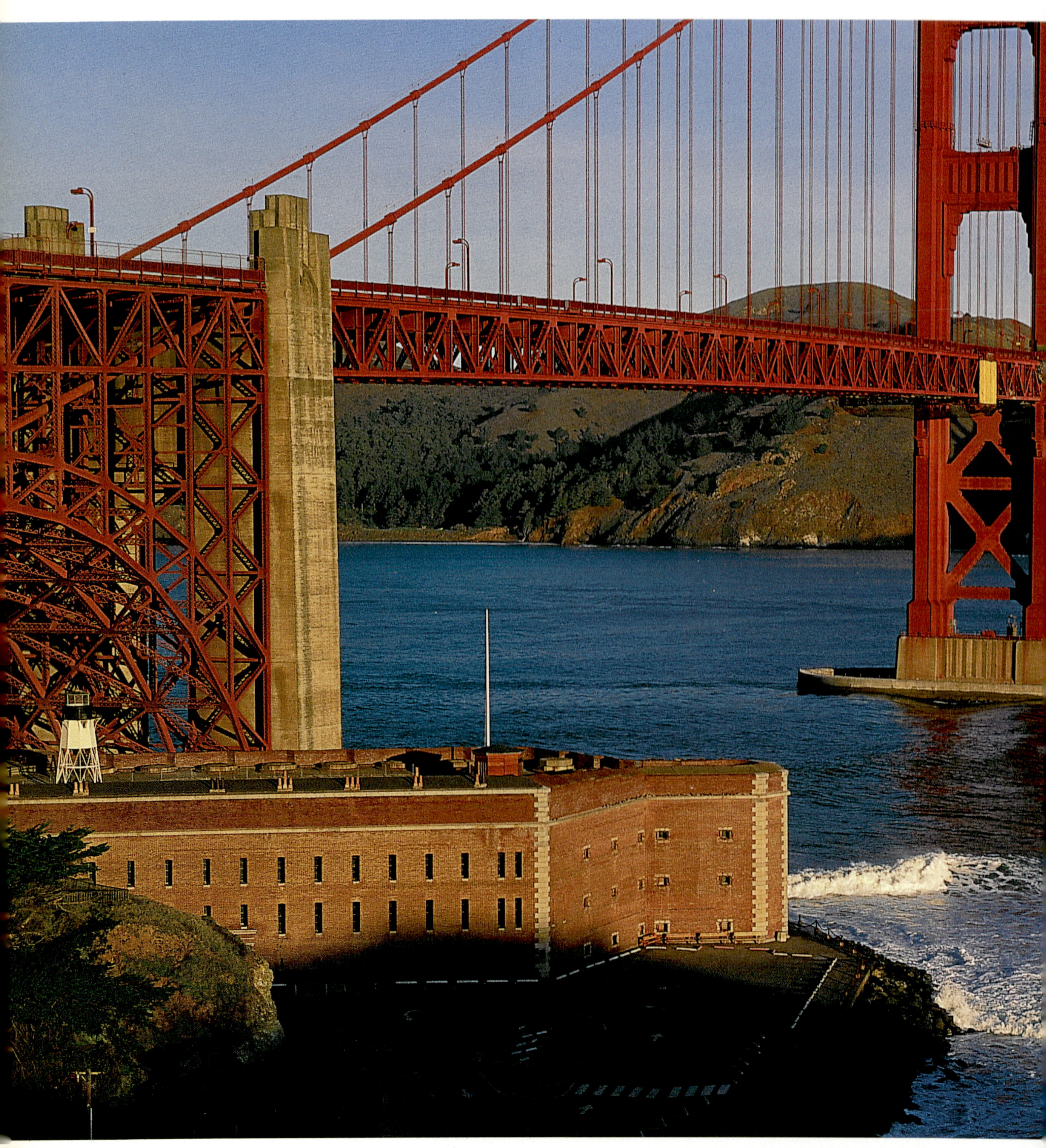

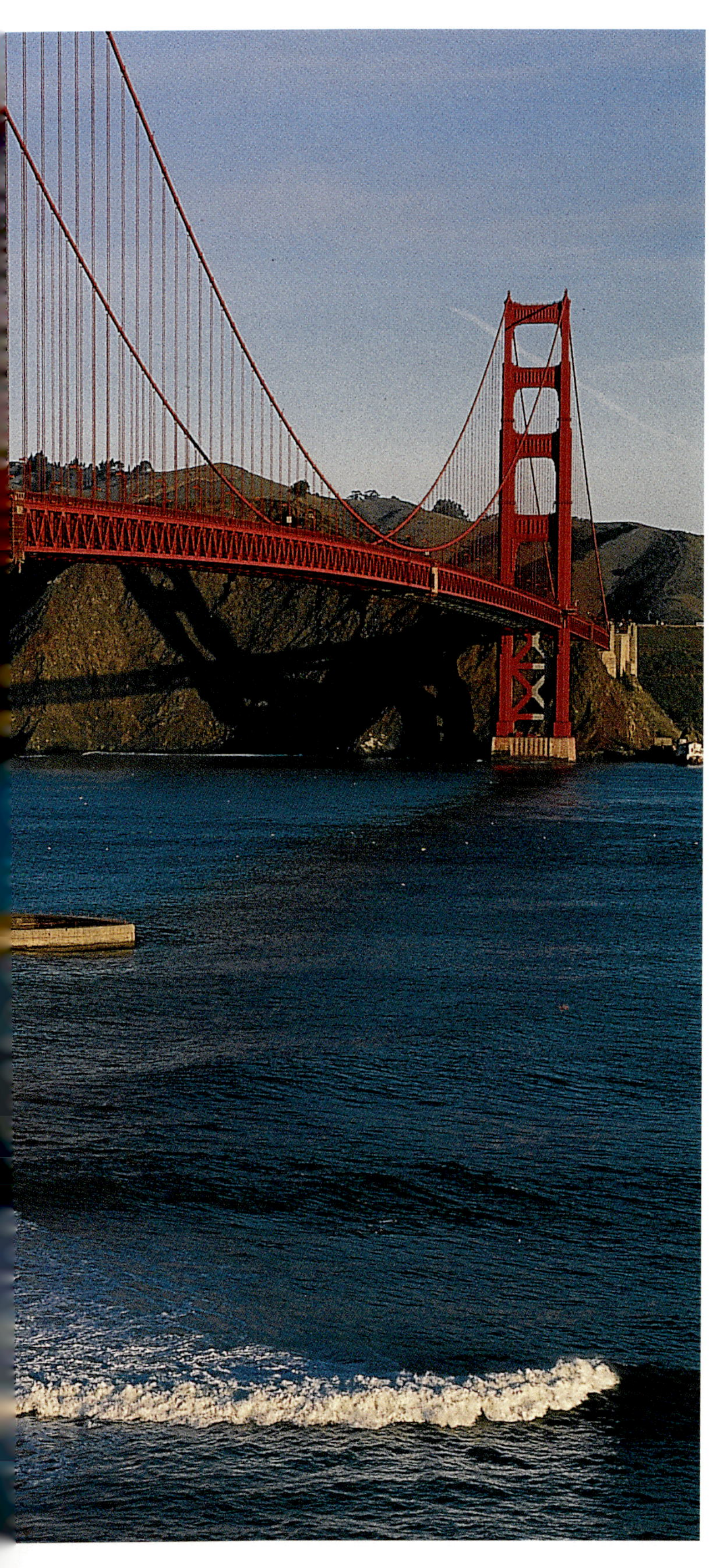

SAN FRANCISCO: TRADING VILLAGE TO URBAN METROPOLIS

1. SAN FRANCISCO BEFORE THE GOLD RUSH

San Francisco's beginnings in June 1776 consisted of a presidio and a mission called San Francisco de Asís (or, popularly, Mission Dolores), built by Spain on the peninsula that formed the southern part of the Golden Gate entrance into San Francisco Bay.

For the four and a half decades of Spanish rule, San Francisco was a somnolent outpost of the crumbling Spanish Empire. Only six foreign ships entered the bay during this period. Their reports tell of a neglected, dilapidated military fort and a mission that was facing a desolate future as a result of epidemics that had begun to annihilate the neophyte Indian population.

It was not until mission lands were seized by the government, during Mexican rule in the mid-1830s, that there began a modest urban development. In November 1834, the California territorial assembly officially created a pueblo of San Francisco, which included present-day San Francisco and San Mateo Counties and large parts of Contra Costa and Alameda Counties as well.

◄ *Fort Point was built from 1853 to 1861 to protect the bustling gateway to the Gold Rush.*

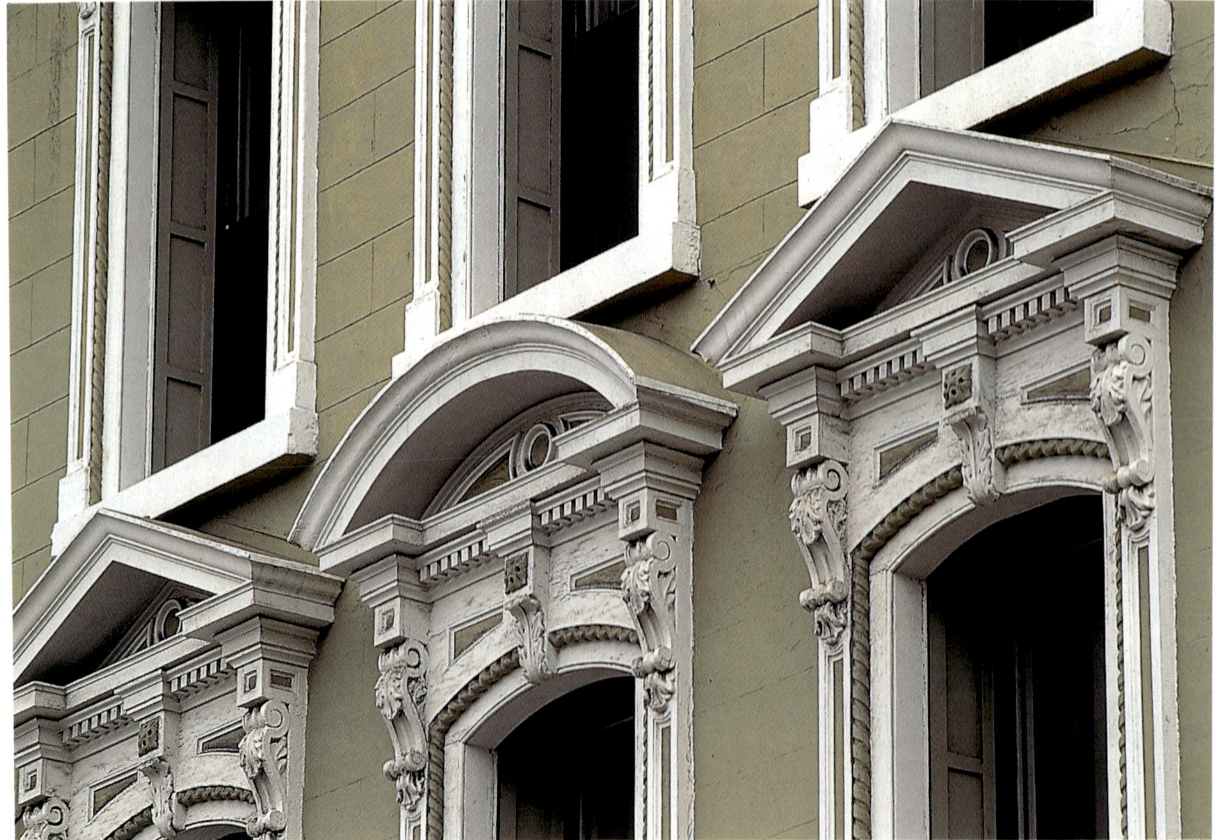

▲ *The Jackson Square Historic District, featuring many Gold Rush-era buildings, offers 1800s architecture and an early San Francisco atmosphere.*
➤ *Striking details adorn the restored 1851 Belli Building in Jackson Square (the late Melvin Belli's law office).*

A few months later, William Richardson—an English seaman who had jumped ship in San Francisco in the early 1820s, married a local señorita, and moved to Southern California—returned to San Francisco to take the appointed post of customs collector. He built a shack on the Yerba Buena Cove (roughly at the corner of today's Clay and Montgomery Streets) and a house a short distance away (on today's Grant Avenue).

From this modest beginning would develop the urban metropolis of San Francisco. Within somewhat more than a decade, the population in this Yerba Buena settlement grew to about two hundred. Ships anchored in the cove, drawn by the hide and tallow trade that was the staple of California's economy. The city built itself around the plaza, today called Portsmouth Plaza, which became the center of San Francisco life for two decades.

In 1846, the news reached San Francisco that Mexico and the United States were at war. Captain John B. Montgomery, U.S.N., raised the U.S. flag in Portsmouth Plaza on July 9, 1846, signaling that the settlement was now part of the United States.

The next year, 1847, the *alcalde,* Lieutenant Washington Bartlett, officially changed the name of the settlement from Yerba Buena to San Francisco. During that same year, the first newspaper in San Francisco went to press, and the first book was published. The town's need for public funds was temporarily resolved by the auction of lots from the public domain—from the area around the Yerba Buena Cove, as well as lots in the actual cove, and from the area around what is today Union Square.

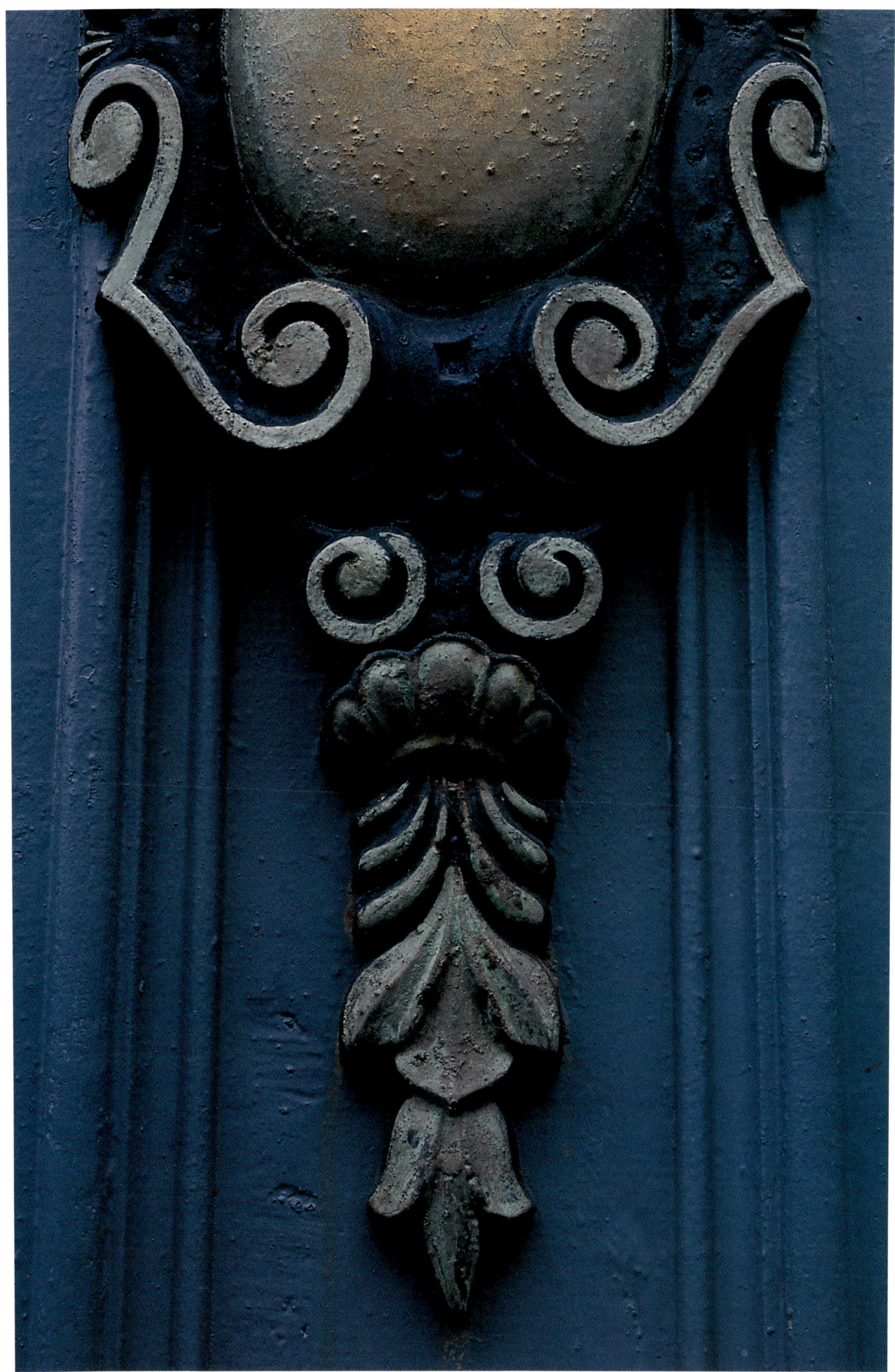

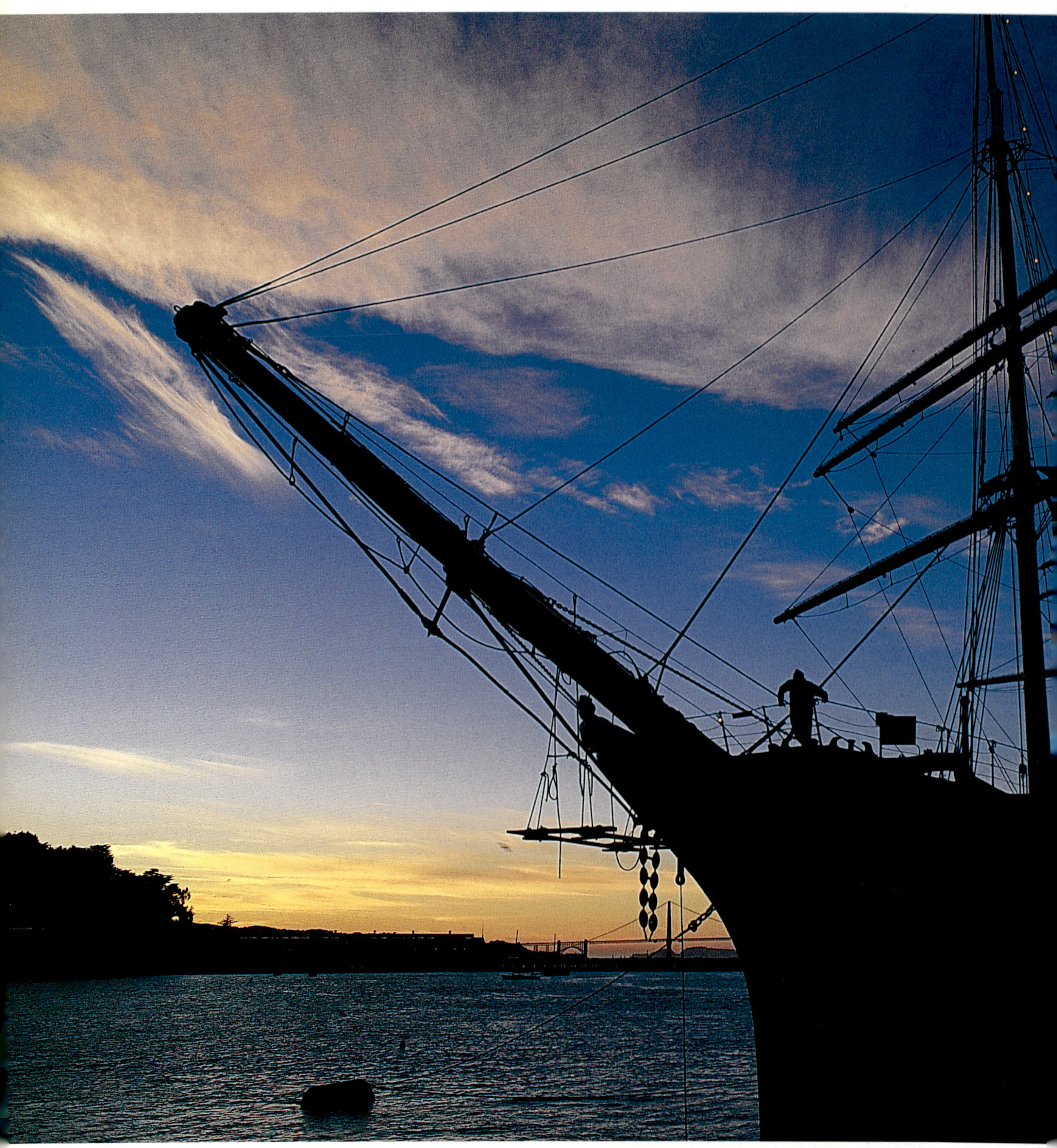

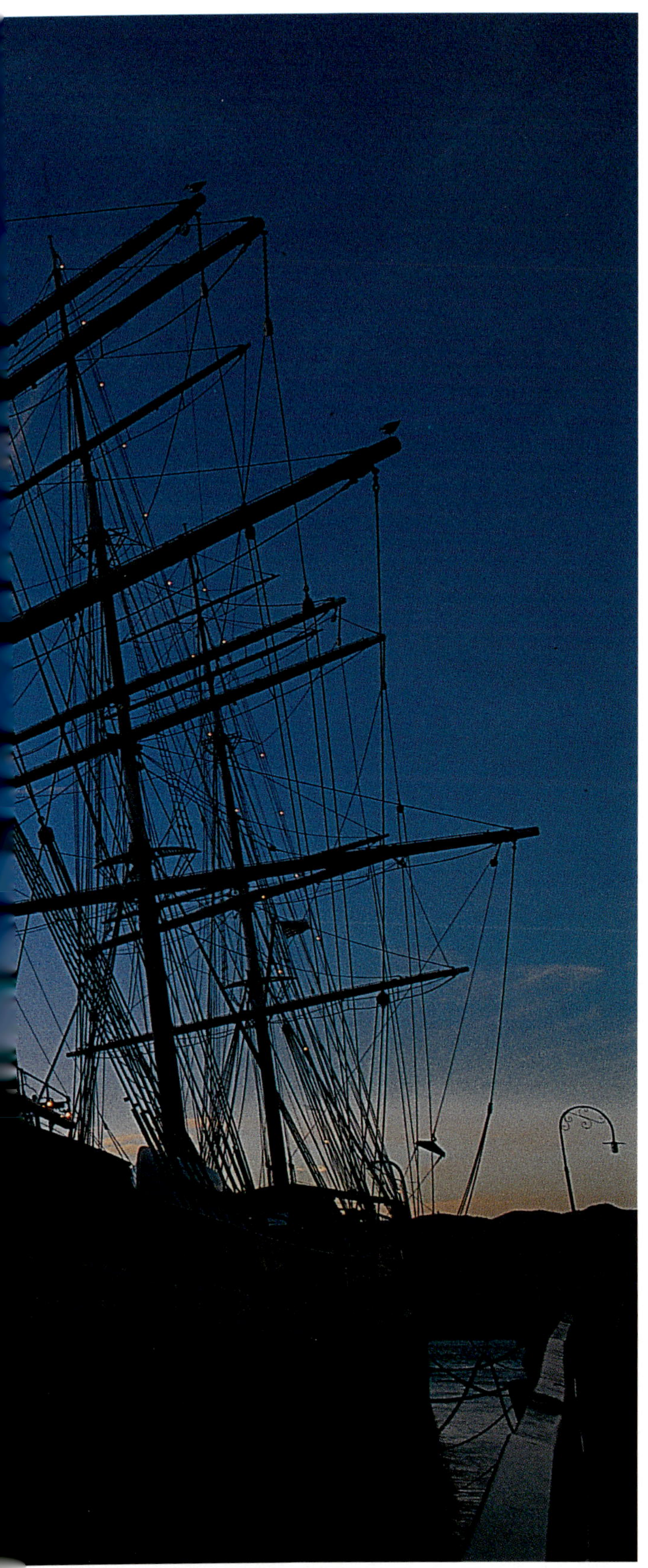

◄ The 1886 Balclutha rests at Hyde Street Pier in the San Francisco Maritime National Historical Park. Tall ships similar to this one lined the bay during the Gold Rush.

The lots had been mapped out by a survey made by Jasper O'Farrell. He created a broad street called Market Street, which was aligned from the Yerba Buena Cove to Twin Peaks. O'Farrell also surveyed a large area south of Market Street, where the lots and blocks were twice the size of those north of the street.

A census of mid-1847 showed that the newly named town had a population of almost five hundred. All thought that the trading village would prosper nicely in the coming years.

2. THE IMPACT OF THE GOLD DISCOVERY

The fortunes of this modestly growing trading town would change dramatically as a result of the discovery of gold at Sutter's Mill in late January of 1848.

It was not until March 15—almost two months after the discovery of gold—that a brief, matter-of-fact mention of the find appeared on the back page of the *Californian,* one of San Francisco's two newspapers.

The *California Star*'s editor had reported there was nothing to the rumors of the gold find at Sutter's Mill. But the rumor persisted, fueled by the appearance in town of a prospector who paid for purchases with eight ounces of gold. On May 27, the formerly skeptical editor of the *California Star* wrote: "... the stores are closed and places of business vacated, a large number of houses tenantless, various kinds of mechanical labor suspended or given up entirely...."

The author of *The Annals of San Francisco,* published in 1856, wrote about the initial gold rush from San Francisco:

About the end of May we left San Francisco almost a deserted place, and such it continued during the whole summer and autumn months. Many ships with valuable cargo had meanwhile arrived in the bay but the seamen were deserted. The goods at great expense had

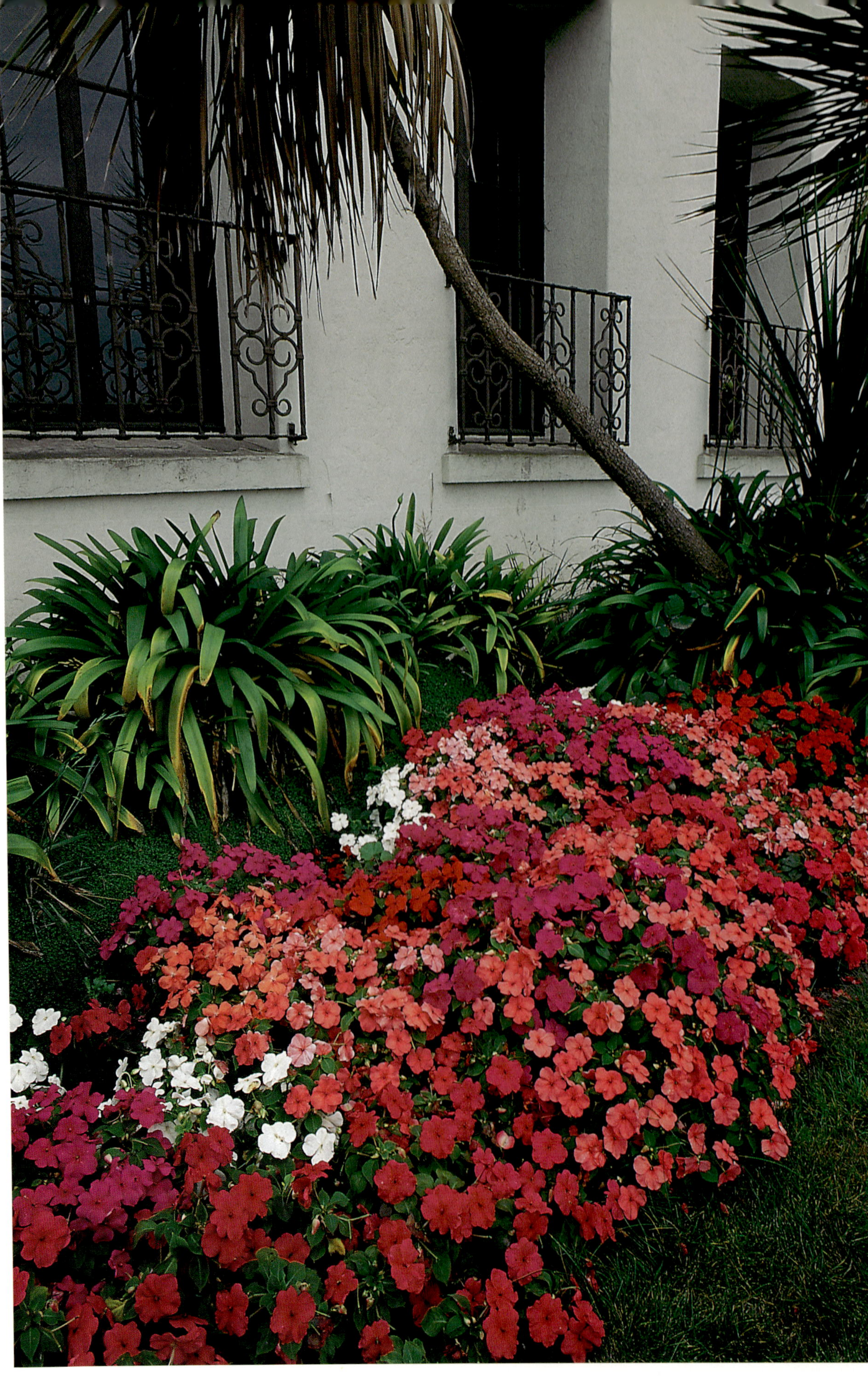

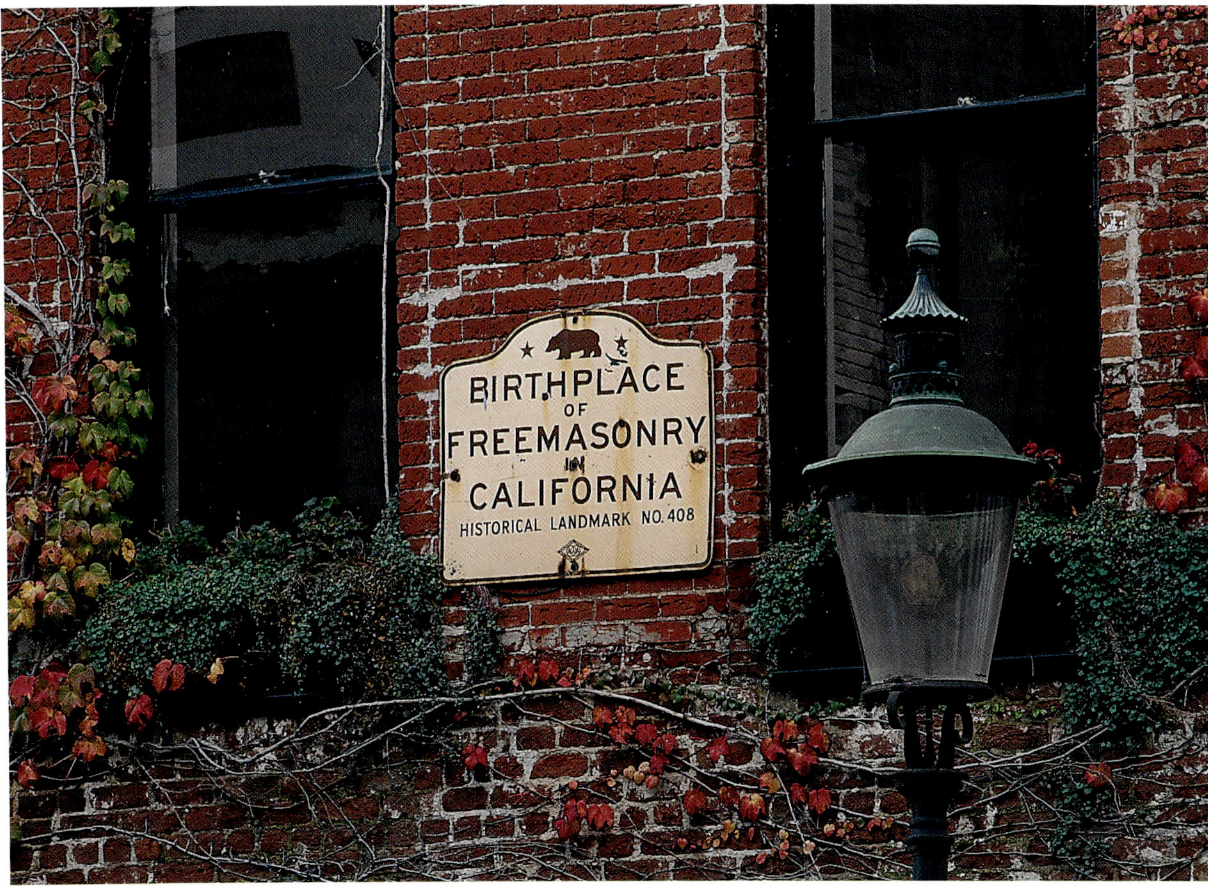

◄ *Under Spanish and Mexican rule, this much-remodeled building served as the Presidio commandant's quarters.*
▲ *The Genella building, in Jackson Square, is on the site of the Masonic Lodge's first California meeting in 1849.*

---

*somehow been landed, but there was nobody to take care of them, or remove them from wharves where they lay
exposed to the weather. The merchants who remained were in a feverish hustle. They were selling goods at high
prices, but could get no hands to assist them in removing and delivering the articles.... Hence, therefore, as at the
mines, the prices of labor and all necessities rose exceedingly. The common laborer, who had formerly been content
with his dollar a day, now proudly refused ten; the mechanic, who had recently been glad to receive two dollars,
now rejected twenty for his days services.*

3. GOLD RUSH BOOM

It was as if a pebble had been dropped in a pond: confirmations of rumors of great riches brought an increasing
number of gold seekers, first from the area nearest to the expanding gold fields, the settlements and farms around
San Francisco Bay, then from more distant areas—Oregon, Southern California, the Hawaiian Islands, Northern
Mexico, the ports of Western South America.

Letters from Californians to friends and family began to find their way into newspapers in the United States and
abroad. Excitement began to mount. President Polk's announcement of the discovery of gold gave the rumors an

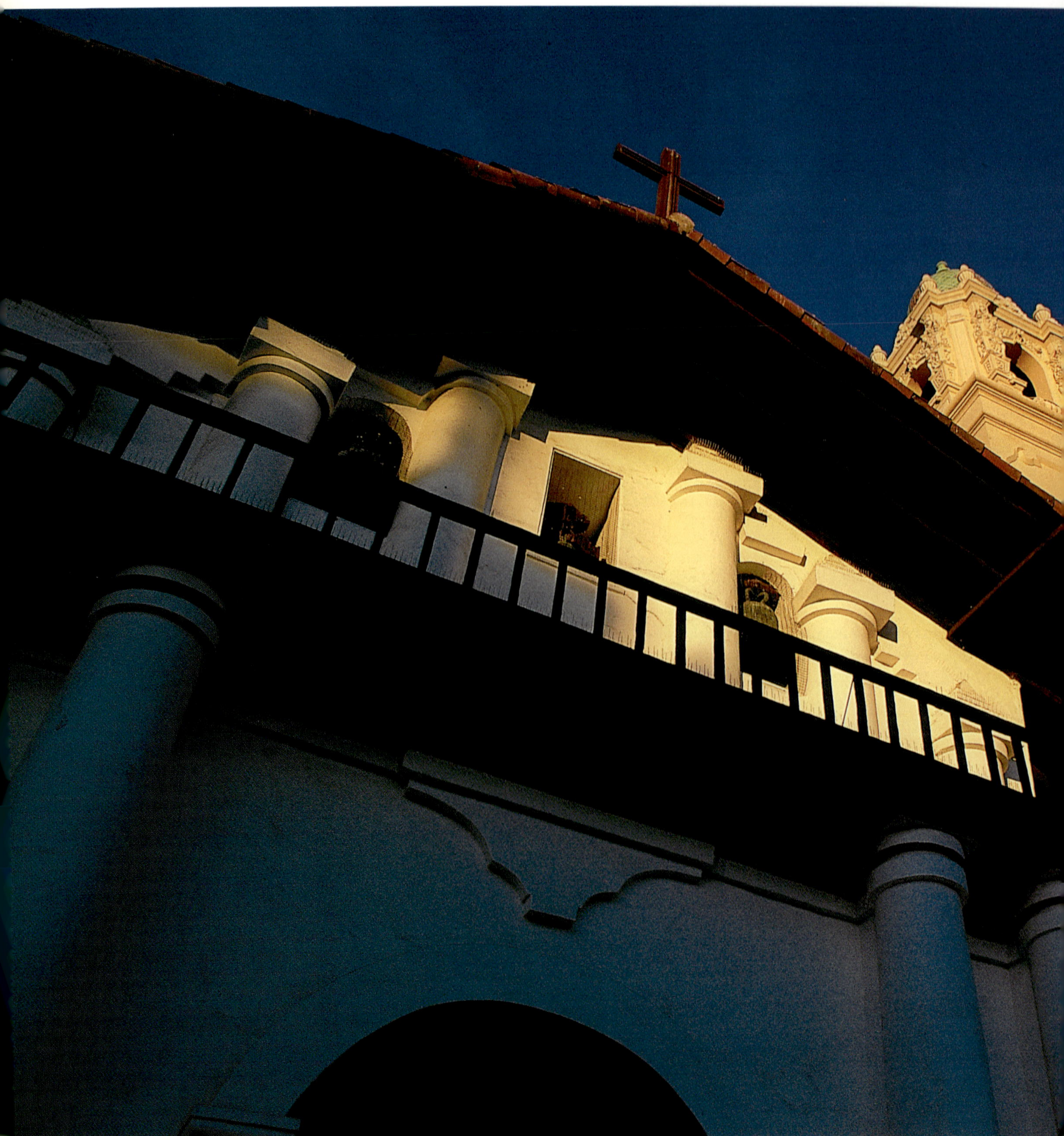

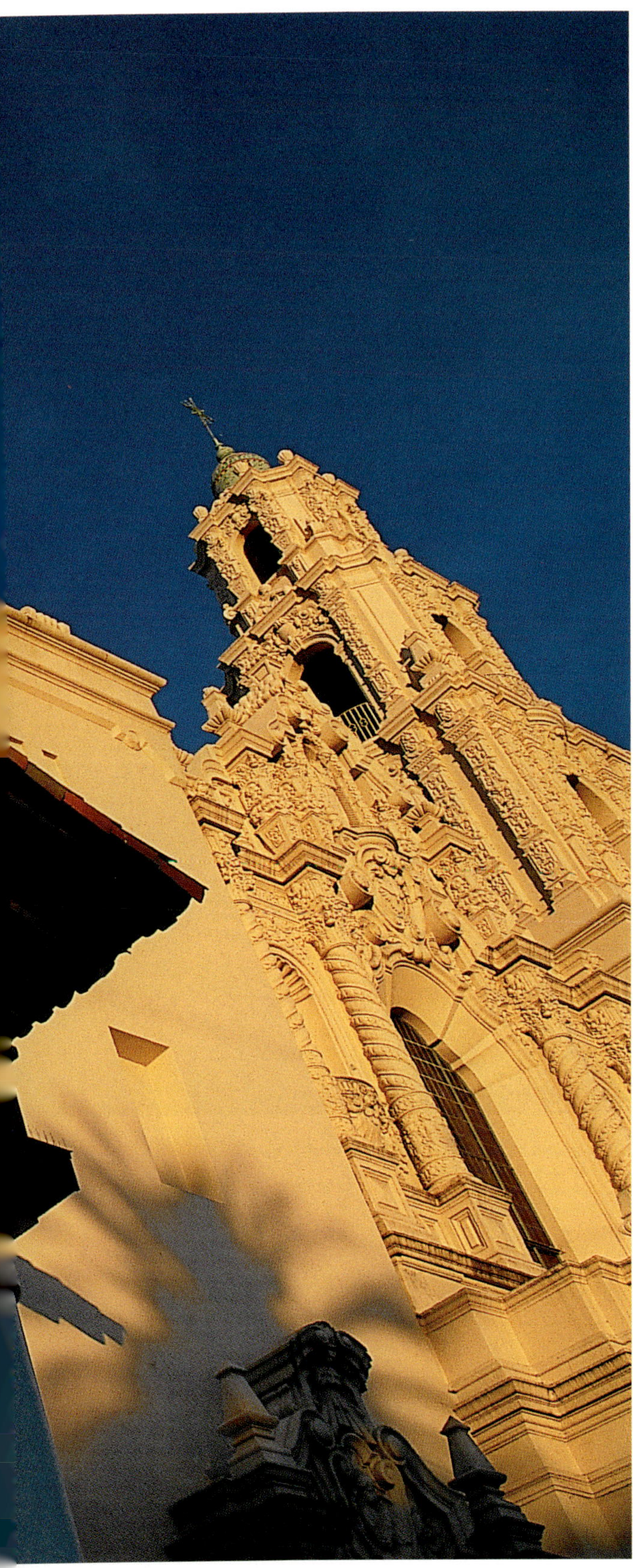

official imprimatur and set off wild excitement across the nation and around the world. Suddenly, thousands upon thousands of young men in towns and farms throughout every area in the United States, in Europe, Asia, and South America set off for California.

The harbor of San Francisco bristled with the masts of ships bringing *argonauts* to the gold fields to seek their own version of Jason's Golden Fleece. The harbor, which had earlier seen the occasional whaler, naval ship, or trading vessel, now saw hundreds of ships sailing through the Golden Gate. (In the month of February 1849, some 130 ships left Atlantic ports for San Francisco.) Every "tub" that could float was pressed into service. And when the ships arrived in San Francisco Bay, crowded together in the Yerba Buena Cove, not only did the passengers leave, but even the crews deserted. (A daguerreotype panorama of San Francisco, taken between October 1850 and April 1851, shows a forest of hundreds of masts of abandoned ships in the cove. Their hulls are still being found beneath the streets of San Francisco.)

Once off the ships, the passengers and crews alike did not linger long in San Francisco, but set off almost immediately for sites where rumor or factual accounts indicated gold had been found.

The hard facts of life were learned rather quickly in the gold fields. Many of those who had passed through San Francisco, full of dreams on their way to the mines, returned crestfallen, to head home or to seek their fortune in San Francisco as doctors, lawyers, bankers, merchants, teamsters, laborers—anything to cash in on the Gold Rush boom that was taking place.

The town that in 1847 had a population of about five hundred situated around the plaza and the cove, now mushroomed into a city comprised of tens of thousands. Large sections of the city adjacent to the cove—Telegraph Hill and Happy Valley, for example—blossomed with tent cities. At one point in 1849, the population doubled every ten days.

San Francisco was the principal seaport and trading settlement on the west coast of the United States and the

◄ *The eighteenth-century adobe church of Mission Dolores features Indian and Spanish art and a garden cemetery.*

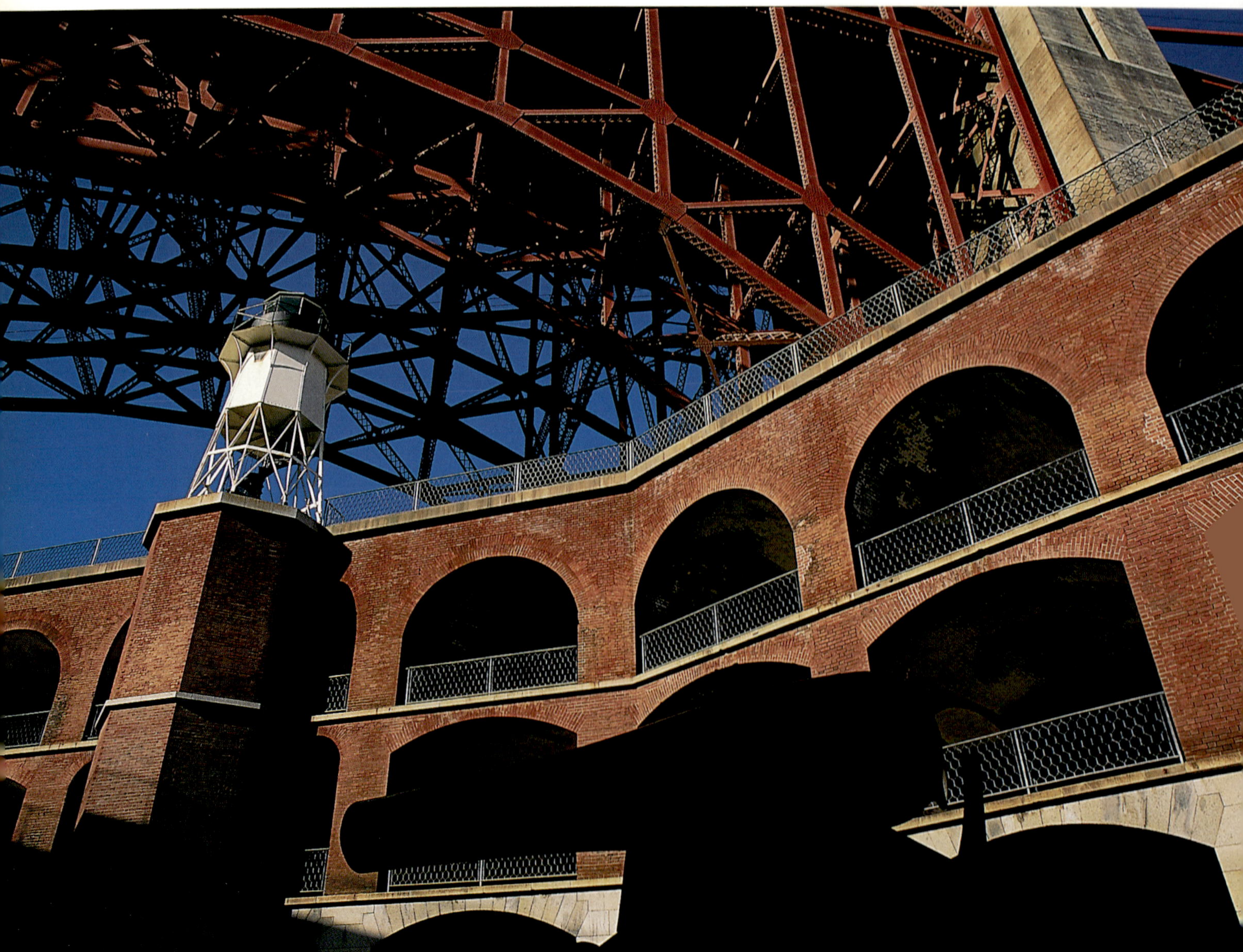

▲ *Fort Point National Historic Site offers an example of a pre–Civil War brick fortress, with exhibits and interpretive tours by rangers who explain its past.*

harbor closest to where gold had been found. Thus, it was to San Francisco that immigrants, from every nook and cranny of the United States and from every part of the world, converged on San Francisco in that short period of the Gold Rush. This mix of nationalities, races, and classes created an instantaneous city—a bustling cosmopolis that knew no "first families." This effervescent society developed a patina of egalitarianism and a promise of limitless possibilities.

It was this urban maelstrom that welcomed Bayard Taylor in 1849. A correspondent of the *New York Tribune*, Taylor later wrote a book about his adventures in San Francisco and California. This passage, describing his landing in Yerba Buena Cove, illustrates the exotic beginnings of San Francisco:

A furious wind was blowing down through a gap in the hills, filling the streets with clouds of dust. On every side stood buildings of all kinds, begun or half-finished, and the greater part of them were canvas shacks, open in front, and covered with all kinds of signs, in all languages. Great quantities of goods were piled up in the open air, for there was no place to store them. The streets were full of people, hurrying to and fro, and of as diverse and bizarre a character as the houses: Yankees of every possible variety, native Californians in serapes and som-breros, Chileans, Sonorans, Kanakas from Hawaii, Chinese with long [pig] tails, Malays armed with their everlasting creeses and oth-ers on whose embowered and bearded vis-ages it was impossible to recognize any special nationality.

Such growth, however, caused much economic hardship. There was a shortage of goods. Labor was expensive. Prices skyrocketed. Real estate inflation was marked: a lot was bought for $16 in 1847, sold for $6,000 in spring 1848, and re-sold for $45,000 by the end of the year; another was traded for a barrel of whiskey and sold a short time later for $18,000.

Rents stunned those recently arrived from other parts of the United States. A one-story build-ing at the corner of Kearny and Washington Streets was leased to a banking firm for $6,000 per month; one-room offices brought $1,000 a month; tiny basement rooms rented for $250. Gambling establishments often rented by the table or twelve-hour shift of operation.

Walter Colton, a naval chaplain who arrived in California in 1846, wrote a book of reminiscences entitled, *Three Years in California*, recording his amazement at the prices that became prevalent after gold discovery:

But you are hungry—want a breakfast—turn into a restaurant—all for ham and eggs, and coffee—then your bill— six dollars! Your high boots, which have never seen a brush since you first put them on, have given out; you find a new pair that can replace them—they are a tolerable fit—and now what is the price—fifty dollars! Your beard has not felt a razor since you went to the mines—it must come off, and your frizzled hair be clipped, you find a barber; his dull shears hang in the knots of your hair like a sheepskinners—his razor he strops on the leg of his foot, and then hauls away—starting at every pull a new fountain of tears—you vow you will let the beard go—but by then one side is partly off and you try the agony again—what is the charge for this torture—four dollars!

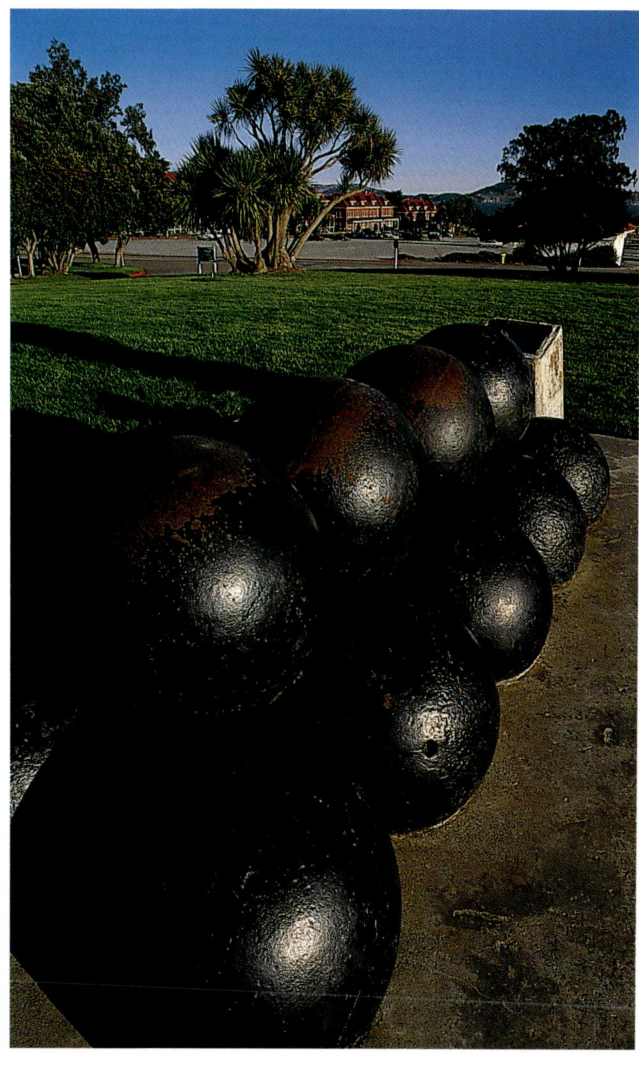

▲ *From 1776 to 1994, when it became a national park, the Presidio of San Francisco operated as a military garrison.*

THE FRENCH

Natives of France arrived in California in sizeable numbers during the Gold Rush. Following the overthrow of the French king and the proclamation of a republic in 1848, the lure of gold captivated France.

The emerging leader of France after the revolution, Louis Napoleon was proclaimed emperor in 1851. He decided to divest Paris of

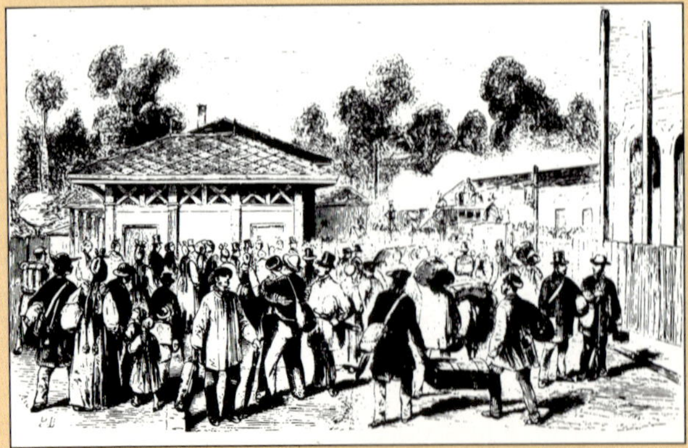

its prostitutes by putting them on ships bound for California, where they brought a certain eclat to the virtually all-male society.

The presence of French gold miners in California is witnessed by the names of mining claims: French Camp, French Corral, French Gulch, French Hills, Frenchmen's Bar, French Ravine, and Frenchtown. These miners, whose lifestyle and language were a source of merriment to the Anglos from the United States, frequently became merchants in the towns and cities of California.

Two such merchants, François Pioche and Romain Bayerque, began a general merchandise store in San Francisco. Within a couple of years, they owned large tracts of real estate. They helped finance California's first railroad and were active investors in various mining and public utility ventures. Pioche even secured French chefs to begin restaurants in California.

4. A TIME OF TROUBLE

John Geary—an ambitious politician sent to San Francisco first to act as its postmaster, then elected the last *alcalde* of the city, and in 1850, became its first mayor—gave this assessment of the city's condition in a speech:

> *At this time we are without a dollar in the public treasury and it is to be feared that the city is greatly in debt. You have neither an office for your magistrate, nor any other public edifice. You are without a single police officer or watchman, and have not the means of confining a prisoner for an hour; neither have you a place to shelter, while living, sick and unfortunate strangers who may be cast upon our shores, or to bury them when dead. Public improvements are unknown in San Francisco. In short, you are without a single requisite necessary for the promotion of prosperity, for the protection of property, or for the maintenance of order.*

By the mid-nineteenth century, many American cities had begun to feel the upheaval caused by the legions of poor immigrants that arrived at their doors. Westward expansion had created hundreds of communities with neither the homogeneity nor the settled traditions of long-established communities. Every individual was scrambling for some economic advantage that would bring him solidity, even wealth, in the expanding country.

Given San Francisco's sudden transformation from trading village to metropolis, its disparate composition, and the greed and ambition that played a large part in its creation, it is not surprising that the urban ills of the United States in the mid-nineteenth century would be *writ large* in this city.

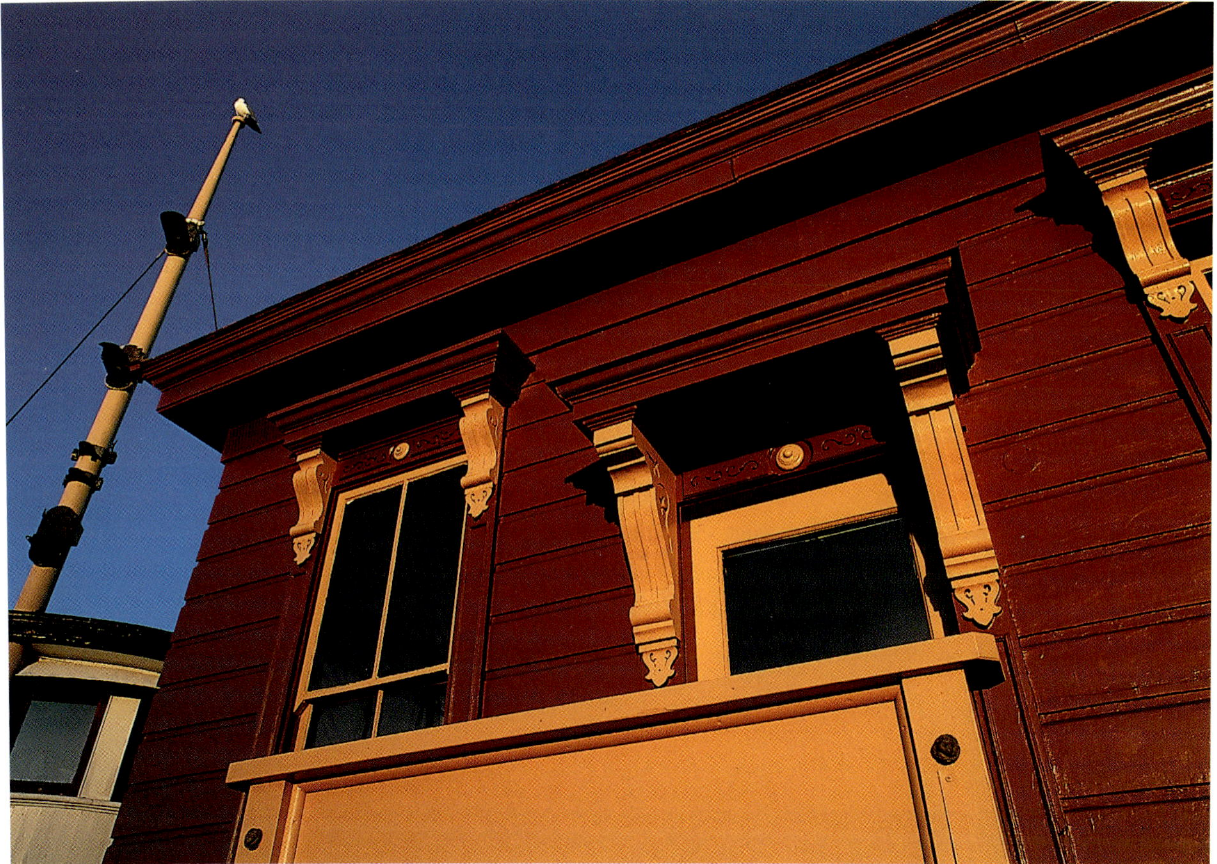

▲ *The 1850s Tubbs Cordage Building serves as an example of early San Francisco's industrial architecture.*

San Francisco did go about seeking to redress the problems enumerated by Geary, albeit in its own fashion. The city hired a couple of constables as the beginnings of a police force; it established the first city cemetery (on the site of the new Asian Art Museum in what is today the Civic Center); and it solved the problem of caring for the indigent sick by hiring Dr. Peter Smith to tend them—on whatever premises he chose to rent, on a per head, per diem basis.

When the city did not pay Smith's bills, he filed suit for payment. The city did not defend the lawsuit, and Smith was given a judgment. When the city still refused to pay, Smith proceeded to have the sheriff set up a series of auctions of city-owned lands. The "city fathers," rather than responding to the claim, asserted that such sales were illegal. Because buyers could not be certain of obtaining clear title, the land was sold for a fraction of its value. In all, during 1850 and 1851, some two thousand acres had to be sold off to satisfy Peter Smith's judgment. It should not come as too great a surprise that much of the land was purchased at those distressed prices by the same "city fathers."

Although amenities may have been in short supply, what most affected San Francisco's citizens was the constant state of turmoil, violence, and lawlessness. This might be expected in a raw frontier town in constant flux, peopled almost entirely by young males, including a number of "toughs" and criminals, far from their homes and families. It was the lust for gain that had brought them to California, an ambition that tended to subordinate all other considerations.

The first major outbreak of violence took place in midsummer 1849. Quasi-criminal groups known as the "Hounds" had been making repeated forays into a tent city of Chileans at the base of Telegraph Hill. One night, however, they destroyed the camp, beating up its denizens, looting, raping, and finally burning the tents.

Even for the violence-inured San Franciscans, this evening of rampage was excessive. Citizens rallied in Portsmouth Plaza to raise funds for the victims and recruited more than two hundred men who armed themselves and offered their services to the authorities. They formed an extrajudicial posse which rounded up those responsible for the attack, tried them, and sentenced them to fines and prison. However, lacking the means for imprisoning the criminals, they ended up letting them go.

This ineffectual attempt by San Franciscans to curb crime may have left the criminals with the impression that their deeds would go unpunished, but it also planted the idea among law-abiding citizens that such activism, if better organized, might amount to something.

An opportunity to demonstrate the validity of this idea came in 1851. The "Hounds" had been joined in their hooliganism by the "Sydney Ducks"—former prisoners from Australia. Already beleaguered by a severe economic recession and the corrupt collusion between some of the city's politicians and businessmen, the citizenry of San Francisco came to the end of its collective patience.

In February 1851, a popular merchant by the name of Jansen was set upon, beaten, and robbed. There was a flurry of protest, and a number of the victim's friends insisted that the suspects not be released (as was usual), but

▼ *Before Ghirardelli became the San Francisco chocolate king, he ran this Gold Country store in Hornitos.*

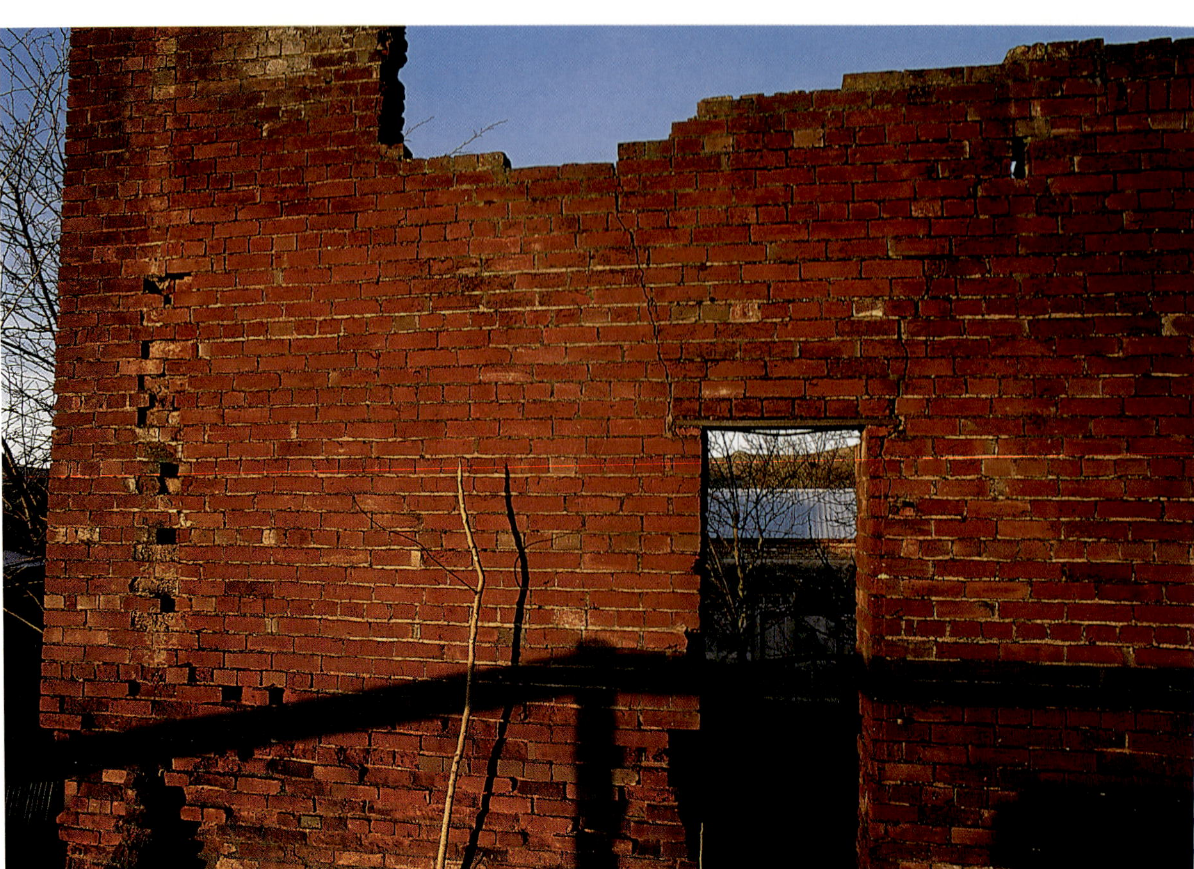

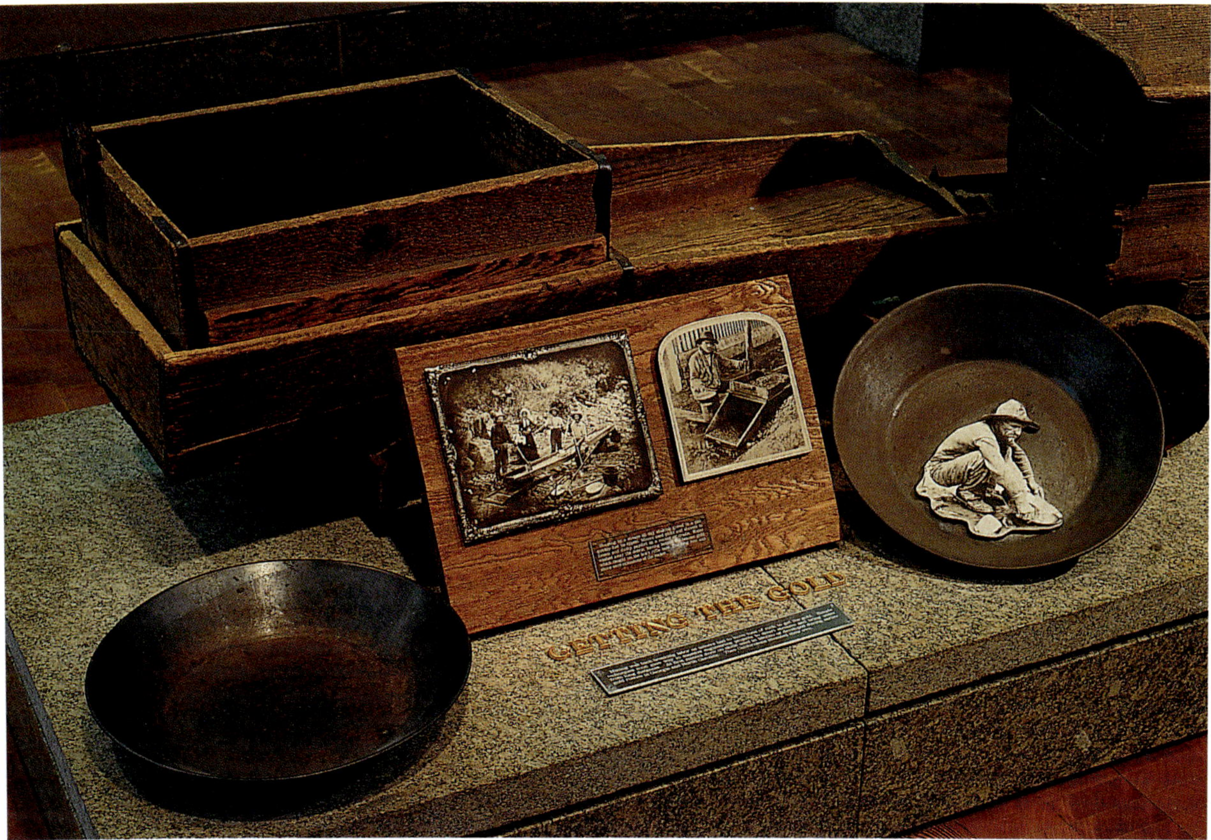

▲ *The Wells Fargo History Museum in San Francisco covers the Gold Rush era from the perspectives of banking, assaying, and transportation.*

be made to stand trial. Despite the demands, the suspects were released. But this time, they were re-arrested by a group of citizens and tried. The suspects were eventually released for lack of compelling evidence.

A few months later, more than two hundred merchants and professionals banded together to form a vigilante committee, signing articles stating that they pledged themselves to maintain law and order in San Francisco: "… we are determined that no thief, burglar, incendiary or assassin shall escape punishment, either by the quibbles of the law, the insecurity of prisons, or the laxity of those who pretend to administer justice."

This defiant challenge to the legally constituted authorities faced an immediate test. The day after these articles were signed, a burglar, John Jenkins, was apprehended by two committee members while robbing a store. He was taken to a building used by the vigilante committee on Sansome Street near Bush. The tolling of the bell at the nearby Monumental Engine Company firehouse called the committee members to the headquarters, where a trial was held and Jenkins found guilty. Led by the irrepressible Sam Brannan, the vigilantes took Jenkins to Portsmouth Plaza and hanged him from the adobe customs house.

There was considerable protest against the extra-legal activities of San Francisco's vigilante committee, but the prominent status of the vigilantes and a general opinion that the police were weak and corrupt gave it popular support. During its reign, the committee searched incoming ships for possible criminals, and those who were suspected of being such were forced to stay on board and return with the ship. The vigilantes deported others and warned lawbreakers to leave the city of their own accord. Complaints of criminal acts were investigated and suspects were

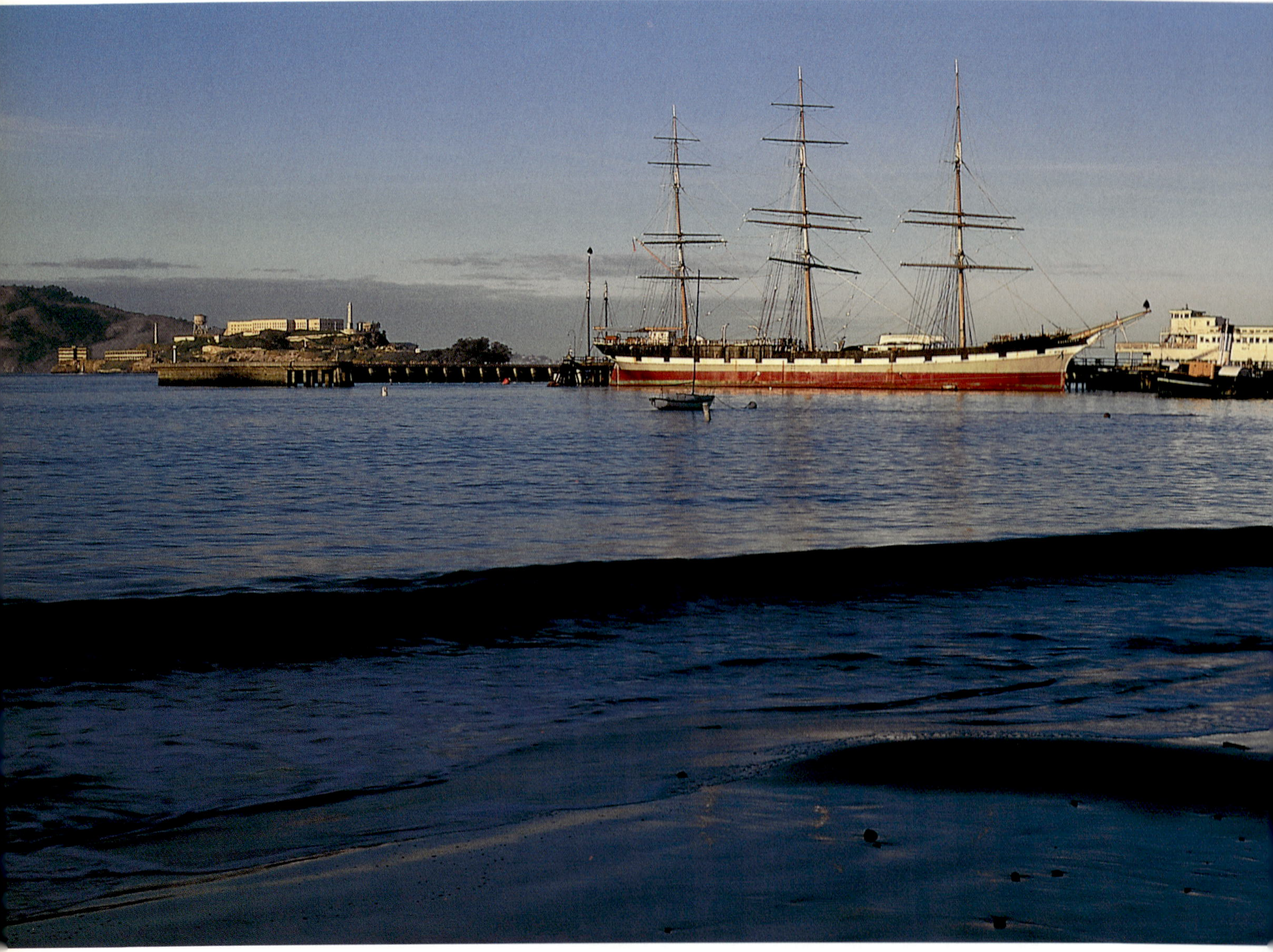

▲ *The San Francisco Maritime National Historical Park includes the Hyde Street Pier and a museum that chronicles San Francisco's Gold Rush role.*

apprehended and tried. If they were found guilty, they were fined, deported, or—in the case of John Jenkins and three others—hanged.

The vigilante committee remained in power for ten weeks. Soon after it voluntarily dissolved, political and business corruption and lawlessness returned to San Francisco. Another five years went by before a larger and more powerful vigilante committee seized the reigns of power.

Crime was not the only problem that afflicted San Francisco during the Gold Rush. Another was that plague of nineteenth-century cities—fire. San Francisco was especially vulnerable to this destructive force, for most of the city had been constructed of flimsy materials in crowded blocks, and lawless elements frequently set fires in order to distract attention from their nefarious pursuits.

Between Christmas Eve 1849 and June 1851, just a year and a half, six major fires destroyed substantial portions of San Francisco. One after another of the city's landmarks—Richardson's house, the Parker House (largest and best known of the city's hotels), the customs house on Portsmouth Plaza—were consumed by flames.

The city authorities responded by appropriating funds for digging additional wells and constructing a reservoir. They also passed laws requiring building owners to keep six buckets of water on the premises at all times, forbade the construction of buildings with canvas, and levied fines on those who refused to offer their services in fighting a fire.

With the first fire, volunteer fire companies began to organize. Such companies had been operating for many years in the major cities of the East, Midwest, and South. San Franciscans now replicated them in their own city and, until they were disbanded and a paid municipal fire department begun in 1867, they were an important social, political, and economic component in the city.

The volunteers were often men of prominence and wealth who did not stint in providing funds for elaborate firehouses and modern fire-fighting equipment. The firehouses were equipped with card and billiard tables, a library, a bar, and other recreational facilities. In masculine Gold Rush San Francisco, they became the counterpart of today's men's clubs.

The men of the fire companies went to great effort to get fellow members elected to political office; as a result, the companies became major political forces in city and state elections. Each fire company consisted of men originating from the same locale (in other words, those from New York City gravitated to the Knickerbocker Engine Company Number 5; those from Baltimore, to the Monumental). Fierce competition existed between them, leading to much of San Francisco's lore. The most famous of such stories tells of the relationship between the Knickerbocker Engine Company Number 5 and Lillie Hitchcock Coit, whose family hailed from New York. Lillie was such a fan that she would rush to fires to cheer the company on. For her loyalty, she was presented with a diamond brooch in the shape of a 5. She even had a gold fireman's hat made for herself with a number 5 stamped onto it. She died in 1929 leaving money to the city to create a memorial to the volunteer firemen—a memorial that still stands in Washington Square.

5. LIFE IN THE GOLD RUSH CITY

The pulsating, expanding city soon exceeded the boundaries that had been set in 1847, and the town council ordered the city surveyor, William Eddy, to conduct a new survey. Eddy's map extended the city to Larkin Street north of Post Street and to Leavenworth and Eighth Streets south of Post Street. Once again, the city authorized an auction to sell the newly surveyed lots.

The nineteenth-century historian of San Francisco, J. S. Hittell, wrote about the city of mid-1849:

In the summer of 1849 San Francisco was a remarkable town. It covered an area of about half a mile square, the boundaries being California, Powell and Vallejo Streets, and the water line, which for nearly a quarter of a mile south of Jackson Street was near Montgomery Street. Many of the people lived in tents and most of the remainder in shanties or mere shells of houses. The tents and shanties were in some places built along the sides of trails or roads over the hills, without regard to the lines of the streets. The hill from Vallejo to California Street above Stockton had much chaparral. There was no grading, planking, or paving in any of the streets; nor was there any wharf extending out to deep water.

The winter of 1849-1850 was an exceptionally rainy one. Horses and mules, as well as men, sank into the mud of the streets, some to die in the urban bog.

But these primitive conditions would not last long. The millions of dollars of gold dust passing through San Francisco created great affluence.

Soon, the tents and shanties gave way to substantial wooden and brick buildings. Wharves began to reach out into the cove and into the deep water, and these became very lucrative businesses for their builders and investors. Sand dunes were cut down and the sand poured into the cove, which began to fill in 1849—a process that continued for six years. The abandoned ships, beached by filling in the cove, were used for various purposes, including warehouses and even a hotel.

Postal service was inaugurated in 1849, the first bank began in 1849, and lawyers and doctors established practices. There were general merchandise stores, bakeries (one of them, Boudin Baking Company, dating from 1849, continues to make San Francisco's famous sourdough bread), blacksmith shops, boarding houses, and shops of all kinds.

Planking was laid down on the streets, and the more affluent citizens built elaborate houses on Stockton Street, just above the hurly-burly of the cove and the area surrounding Portsmouth Plaza. Stockton Street would become San Francisco's first premier residential area.

Established soon after the discovery of gold, the myriad saloons and gambling houses were at first makeshift operations, housed in tents; the gaming took place on planks placed on top of empty barrels. Twenty-four hours a day, using the light from coal oil lamps when night fell, prospectors who would soon leave for the mines or who had just come come back from them gambled steadily.

The tents were soon replaced by brick gaming halls, which were stocked with fine wines and liquor. Gaudy, lascivious paintings and elaborate furniture made up the interior decor. What money the gaming tables did not take would certainly be snapped up by the ubiquitous prostitutes.

The city's two newspapers, which had briefly suspended publication when gold fever emptied San Francisco in 1848, merged and became a daily in 1850. Many other newspapers and magazines, in the variety of languages that had been brought to the city, started up during the Gold Rush.

The newly wealthy adventurers, far from being satisfied only with work, whisky, and cards, demanded entertainment, and had the money to pay for it. The affluence gold had brought to Northern California attracted all sorts of entertainers to San Francisco and to the burgeoning boomtowns of the Mother Lode.

An assortment of entertainment, the constantly expanding repertoire of plays, and music of all sorts—including opera (first performed in 1851)—provided a rich fare for entertainment-hungry San Francisco. The first real play was performed in San Francisco in January 1850. Several theaters were built that year and the next. One of the most famous was the Jenny Lind Theater (the first of three successive Jenny Lind Theaters that were each destroyed by fire), built by impresario Thomas Maquire. A boat ride across San Francisco Bay to bucolic Oakland for picnics, excursions across miles of sand to view Seal Rocks, or a horse ride out the newly planked Mission Road to crumbling Mission Dolores to watch a bull-and-bear fight were among the entertainment options available to San Franciscans.

The peculiar demographic composition of Gold Rush San Francisco led to a very different style of life. The almost entirely male population required unusual domestic arrangements with regard to cooking and housekeeping. Living arrangements revolved around the boarding house, although owners and employees of businesses sometimes slept on their business premises.

It was these arrangements, coupled with the extraordinary affluence that gold had brought, that gave rise to San Francisco's host of restaurants. There were numerous ethnic restaurants—Chinese, Italian, French, German—

that served their communities. There were also modest establishments that served the ordinary fare expected by the United States in the mid-nineteenth century. And before long, expensive, fine restaurants with elaborate cuisines came into existence.

These multi-ethnic restaurants have served a very special function in San Francisco, aside from the purveying of food and spirits. They became the places where business deals were made, political strategies formulated, and social relationships played out. To the present day, the restaurant continues to play a prominent role in the economic, political, and social life of San Francisco.

And so began the city of San Francisco—not the steady, slow development that had characterized the older cities of the Eastern United States, but rather a chaotic, volcanic eruption that gathered energy from the vital mix of diverse peoples that flowed over its hills.

The swarming numbers, living and doing business in tents and shacks placed in the haphazard order that marked the early days of San Francisco's Gold Rush were soon better housed and conducting business in the typical narrow brick commercial buildings of the time. The abandoned ships were forgotten, sunk in the bay mud, and the cove filled in. Streets were planked and toll roads built to outlying parts of the city.

Fitfully, the wide-open, lawless town began to yield to law and order, and the institutions that brought about official law and order were established. Theaters, churches, and public buildings were constructed.

But whatever changes have taken place over the past hundred and fifty years, the city of San Francisco still derives much of its character—even today—from its beginnings as a Gold Rush boomtown.

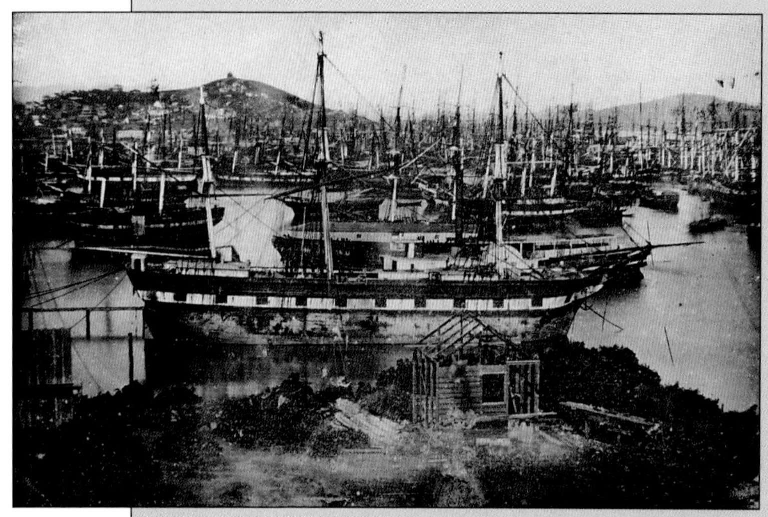

SAN FRANCISCO

Since January 1847, when Yerba Buena was renamed San Francisco, the small trading village was poised to become the principal destination for ships to Northern California. So, after the discovery of gold, gold seekers coming to California by sea landed in San Francisco. Every ship that could float was pressed into service, either for the voyage to Panama or Nicaragua or around the tip of South America.

When the ships arrived in San Francisco, passengers and crews alike disembarked. Hundreds of ships lay abandoned in the Yerba Buena Cove. Many rotted and sank in the bay mud, to be covered over when the cove was filled in between 1849 and 1855. Some of the ships were dismantled for much-needed lumber. One was used as a hotel, another as a prison ship; yet another saw service as a warehouse.

The port of San Francisco soon became the third-busiest port in the United States. Today, very little remains of its maritime preeminence.

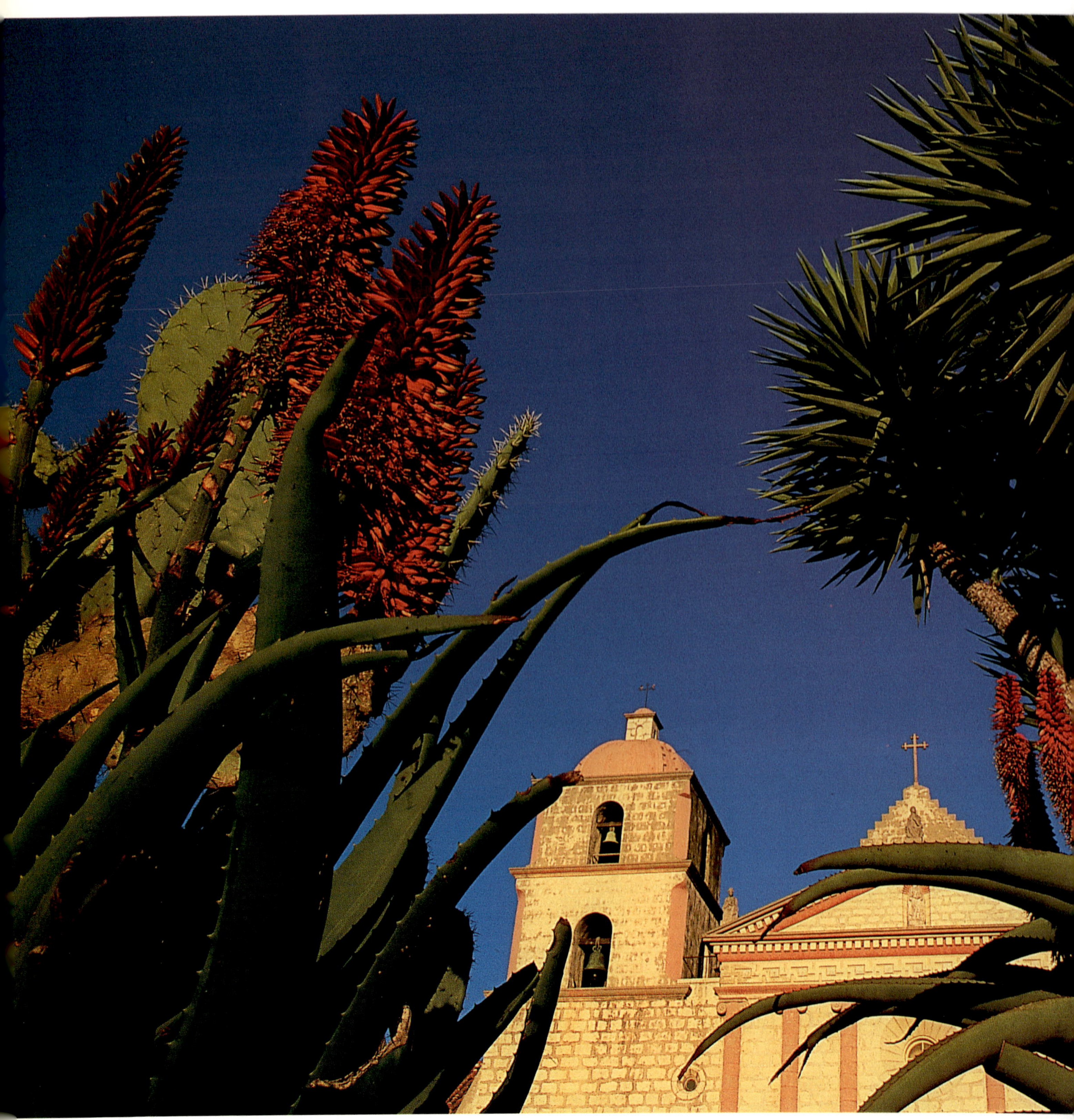

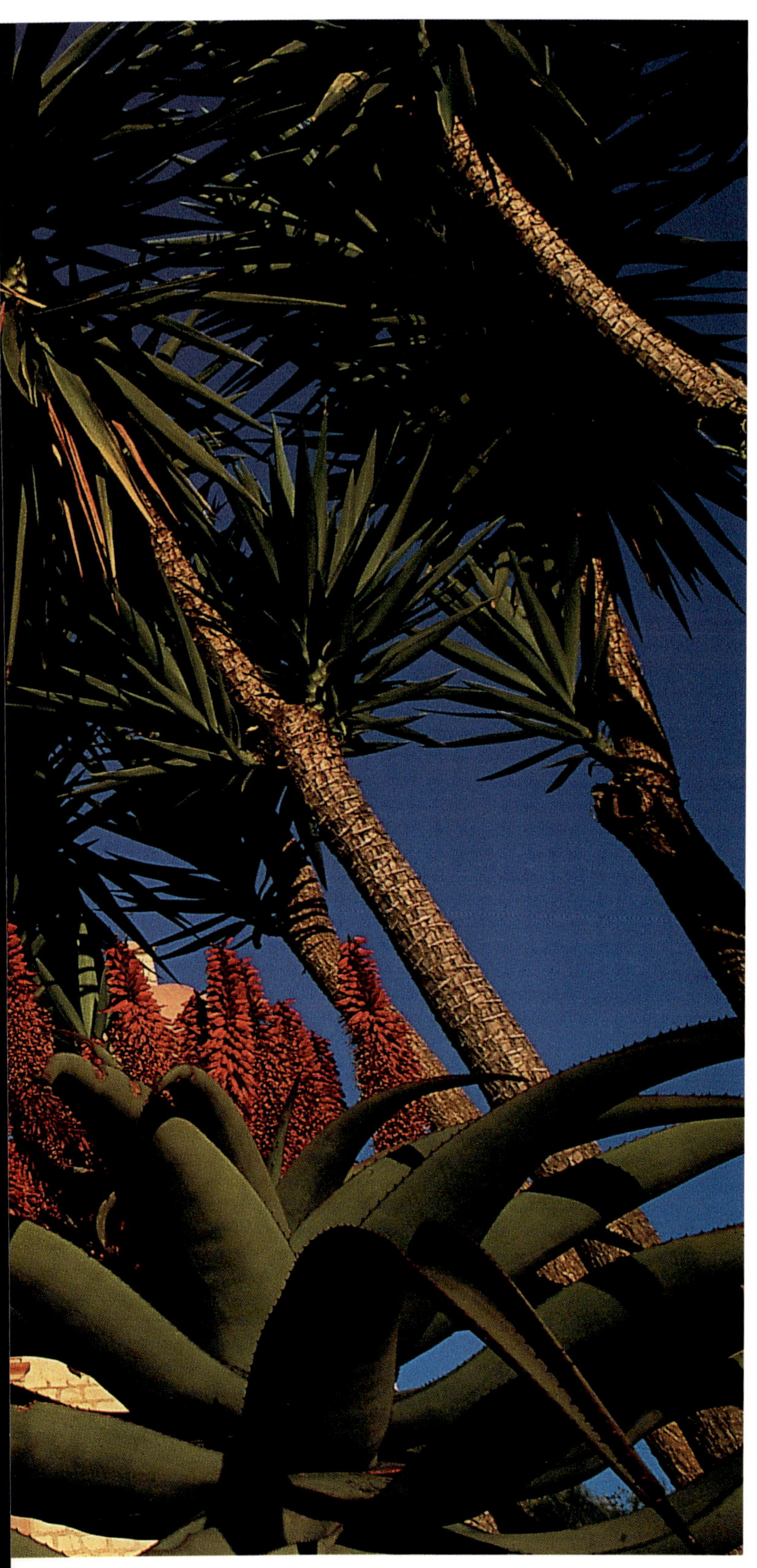

THE SOUTHLAND

4

1. NORTH VERSUS SOUTH

The sharp contrast today between Northern and Southern California was evident from the eighteenth century, when Spanish colonizers began to settle in both areas. Even after the discovery of gold brought tens of thousands of adventurers into California, turned San Francisco into a rambunctious metropolis, and saw mining camps transformed into burgeoning cities, Southern California remained a sleepy ranching and agricultural hinterland, dominated by its Hispanic traditions.

The towns and cities of Southern California today are the legacy of the original Spanish settlements: the mission, the presidio, and the pueblo. Los Angeles, the third most populous city in the nation, traces its beginnings to the creation of a pueblo in 1781. San Diego was founded in 1769 as a presidio and as a mission. Santa Barbara also began as a presidio (1782) and a mission (1786). Other missions that were sprinkled along the coast of Southern California, such as Mission San Luis Obispo and San Juan Capistrano, provided the beginnings for yet other towns.

◄ *Many Southern California cities, including Santa Barbara, show their Spanish legacy.*

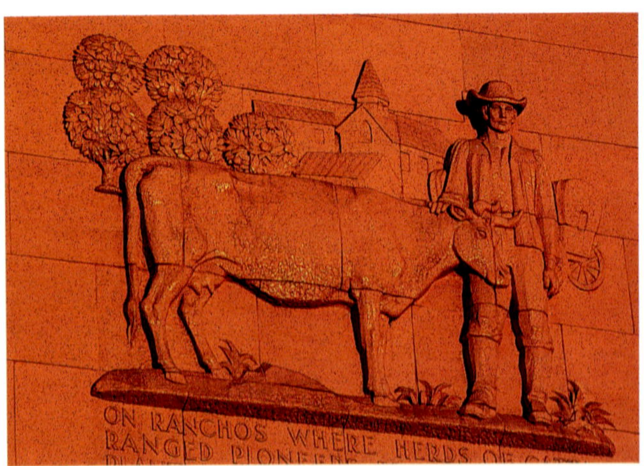

▲ *Fort Moore Pioneer Memorial in Los Angeles honors the area's ranchos and the 1847 raising of the United States flag.*
➤ *The Old Town San Diego State Historic Park displays buildings from the Mexican period and early American era.*

The on-going rivalry between the northern and southern parts of the modern state—at times feigned for amusement, at others representing the clash of real interests—dates back to the Mexican period. The rivalry centered on whether to move the capital of the province from Monterey to Los Angeles—essentially, a battle between Southerners and Northerners for political power.

With the advent of Mexican rule in the early 1820s, a new generation of Californios began to assert political and economic dominance. These were the *rancheros*, those who had received one of the huge parcels of land that had once been under the trusteeship of the missions. Beginning in the mid-1830s, these lands were confiscated from the missions and given as huge *ranchos*, or ranches, to the descendants of the Spanish soldiers who had settled in California, as well as to a smattering of Mexican colonists and a small number of foreigners (mostly British and American) who had become naturalized citizens of Mexico.

Rancho life is recorded by historians as a romantic and pastoral era, and indeed it was. Despite the background cacophony of incessant political squabbles, the rancheros led idyllic lives. They had numerous Native laborers available to work their farms and ranches. The rancheros produced large families, built gracious adobe haciendas, cultivated an elaborate hospitality for neighbors and family, and developed exquisite skills in horsemanship and other recreations.

The economic basis for rancho life during the 1830s and 1840s was the huge herds of cattle that roamed the rolling hills of Southern California. Once a year, the rancheros slaughtered cattle and prepared hides and tallow for the foreign trading vessels that sailed into the ports along the coast. The traders acquired thousands of hides to be made into leather goods and huge pouches of tallow for candles, bartering for them with manufactured goods, such as furniture and household utensils. This trade allowed the rancheros to live in simple magnificence. (The hide and tallow trade during the mid-1830s is exquisitely described in Richard Henry Dana's *Two Years Before the Mast*.)

This bucolic life began a transformation with the occupation of California during the Mexican-American War. After raising the flag in Monterey and San Francisco in July 1846, U.S. forces seized the southern towns of Los Angeles, Santa Barbara, and San Diego, overcoming Mexican loyalist resistance in each.

Gold was discovered a year later. Nevertheless, despite the influx of immigrants heading toward the gold fields, the three Southern California towns remained small and sleepy. For a time, rancho life continued as it was; its almost feudal baronial style lasted until the 1860s.

Rather early in the Gold Rush, the Northern California rancheros began to lose their land grants to squatters and to legal challenges. The rancheros of Southern California retained their holdings for another decade and a half. One reason for this difference was that Southern California was not as aggressively overrun by gringo gold seekers as was the North. But the principal reason was that Southern California's rancheros began to make substantial sums of money after the discovery of gold, allowing them to better afford the legal fees and expenses of defending the title to their

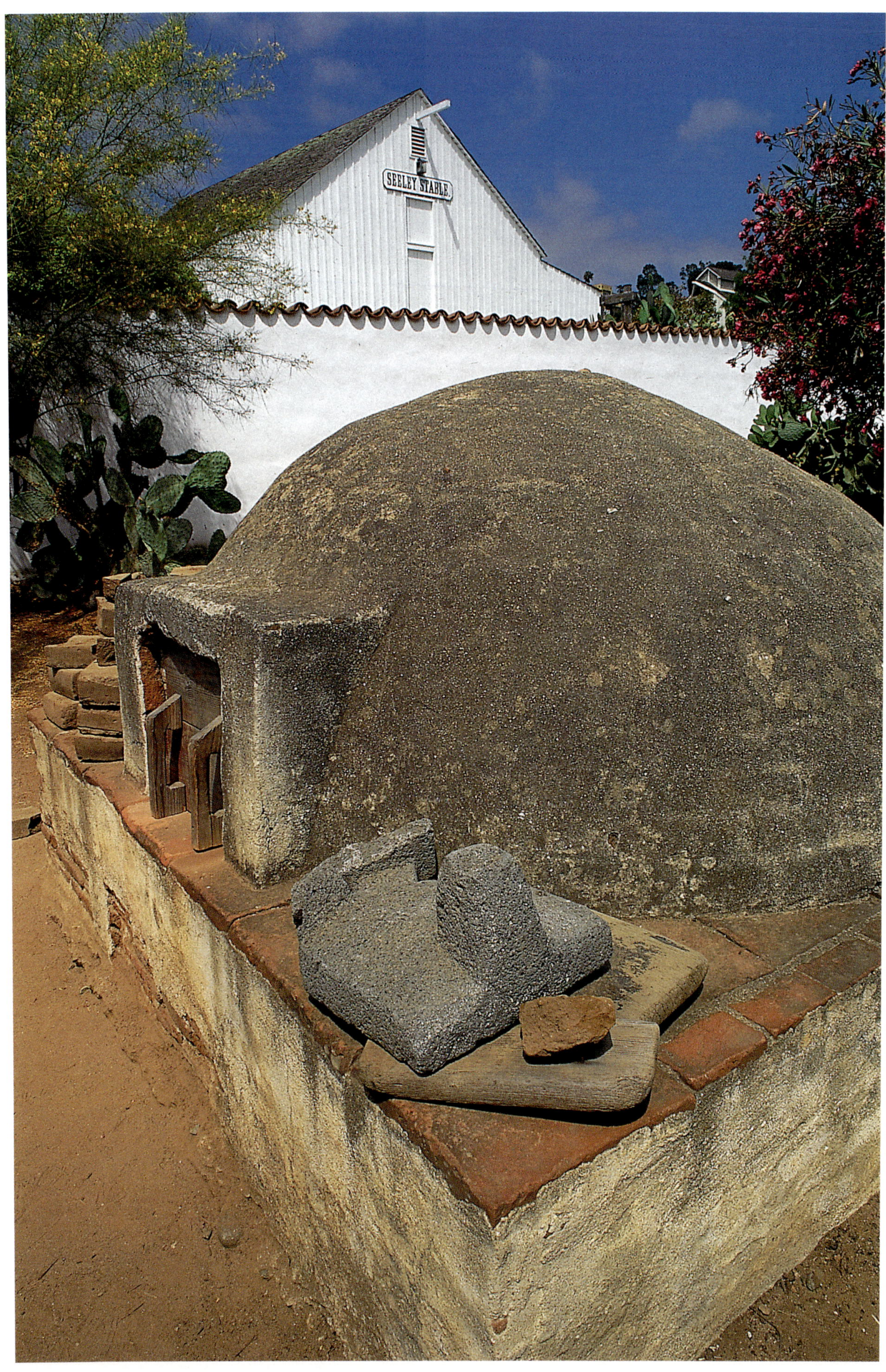

SEELEY STABLE.

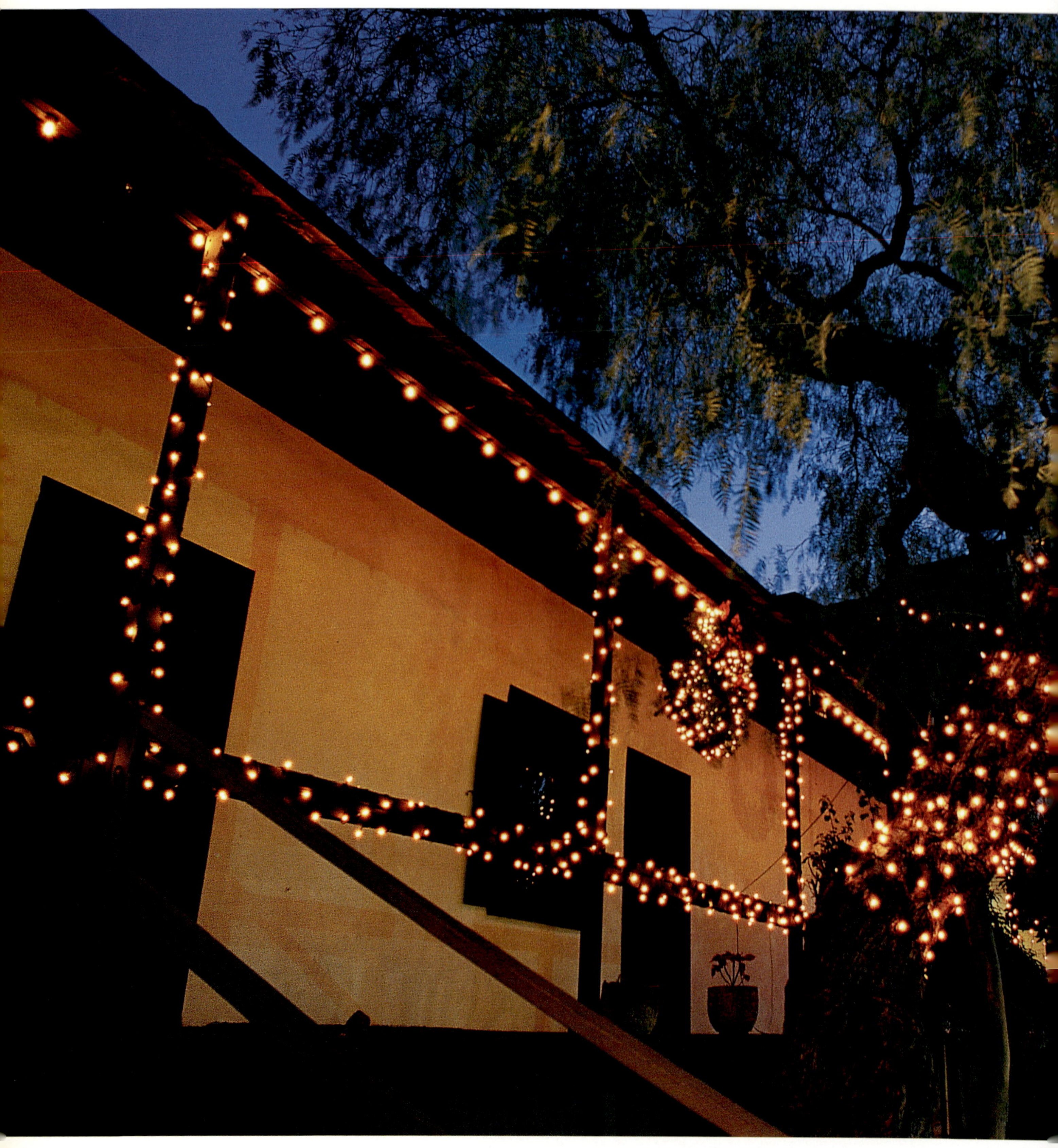

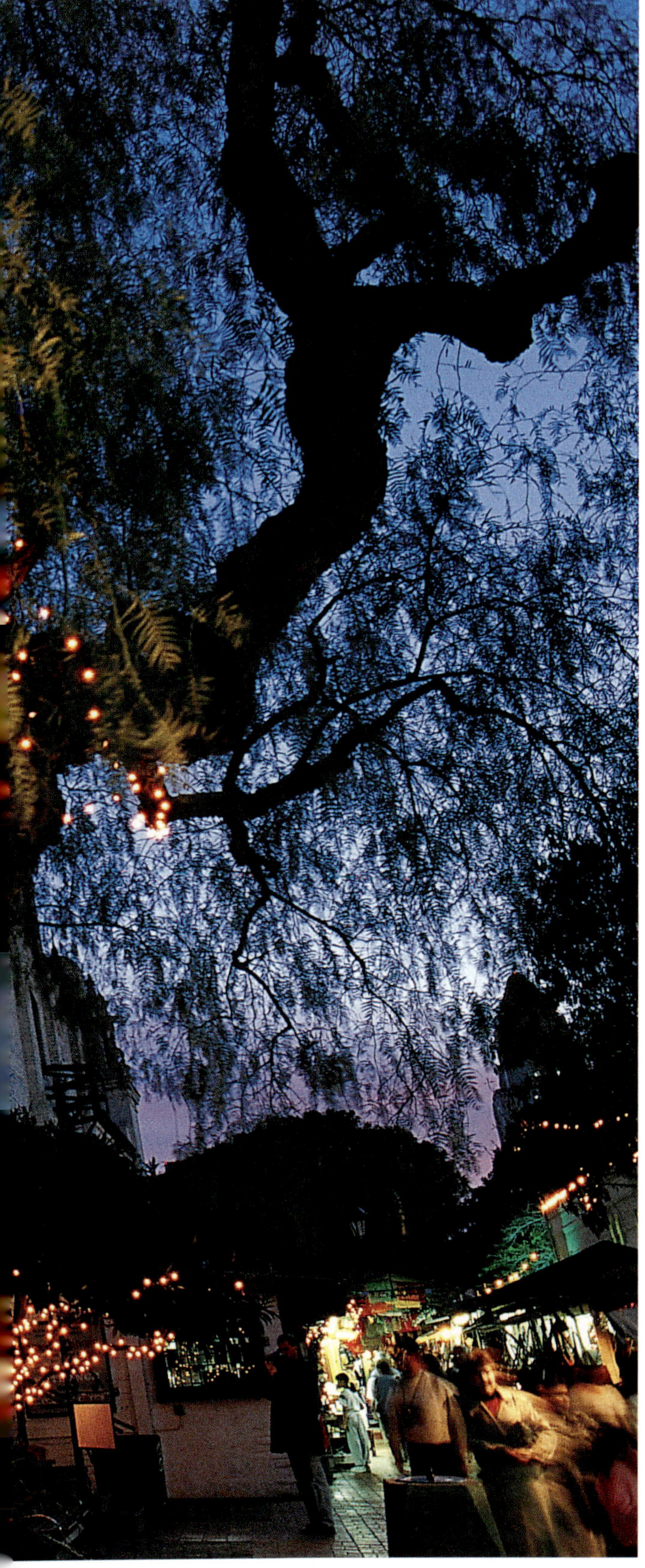

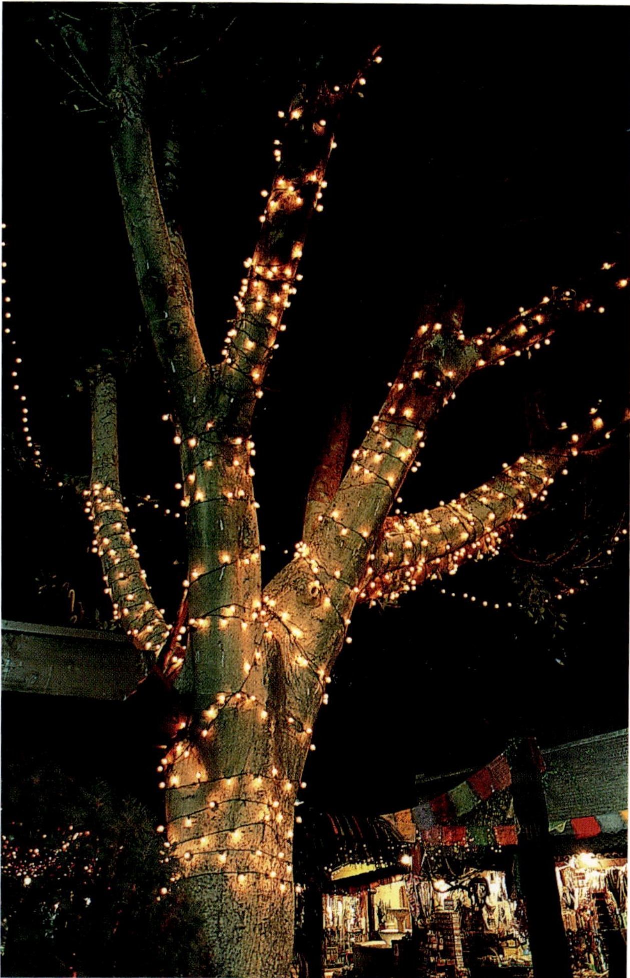

properties. The source of this substantial income was their herds of cattle.

Before 1849, cattle were valuable only for their hides and tallow. A full-grown steer seldom sold for more than four dollars. But the Gold Rush created a huge demand for beef. Not only had inflationary pressures pushed up prices for tallow and hides, the skyrocketing population's carnivorous appetite created an entirely new and profitable demand for meat.

Great cattle drives that continued until the mid-1870s brought beef up from Southern California to the north, along the coast or through the San Joaquin Valley. As Robert Glass

Cleland writes in his definitive *The Cattle on a Thousand Hills*: "In economic significance and picturesque detail, the traffic was comparable to the great cattle drives over the Bozeman Trail of Montana or the Abilene Trail of Kansas."

It cost two to four dollars a head to drive the cattle to the slaughterhouses in Northern California, where beef cattle would fetch as high as seventy-five dollars and small calves thirty to forty dollars per head.

This sudden prosperity drove the rancheros to a frenzy of spending. Their diversions became more lavish and costly. Their simple adobe houses were filled with expensive laces, carpets, and furniture. Horses wore saddles trimmed with solid silver. Spurs were made of gold; bridles, with silver chains. Betting reached extraordinary sums.

Horace Bell, whose book of reminiscences of Southern California during the early 1850s offers an intimate picture of life at that time, writes:

The streets were thronged throughout the entire day with splendidly mounted and richly dressed caballeros, most of whom wore suits of clothes that cost all the way from $500 to $1,000 with saddle and horse trappings that cost even more.... Of one of the [rancheros], I remember, it was said his horse equipment cost over $2,000. Everybody in Los Angeles seemed rich, everybody was rich, and money was more plentiful at that time, than in any place of like size, I venture to say, in the world.

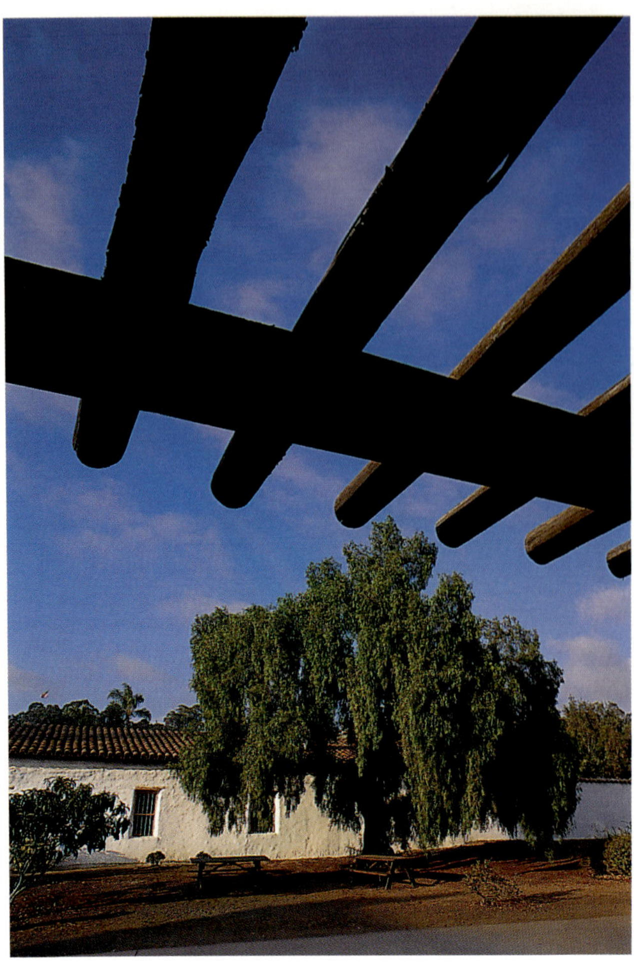

▼ *La Casa de Estudillo, in Old Town San Diego, houses a museum profiling a prominent family of the Mexican era.*

The prodigality and ostentation, the improvidence and luxury of the rancheros took its toll. They spent as if the current high prices would last forever. And if their substantial income was not sufficient to maintain their extravagant lifestyle, they borrowed from bankers and moneylenders in San Francisco. But this incredible prosperity could not last.

Seeing the profit to be made in the California trade, livestock owners in the Midwest began to drive herds of cattle into the Sacramento Valley, and in the early 1850s, the business of raising cattle for beef became well-established.

In addition, by the mid-1850s, the growth of the sheep industry in California and the importation of sheep from New Mexico led to a further decline in the profitability of the cattle trade.

The impact of paying from 3 to 10 percent interest per month on loans began to take a major toll on the rancheros. Relatively small loans, left to compound, suddenly became a huge, burdensome indebtedness that could not be shaken. Foreclosures began to reduce the holdings of land belonging to the rancheros.

Then nature added a crowning blow to the ruin of the rancheros. The winter of 1861-1862 brought disastrous flooding: it is estimated that

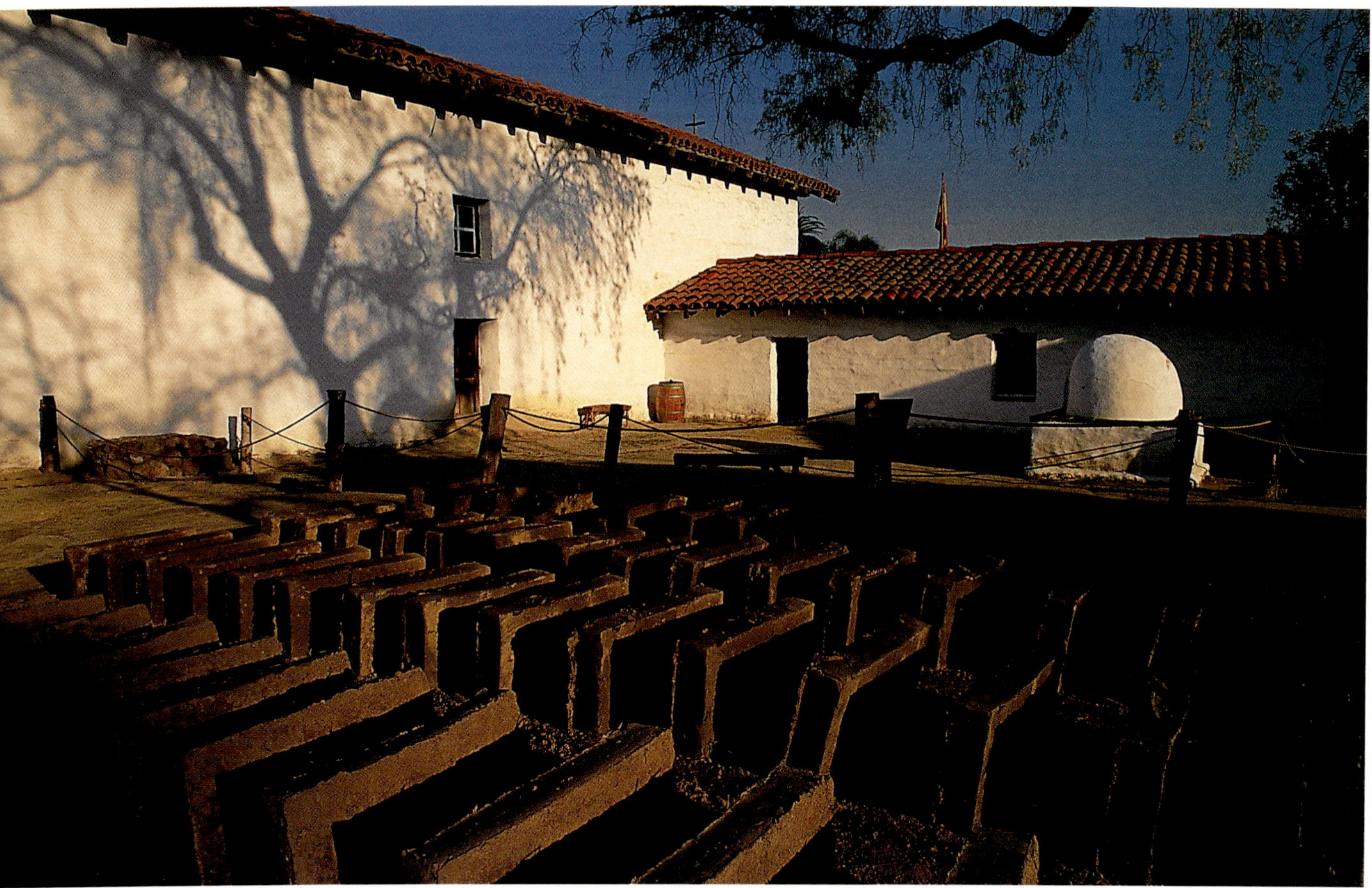

▲ *At El Presidio de Santa Barbara State Historic Park, part of the original quadrangle has been restored. Here, new adobe bricks are drying.*

some two hundred thousand head of cattle were swept away by the waters. The next two winters brought no rain, and in the resultant drought, vast herds died off. This spelled the end of the ranchos.

The ruined rancheros watched their lands fall into the hands of speculators, who divided these enormous holdings into small parcels. The end of this romantic period ushered in the land boom of the 1880s, the subsequent rise of citrus agriculture, the influx of immigrants, and the eventual wealth of Southern California.

2. LOS ANGELES

Today's sprawling city of Los Angeles bears no resemblance to the modest roots of its beginnings in 1781, when forty-four colonists from Mexico established the second of three officially sanctioned pueblos in Spanish California.

The town, dedicated to Our Lady Queen of the Angels, was established on the Porciúncula River by a group of settlers who had volunteered to migrate to this newest of Spain's provinces. As incentives for them to establish the new town, the settlers were provided, by royal authority, with cash bonuses, a freedom from taxes, and with the provisions necessary to begin life on this frontier.

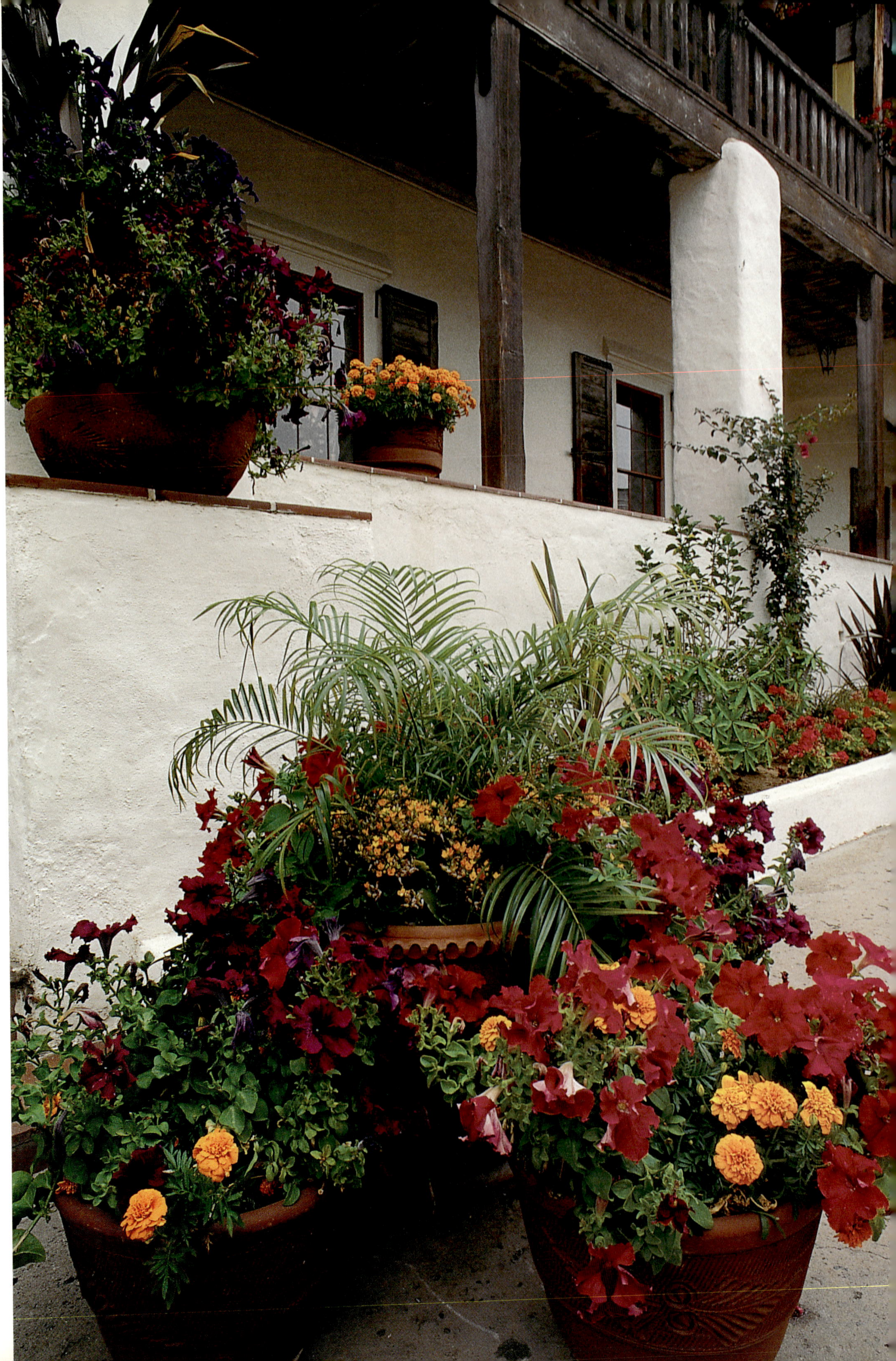

The colonists built tile-roofed adobe homes, a town hall, a chapel, barracks, guardhouse, and granaries around a plaza—all surrounded by an adobe wall. Outside the wall, each resident owned an agricultural plot; and other land was held for the communal use of the town.

The romantic haze that surrounds California's Spanish-Mexican period cannot hide the reality that the pueblo was a windy, dirty settlement with sewage and refuse rotting in its unpaved streets. It was a primitive, insignificant village during its four decades under Spanish rule.

The village grew slowly during Mexican rule. When the wholesale granting of ranchos began in the mid-1830s, Los Angeles was raised to the status of a *ciudad,* or city, and became the urban and commercial center for the surrounding ranchos. In 1845, it became the capital of California—an honor it would retain only during that last year of Mexican rule.

This town provided the most organized and assertive resistance to U.S. occupation. After Commodore Stockton and Captain Frémont had peacefully occupied Los Angeles, they departed, leaving a naval officer by the name of Archibald Gillespie in charge. Gillespie infuriated the *Californios* by enforcing unnecessarily strict regulations on the populace. The outraged citizens besieged Gillespie and his forces until the U.S. occupying troops were forced to surrender and march out of town. An expeditionary force under General Stephen Watts Kearny was also defeated at San Pasqual.

Stockton, Frémont, and Kearny regrouped their troops and marched back into Los Angeles. Their combined forces proved too strong for the insurgents, and the Californios capitulated in January 1847, putting an end to the hostilities.

Then, in 1848, the sleepy town began to wake up, after news of the discovery of gold began to spread. Gold seekers from the Mexican state of Sonora streamed northward, but many got no farther than Los Angeles, where they settled around the plaza. With these new settlers, the small town was infused with a lawlessness it had not known before. Added to these troublemakers were members of a regiment known as the New York Volunteers, sent to California to participate in the Mexican-American War and mustered out in Los Angeles in September 1848.

Gambling, drinking, carousing, and debauchery characterized the adobe-built town. "Mountebanks, cockfights, and liquor shops are to be seen in all directions," wrote one observer in March 1849. "A Californian is a rare sight now on the streets. You never see them parading about on their fine horses as formerly."

The proliferation of crime in the town was so troubling that citizens formed a vigilante group—the Los Angeles Rangers—in 1853. The Rangers had some effect on the town's *desperados*, but violence continued to plague Los Angeles until the 1870s.

Urban violence was mirrored throughout the countryside of Southern California: cattle rustling, horse stealing, robberies, murders, and beatings were endemic in the sparsely populated southern part of the state.

Even after U.S. occupation, Los Angeles—unlike San Francisco, whose phenomenal growth had been fueled by the Gold Rush—retained its Hispanic appearance and traditions. When the city was incorporated by the state legislature, a coterie

◄ *Old Town San Diego preserves adobes like La Casa de Bandini, as well as other historical sites.*
▼ *This romanticized California mission scene adorns a stagecoach at Old San Diego's Wells Fargo Museum.*

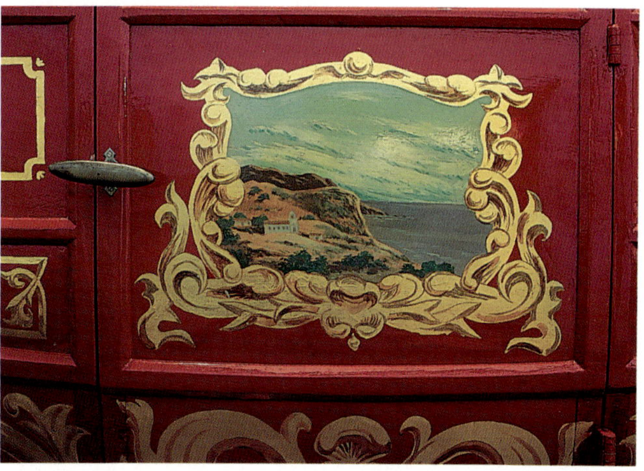

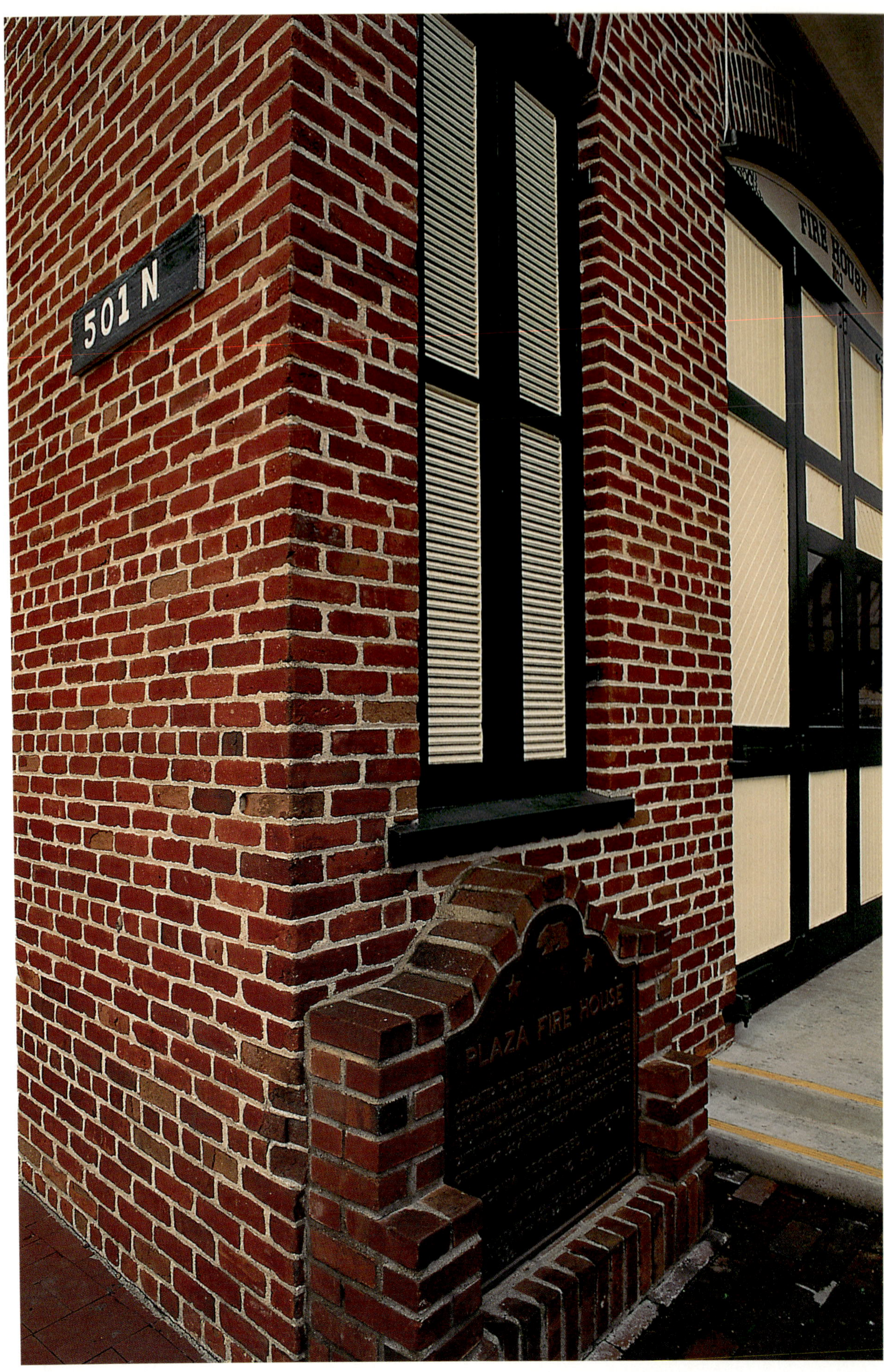

501 N
FIRE HOUSE
PLAZA FIRE HOUSE

of Californios continued to hold the reins of political power. In addition, economic power belonged to them as the result of the surge in prices paid for their cattle.

The political dominance of Los Angeles during the last years of Mexican rule evaporated after United States occupation. The discovery of gold in the northern part of the state provided that region with a substantial population and political power. As a result, the burden of taxation was placed disproportionately on the agrarian south with their enormous holdings of land—an injustice that early-on led Southern Californians to press for a division of the state.

This partition movement lasted as a viable political movement only until the early 1860s, when the Civil War put an end to any interest the federal government had in entertaining the proposal created by the California legislature to divide the state.

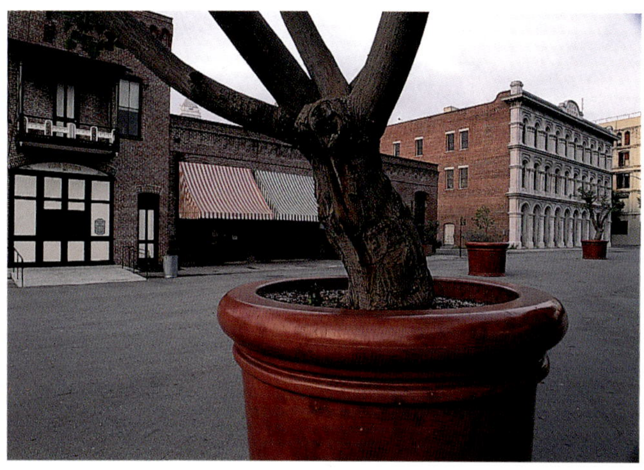

◀ *The Plaza Firehouse stands in El Pueblo de Los Angeles, a tribute to the ethnic groups that built the city.*
▲ *Mexican California's last governor, Pio Pico, built the Pico House (far right) in 1870 in El Pueblo de Los Angeles.*

Changes were wrought slowly in the settlement of Los Angeles. The plaza area deteriorated. This center of the town's Hispanic past, with its bull and bear fights, its Corpus Christi processions, its fiestas and fandangos, did not survive the collapse of the cattle boom. Gradually, the town moved away from the area, leaving behind a slum. Many years would pass before the buildings that remained would be rehabilitated and the plaza revitalized as an urban attraction. By then, the once sleepy center of life in Southern California had become transformed beyond all recognition.

3. SAN DIEGO

Two towns—one to the south of Los Angeles, the other to the north—vied for the position of "number two" town in California's southland. One was San Diego; the other, Santa Barbara. The towns had similar beginnings—as mission and presidio settlements in Spanish California.

San Diego—called by Father Junípero Serra the "Mother Mission" of California—was the 1542 landing point of Juan Rodriquez Cabrillo, the first European to set foot on California soil. The Spanish explorer, Vizcaino, also landed there some six decades later.

In 1770, when Monterey was established as the capital of the new colony, San Diego's mission was charged with evangelizing the Natives of the colony's most southern part, and the presidio guarded its excellent bay. The Natives were, however, unsubmissive and more influenced by the tribes of the interior than by the missionaries. Periodic uprisings were to plague the mission and the presidio for many years.

Shortly after the secularization of mission lands, San Diego was made a pueblo (1835). But this municipal status lasted for only three years until it was decided that the size of its population did not warrant the designation. In 1838, San Diego was made part of the subprefecture of Los Angeles. In 1841, when the first bishop of California arrived in what was to be the seat of his diocese, he found only 150 people in San Diego and moved to Santa Barbara.

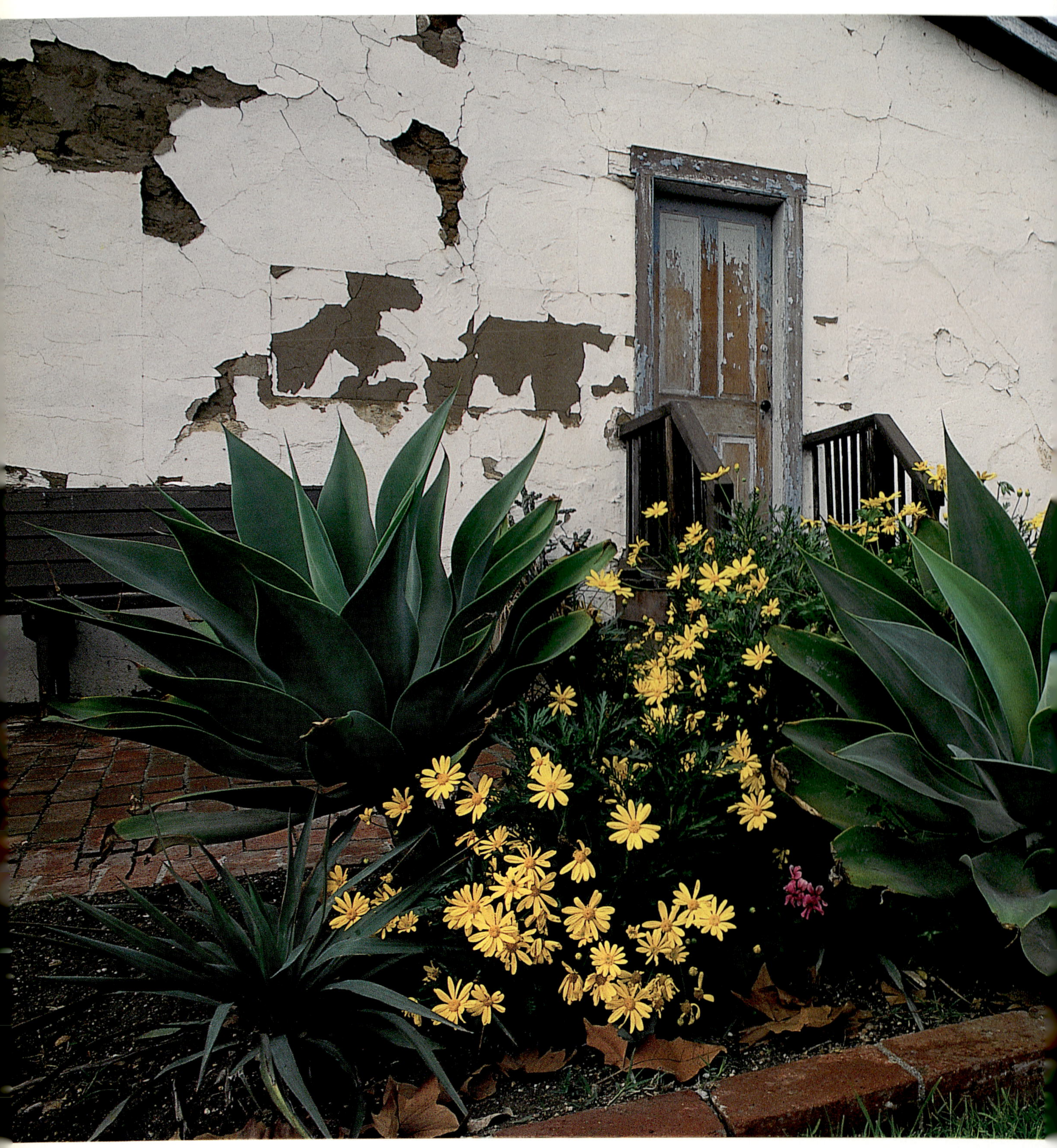

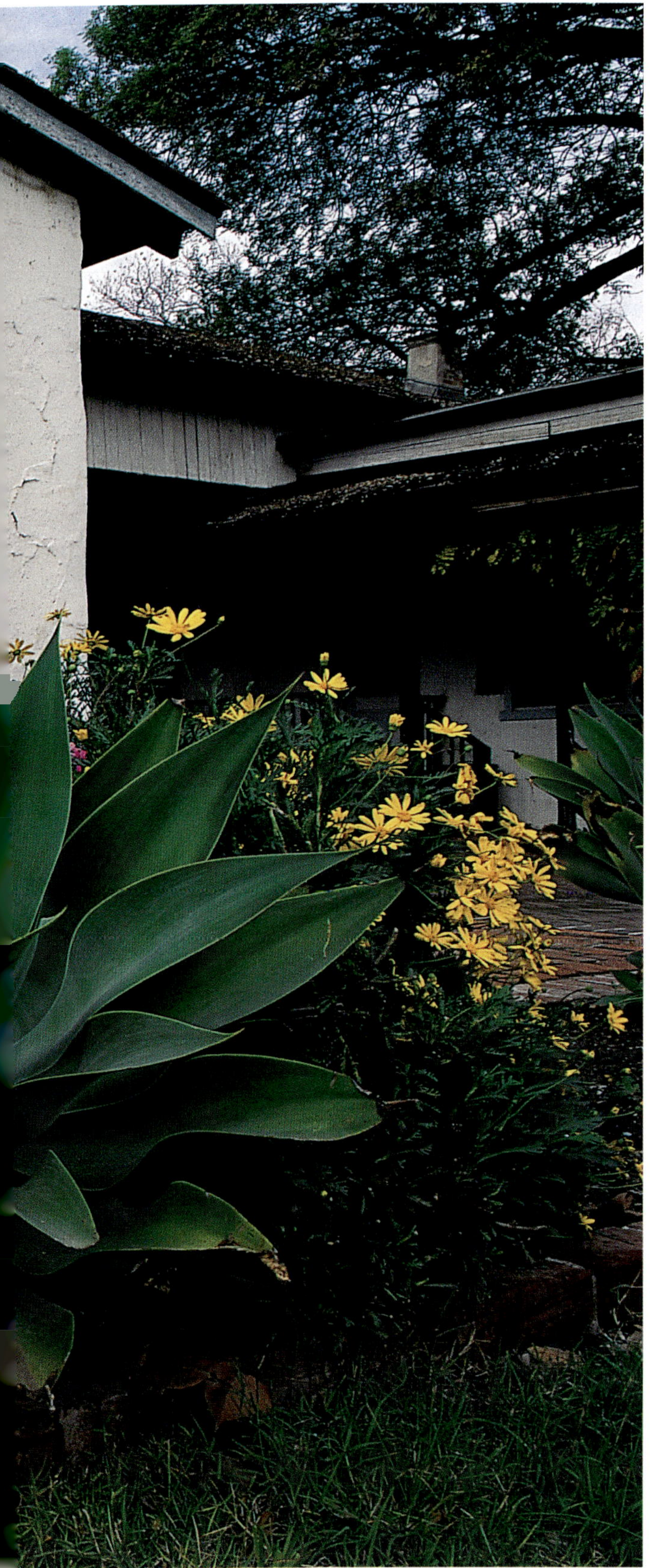

In 1846, Mexican rule ended, and Captain Samuel F. du Pont, U.S.N., raised the United States flag in San Diego; but, as in Los Angeles, there was a Californio counterattack before the town was permanently secured. The U.S. military presence was enhanced by the arrival of the Mormon Battalion in 1847.

When gold was discovered in the north, San Diego shared the boom-and-bust experience common to Southern California's towns. At first, there was every sign that San Diego would enjoy permanent prosperity. San Diego had one resource that could sustain it during the slump of the cattle business—a good harbor.

In 1849, the Pacific Mail Steamship Company began service to San Diego. The rancheros' prosperity stimulated economic activity at the pueblo—called Old Town. In 1850, San Francisco merchant William Heath Davis began a rival settlement on San Diego Bay called New Town. About the same time, an immigrant to San Diego, Agoston Haraszthy, participated in the founding of Middle Town—a settlement, as the name suggests, between Old Town and New Town.

In 1851, the Indians around San Diego again began to grow restive. These Native Americans, who had once enjoyed the protection and security of the missions, despite the drawbacks for them, were in effect disinherited with the end of that system. Outside of the mission system, they saw their lives and way of life threatened by the increasing stream of white settlers in the area and the contempt these settlers showed for them.

Antonio Garra, a Native American, attempted to unify the various tribal groups to destroy the whites in and around San Diego. His group of rebels massacred a number of travelers and settlers in outlying farms and threatened San Diego. But the uprising collapsed when various military and civilian forces captured the ringleaders, including Garra, and executed them.

The Native uprising was not San Diego's only problem with law and order. Criminals, drifters, disaffected Native Americans, and hooligans kept San Diego and the surrounding area in constant uproar. Murders, robberies, beatings,

◄ *Pio Pico State Historic Park in Whittier commemorates Pico and his prosperous Gold Rush-era rancho.*

MINERS

The formal pose of the miners in the adjoining photograph belies their difficult lives. After a long, expensive, often dangerous journey, the miner had to search out a place where he might find gold. Supplies were hard to obtain and very expensive. He worked six days a week, toiling at tedious, back-breaking work in the hot sun and the cold streams of the Sierra Nevada.

In most cases, his efforts were for naught. Most miners barely found enough gold to buy the basic necessities for existence. A good many miners lost their health, and some, their lives.

Some of the gold seekers would spend many years trying to fulfill their dreams of wealth; others returned to their homes; and still others decided to stay in California to engage in occupations other than gold-mining.

Few gold seekers found the gold that had brought them to California. Most suffered loneliness, sickness, hard work, and disappointment. But many former miners eventually turned their hands to other business ventures, continuing to seek their fortunes in the Golden Land.

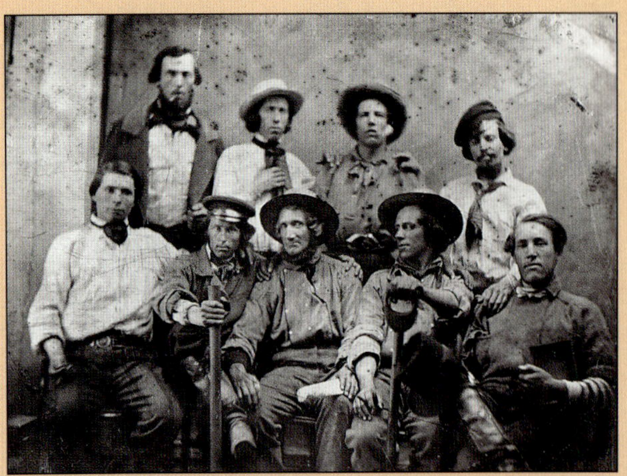

cattle and horse stealing became everyday affairs in both the town and outlying ranches.

The town of San Diego did not fulfill the hopes of its promoters. The town's first newspaper, the *Herald,* began publication in 1851, foretelling great prosperity and growth for San Diego. Nine years later, shadowing the collapse of the regional economy, it ceased publication.

Surveys for a railroad indicated that San Diego was too "hemmed in" to become the terminus for the West. Politics and practicalities dissuaded the stagecoach line to the east from utilizing San Diego. The whaling industry, which began to grow in the early 1850s, providing a temporary boost, died out after several years. Buildings in New Town were abandoned; the wharf there was torn out for its planking.

Many years would elapse before the constellation of circumstances would occur that would shape San Diego into one of California's largest and most thriving towns.

4. SANTA BARBARA

There are certain similarities between the historical experience of San Diego and that of Santa Barbara. Both were visited in 1542 by Juan Rodriquez Cabrillo, and in the early seventeenth century by Vizcaino. Both had their inception as a Spanish colonial presidio and a mission. Both settlements were surrounded by many large cattle ranches and served as the center for a society comprised of both Hispanic and Anglo-American rancheros.

After Commodore Stockton sailed into the town as part of the United States conquest of 1846, Santa Barbara threw out the small band of soldiers positioned there; but Frémont recaptured the town shortly thereafter without firing a shot.

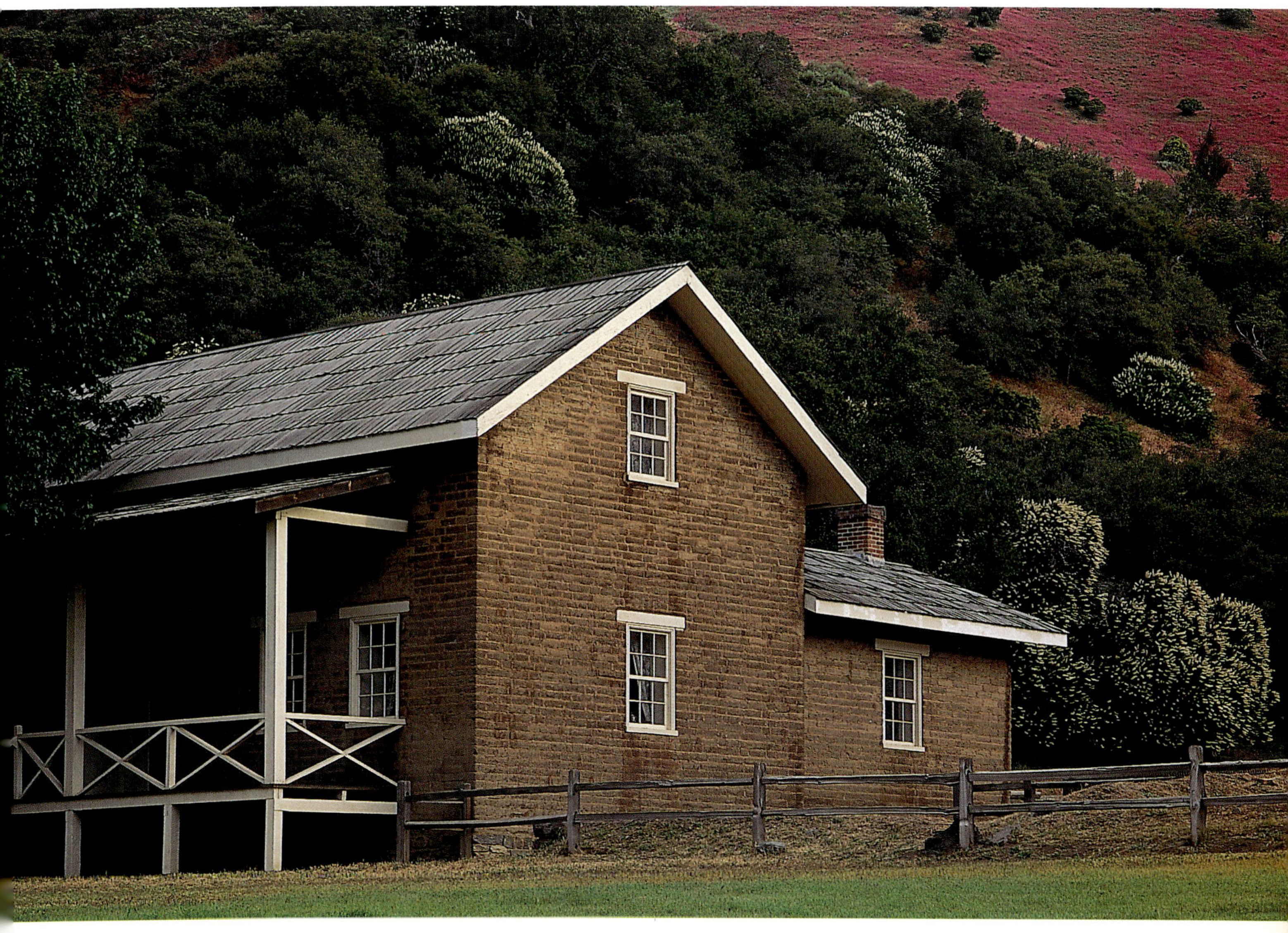

But Santa Barbara's history was a more tranquil one than that of either San Diego or Los Angeles. It has been claimed that its population during the Mexican period was more refined and elegant than that of the other two cities. The fact that the first bishop of California, Francisco Garcia Diego y Moreno, made his residence at Mission Santa Barbara insured that the mission was maintained even after secularization.

Today, Santa Barbara is one of the most beautiful cities in California. Its carefully preserved and burnished Hispanic heritage, its exquisite weather, and the gleaming houses and manicured gardens of its generally well-off residents combine to imbue the area with a sense of well-being. It is difficult to imagine that this was once second in population only to Los Angeles among Southern California towns, and that during the Mexican period its port bustled with trade that centered on the hides and tallow produced by enormous herds of cattle.

No industry and only a slight hint of any commercial activity stirs in Santa Barbara today. Little of the raucous nature of Los Angeles or San Diego marred Santa Barbara during the Gold Rush, and virtually none of the urban problems common to the other cities afflicts it today. Without the ferocious dynamism of Los Angeles or the successful latter-day boosterism of San Diego, Santa Barbara has retained the flavor of California's pastoral rancho past.

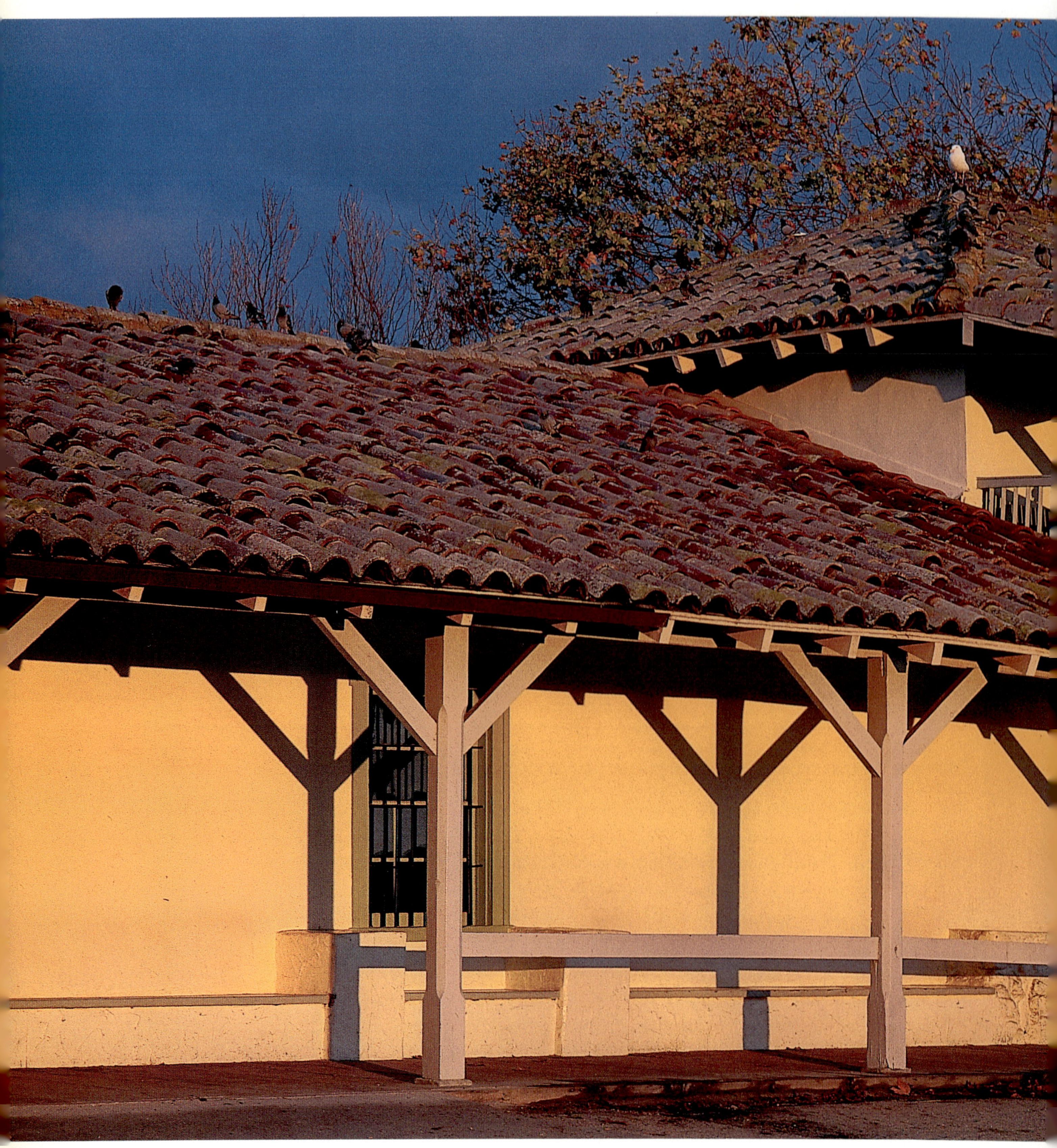

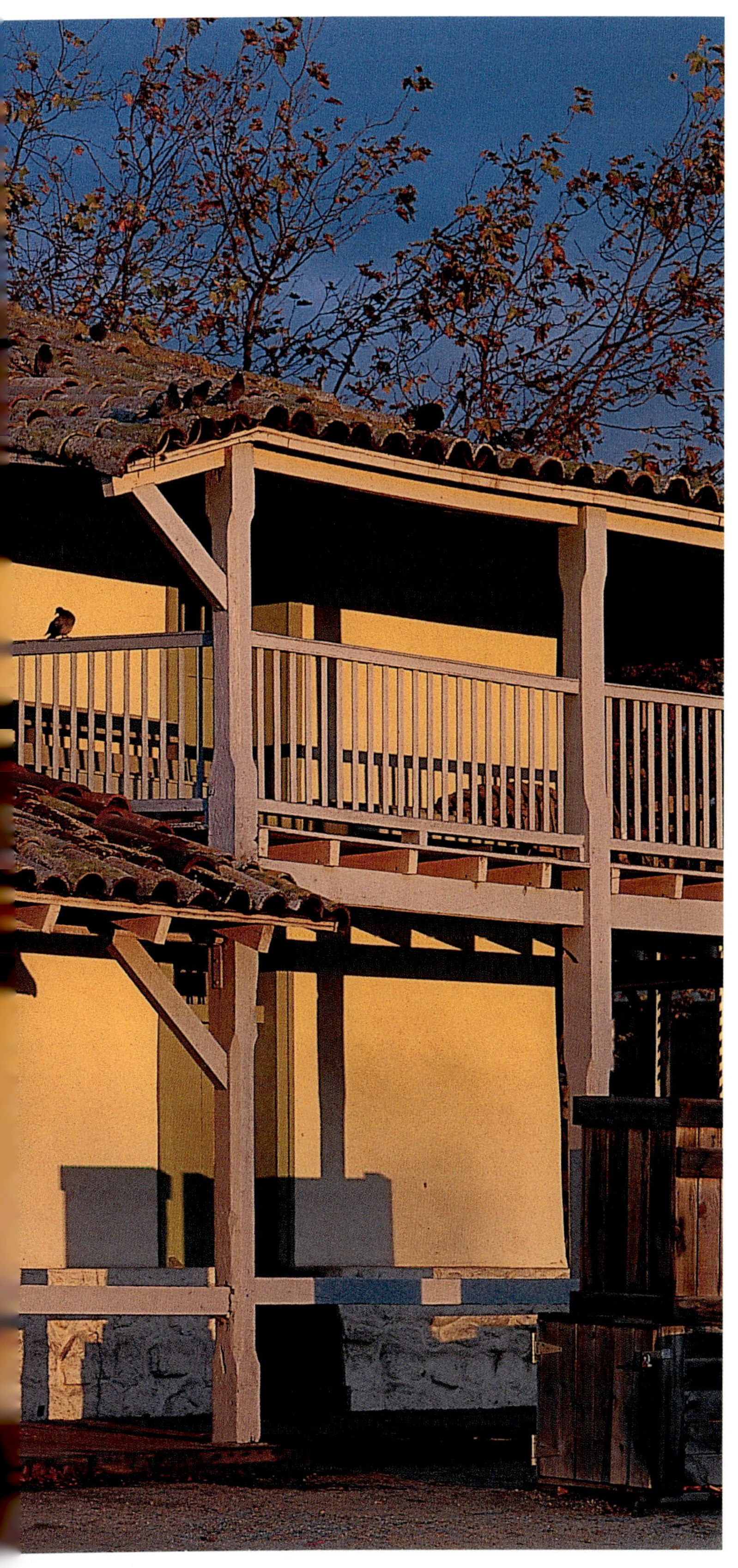

MONTEREY AND STATEHOOD

5

1. THE CONSTITUTIONAL CONVENTION

In the fog-shrouded town of Monterey in early September 1849, forty-eight men gathered to compose a state out of the vast, diverse territory of California. They met in a building named after the first *alcalde* of the U.S. period, Walter Colton, who had constructed it in 1847 as a one-story town hall. Now, a second story had been added to accommodate the delegates who had come together to deliberate on what shape the government of California should take.

In 1849, Monterey was still the administrative capital of California, as it had been since 1770 (and in 1775 became the capital of both Alta and Baja Californias). The Gold Rush had created larger cities to the north, but Monterey had retained its quiet charm, its combined Hispanic and Anglo-American composition, and its position as the seat of government.

Monterey's selection as the capital of Spain's new colony in 1769 stemmed from Vizcaino's exaggerated evaluation of Monterey Bay in his 1602-1603 explorations of California's coast. In 1770, a presidio and a mission were established

◄ *Monterey was California's capital under Spanish, Mexican, and early United States rule.*

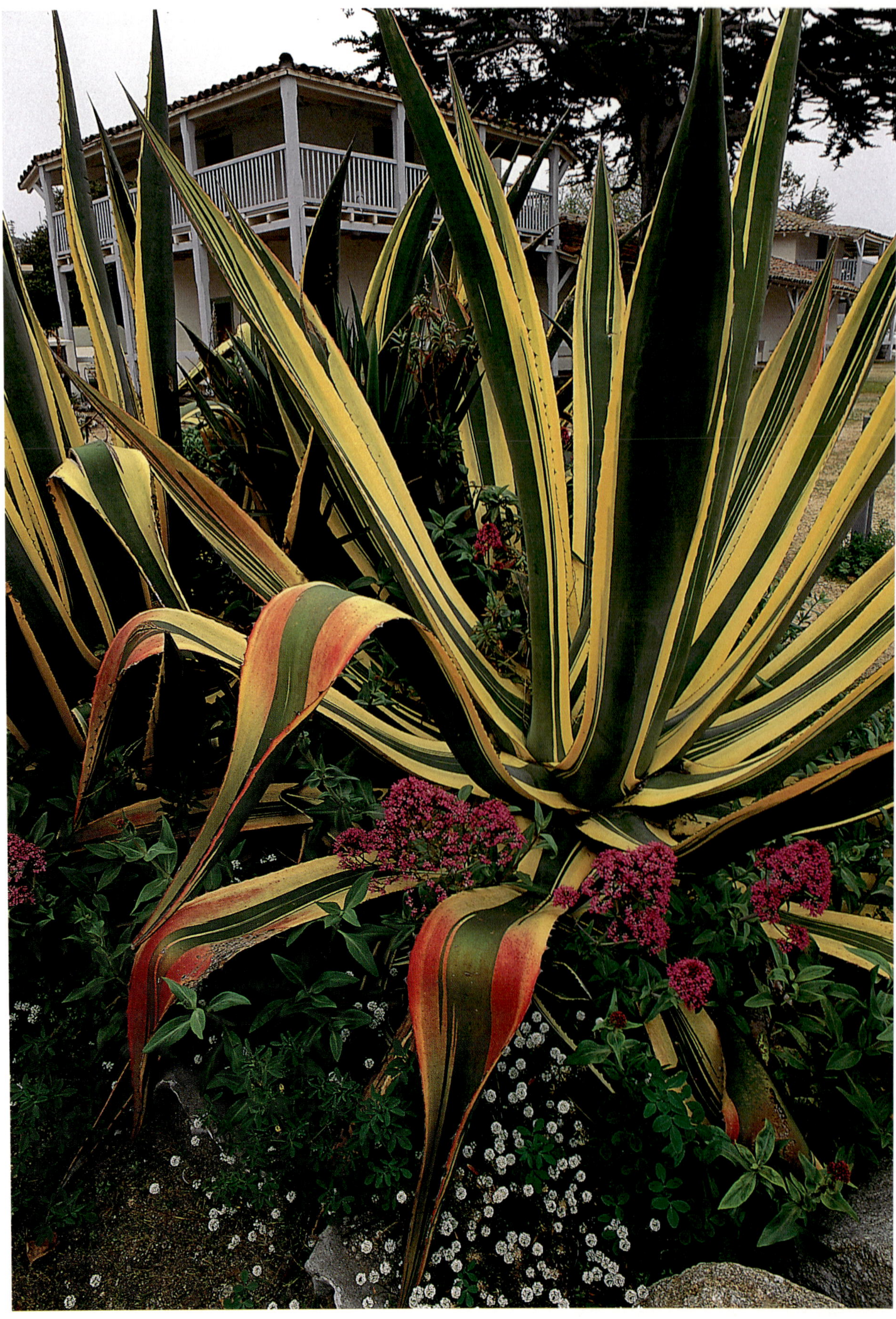

on Monterey Bay. (Shortly thereafter, the mission, San Carlos Borroméo was moved a few miles south to Carmel Bay.) It was from here that the slow growth of Spanish California was directed.

In 1818, the town was seized, looted, and burned by Hippolyte Bouchard, a French-born privateer operating for the insurgent Argentinians who revolted against Spanish rule.

In 1821, California became part of the new republic of Mexico, and its governance emanated from Monterey. An increase in international trade, more foreign immigration into California, and the granting of ranchos brought changes to Monterey, as they did to all of California under the brief period of Mexican rule.

Mexico's tenuous hold on the territory was demonstrated in 1842, when Commodore Thomas Catesby ap Jones, U.S.N., under the misapprehension that Mexico and the United States had gone to war, seized Monterey. The naval officer, embarrassed but unpunished by his government, left with an apology a few days later.

Four years later, war did break out, and Monterey was seized for the United States in July 1846 by Commodore Sloat. But Monterey's days of power were numbered. A report by Lieutenant Edward Gilbert the following year compared the old capital to the upstart trading village of San Francisco:

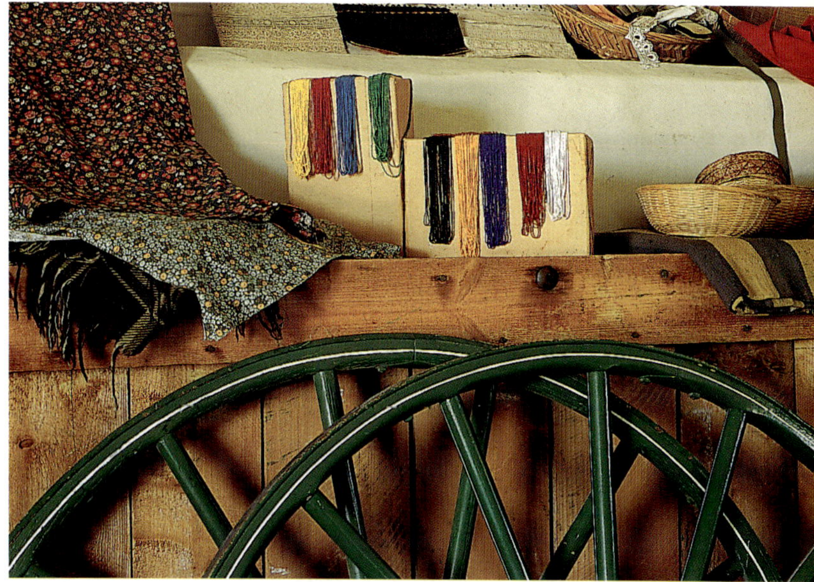

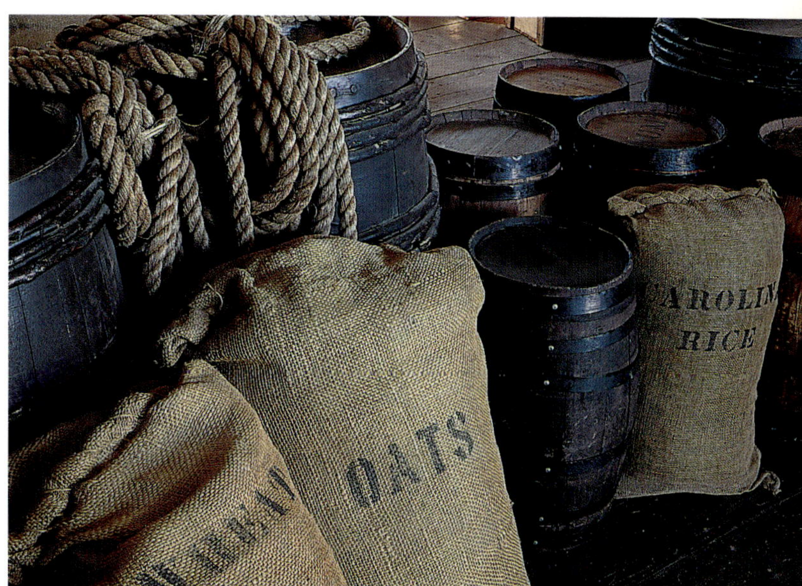

◄ *The Custom House is where Commodore John Sloat raised the American flag, claiming California for the U.S.*
▲ ▲ *The Custom House Museum in Monterey depicts artifacts of California's oldest government office.*
▲ *All supplies coming through Mexico's California port of entry were checked at the Custom House.*

In conclusion I cannot suppress a desire to say that San Francisco is destined to become the great commercial emporium of the North Pacific coast. With the advantages of so hearty and intelligent a race of pioneers, it can scarcely be otherwise. Notwithstanding these conclusions.... I have heard it said that Monterey is destined to outstrip it. That Monterey can never surpass San Francisco, I think the following will clearly establish:

1) San Francisco has a safer and more commodious harbor than Monterey;

2) The waters of the bay afford an easy method of communication and ... transportation between the town and the hundred lateral valleys, which are destined soon to become granaries and hives of plenty;

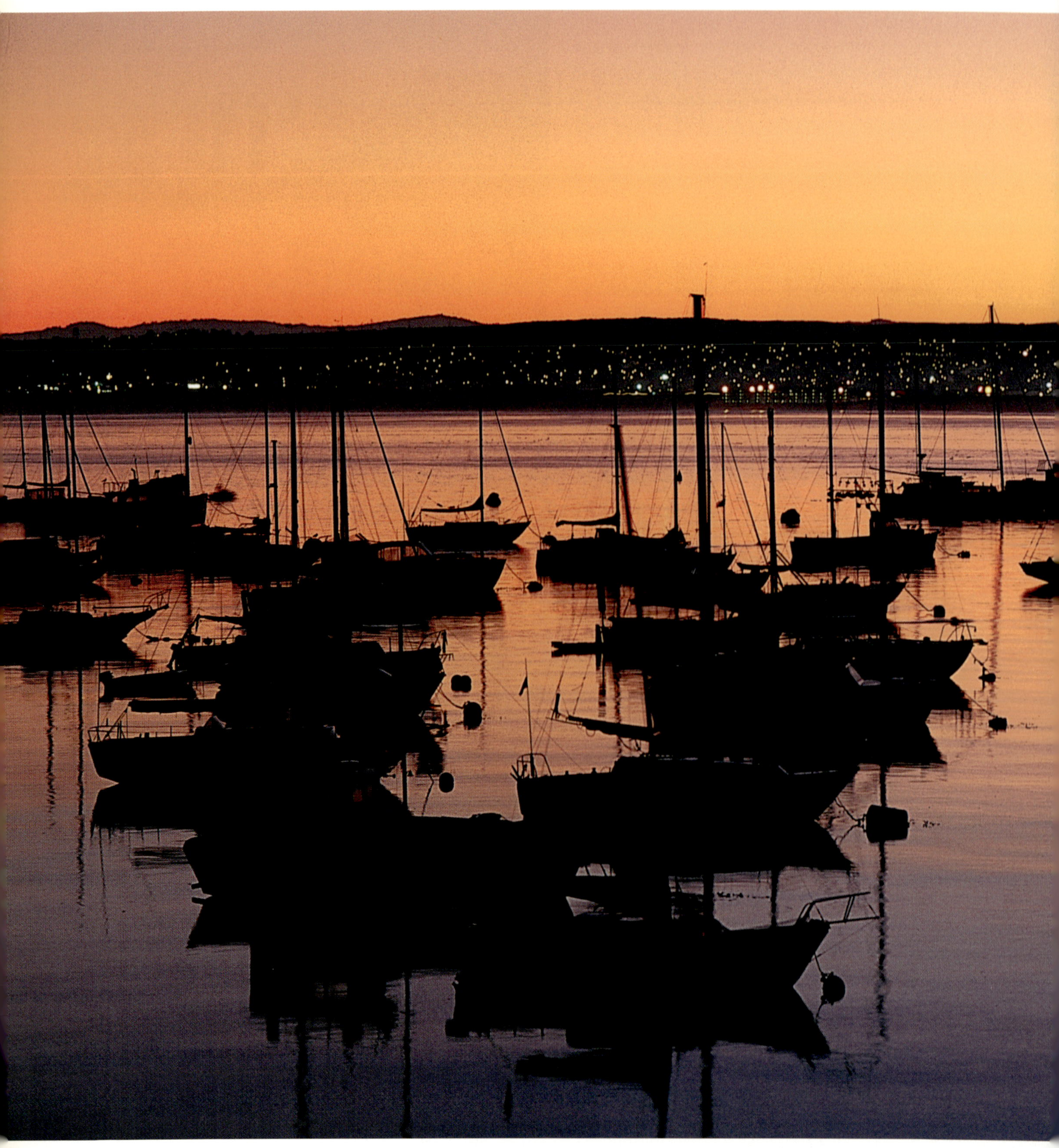

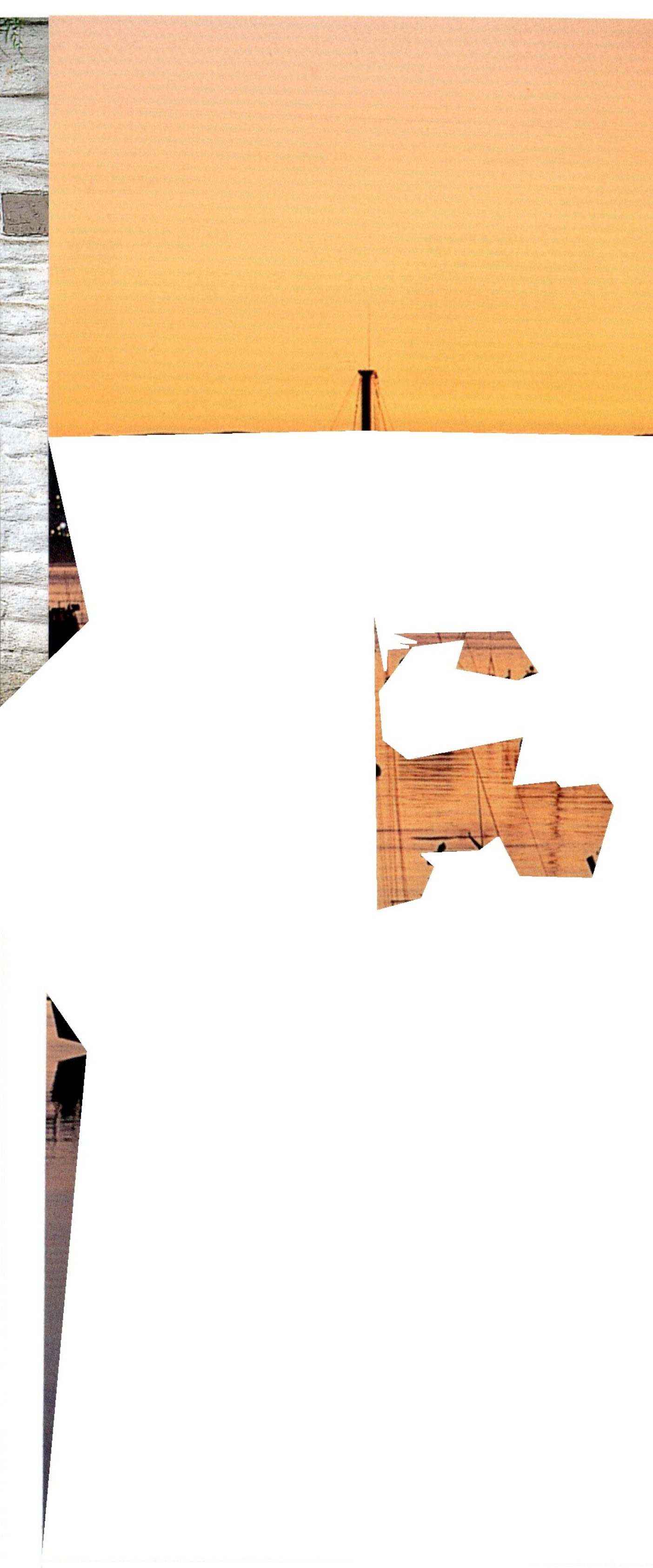

3) It also has a ready means of communication by water with large and rich valleys of the San Joaquin, the Sacramento, and the American Fork, as all of these rivers are tributaries to the bay. So far as my information goes, Monterey, although it has a fine country at its back, has none of the facilities for reaching and transporting the products which San Francisco possesses in regard to the country that surrounds it. This, allowing for all other things being equal, would give San Francisco an insuperable advantage.

Gilbert's perspicacity would be well proved within the next few years. This convention was the last gasp of Monterey's political importance. With statehood, the capital moved; and once cattle prices collapsed, Monterey became a quiet backwater.

But as the convention assembled in 1849, Monterey and its surrounding countryside were prosperous because of the high prices that were being paid for cattle and sheep. The town sparkled with new-found wealth and merriment, as affluent families entertained each other and the visitors who had come to the town to transact business.

The convention had been called at the initiative of General Bennett Riley, military governor of California, for the purpose of creating a civilian government. The U.S. military had seized California in 1846, but the United States made no provisions for governing it. After three years of military rule, Californians agitated for a civil government. Riley, on his own dubious authority, issued a proclamation for an election to be held on August 1, 1849, to choose delegates to a constitutional convention to begin on September 1.

Thus, these forty-eight delegates, most of whom had never met each other, gathered to draft a constitution and create a state government without any direction from, or even the permission of, the federal government. They were a disparate group: only three-quarters were citizens of the United States by birth, and they ranged in age from their twenties to their fifties. Twenty-two were from free states; fifteen, from slave states. Seven were California-born, and

◄ ***This Monterey Bay sunrise scene spreads out from near the spot where Commodore John Sloat landed.***

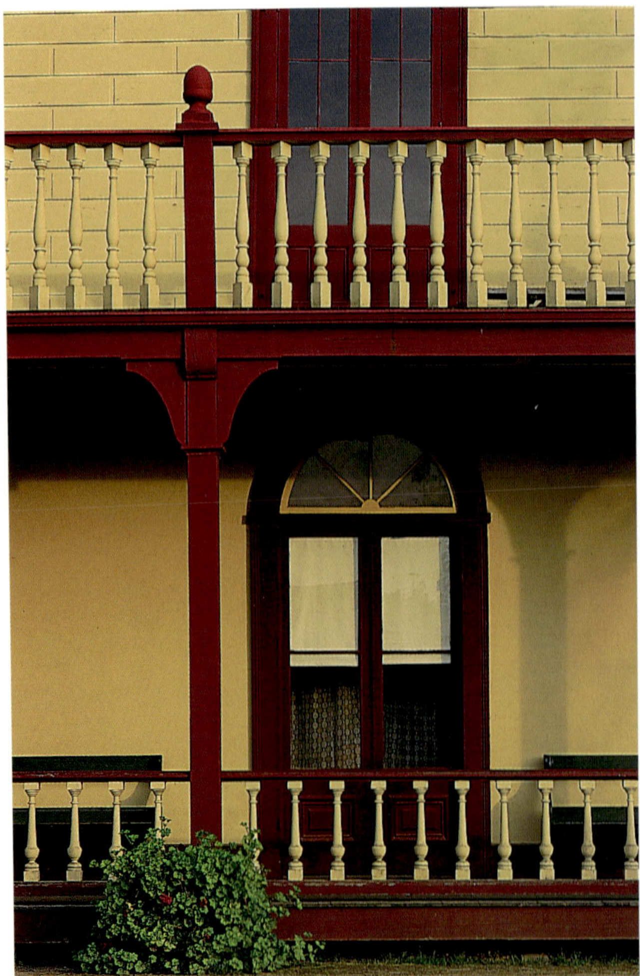

▲ The San Juan Bautista State Historic Park includes Plaza Hall (pictured).
➤ Mariano Vallejo's home, in Sonoma State Historic Park, pays tribute to this early ranchero and civic leader.

In a following election, the state's governor, two members to the U.S. House of Representatives, and other officers were selected. The bicameral legislature (consisting of two chambers) convened on December 15, 1849, and subsequently elected the two United States senators: William Gwin, a Southerner who had been a moving force on the constitutional convention, and John C. Frémont, "the Great Pathfinder."

And so, three-and-a-half months after the delegates first gathered in Monterey, a state constitution was drafted and voted upon, state officers and legislators were elected, and this newly elected government convened to begin to enact the state's business. The elected representatives to the United States Congress were sent off to Washington, D.C., with copies of the constitution and news of what had been accomplished in California; but there was no certainty that Congress would approve of the decisions that had been made in Colton Hall.

2. SAN JOSE AND THE "LEGISLATURE OF A THOUSAND DRINKS"

The town of San Jose had been selected as the capital, and California's legislature assembled there despite the absence of accommodations for a state government. This small town had been California's first pueblo, founded in 1777. It was flanked by two nearby missions, Santa Clara and San Jose (in the present-day town of Fremont).

Governor Peter Burnett sent an inaugural message to the legislature, outlining a myriad of procedural and substantive issues that needed to be decided. The duties of the constitutional officers of the state needed to be defined. And since the state had no source of revenue, a method of taxation needed to be devised. Legislation authorizing a poll tax and a property tax, and a law setting up provisions for state indebtedness were passed by mid-1850.

During the spring of 1850, the legislature tackled the question of organizing the state politically into counties. Twenty-five counties and their seats were created, and provisions for the election of county officers were enacted. Nine cities—Sacramento, Benicia, San Diego, San Jose, Monterey, San Francisco, Sonoma, Santa Barbara, and Los Angeles—were initially incorporated. Also created in this extraordinary burst of legislative industry was a state judicial system: local courts, an appellate court, and a state supreme court. This was followed by the decision to adopt English common law, rather than civil law, as the basis for the state's jurisprudence.

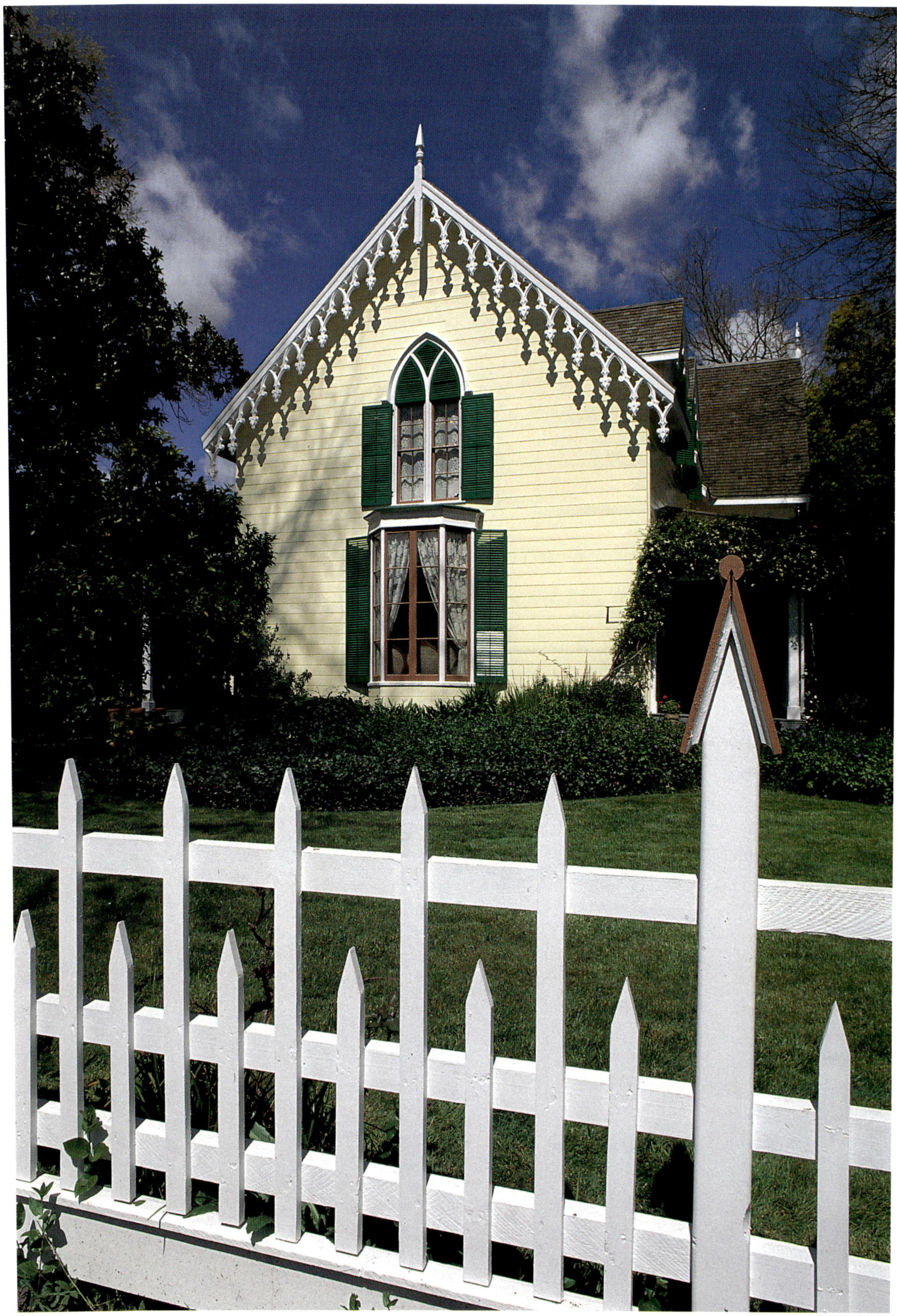

Only Louisiana, it was pointed out, among those states that had formerly been under civil law as the result of having been governed by France and Spain, had retained the use of civil law.

In all, 146 acts and 19 joint resolutions were passed by the two houses and signed by the governor between December 15, 1849, and April 22, 1850, the date of adjournment. This feat was one of great magnitude, creating a state and its government from a wild and distant region, with no money in the treasury and no revenue, and at a time when the state was in the convulsive throes of the Gold Rush.

The prejudices of the mid-nineteenth century could be seen in some of the acts of the first legislature. A bill to prevent the immigration into California of free blacks and other "persons of color" passed the Assembly but was tabled in the Senate. Nevertheless, a law was enacted (which would remain in effect for thirteen years) to prohibit any black or mulatto person or any Indian from giving evidence in any action to which a white person was a party in any court of the state.

The work of California's first state legislature has been disparaged by the impression that it was totally under the sway of lobbyists who saw to it that the lawmakers were kept in liquor—thus the nickname, "legislature of a thousand drinks"—and in riotous living. John Sutter, who was not a member of the legislature, said that one-third of its members were good, the rest bad, and that "they appeared in the legislature halls with revolvers and bowie

---

▼ *At Monterey's Colton Hall, near this early map exhibit, California's first constitution was written—in both English and Spanish—in 1849. Among the constitutional delegates were John Sutter and Mariano Vallejo.*

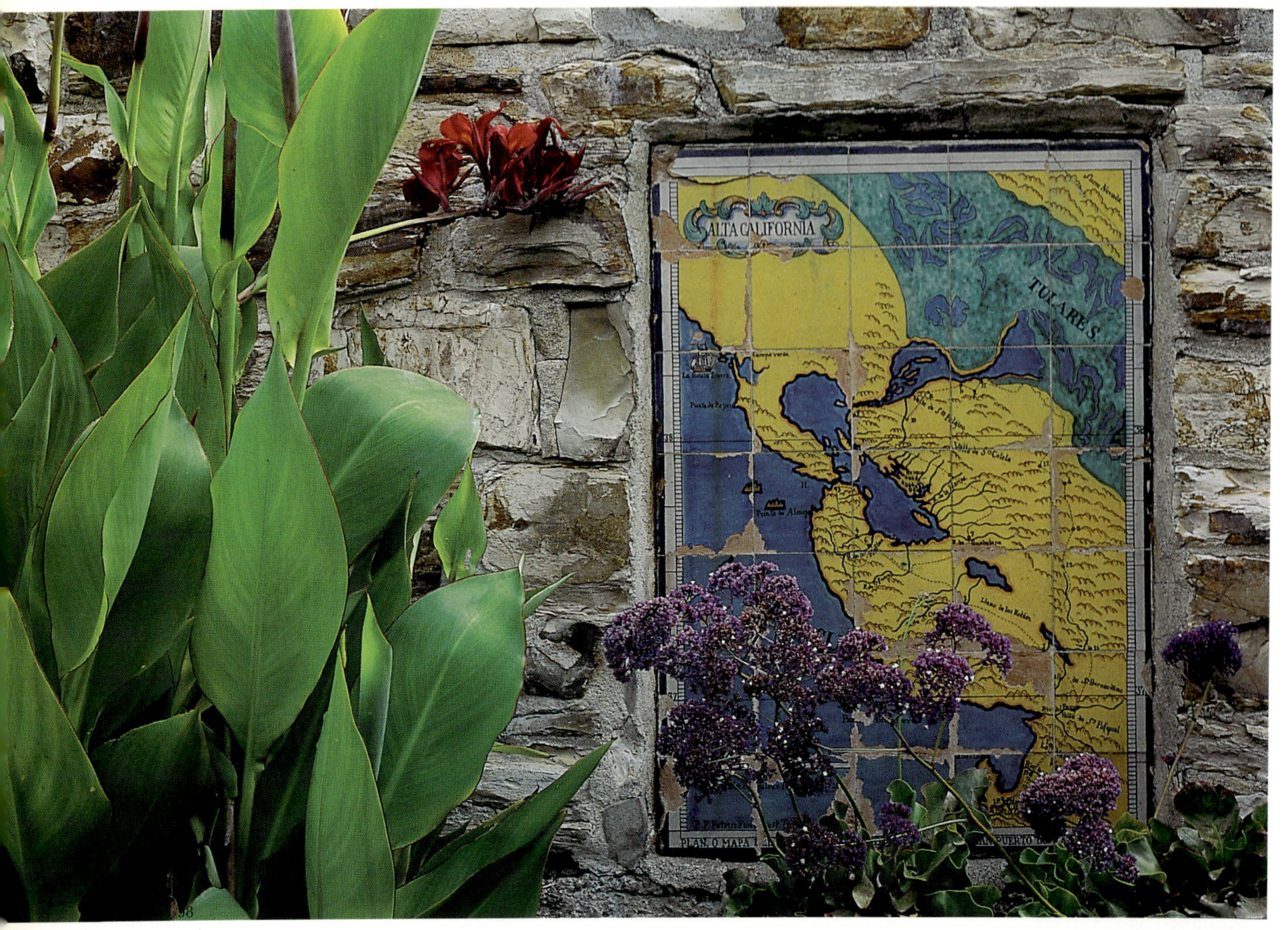

knives fastened to their belts, and were drinking, rioting and swearing nearly all the time."

Actually, the name, "legislature of a thousand drinks," was taken from the invitation of a man by the name of Thomas Jefferson Green to members of the legislature after business hours, "Well, boys, let's go and take a thousand drinks." And Sutter's description must be taken with a grain of salt. Certainly the first legislators were neither prissy nor sedate, but no group of lawmakers as despicable as Sutter makes them out could have accomplished as much as these men did in just four and one-half months.

William Henry Ellison in *A Self-Governing Dominion* gives a more balanced and definitive assessment of the first legislature:

> *It was called together under circumstances that were novel, challenging, and important. In most matters it acted with consummate good judgement. In a region far from the seat of the national government, it discarded old institutions that were adapted neither to the habits, nor to the tastes, nor to the political philosophy of the newly arrived population. New ones were quickly constructed by the talents, understanding, and industry of a small body of young legislators.*

These men may not have perfected what they built, but they did lay a fair foundation of enduring quality. The ability of the state's governmental structure to adapt to changing conditions is a perennial tribute to the devotion and to the political wisdom of those builders who participated in the first legislative session in California.

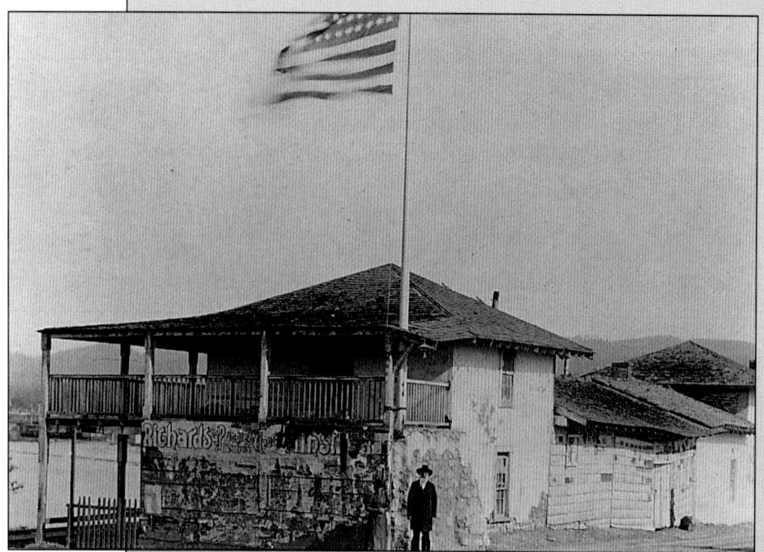

CUSTOM HOUSE

From 1770, Monterey served as the capital of California, the seat of civil and military government and the site of the ecclesiastical governance of the missions.

In 1814, Spain built this adobe customs house in Monterey. When Mexico, following its revolt from Spain in the early 1820s, allowed increasing foreign trade, Monterey (and particularly the Custom House) became the commercial hub of California.

The hides and tallow of California's numerous herds of cattle became sought-after commodities by businesses in Latin America, the United States, Great Britain, France, and Russia. The onerous customs duties—and bribes paid to reduce these duties—were paid at the customs house.

In 1842, Commodore Thomas Catesby ap Jones, U.S.N., raised the U.S. flag at the customs house when he seized Monterey in the mistaken belief that the United States and Mexico were at war.

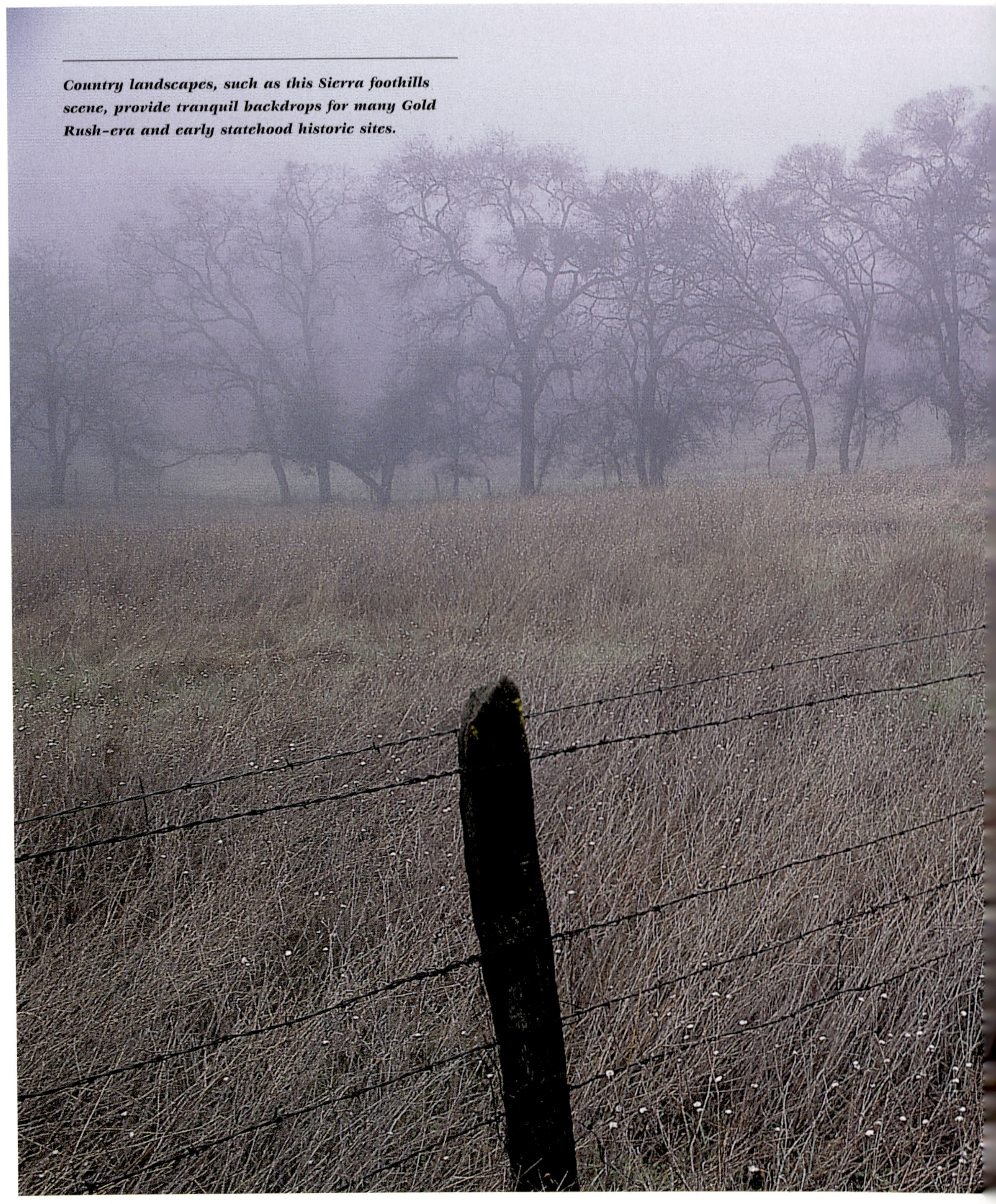

Country landscapes, such as this Sierra foothills scene, provide tranquil backdrops for many Gold Rush-era and early statehood historic sites.

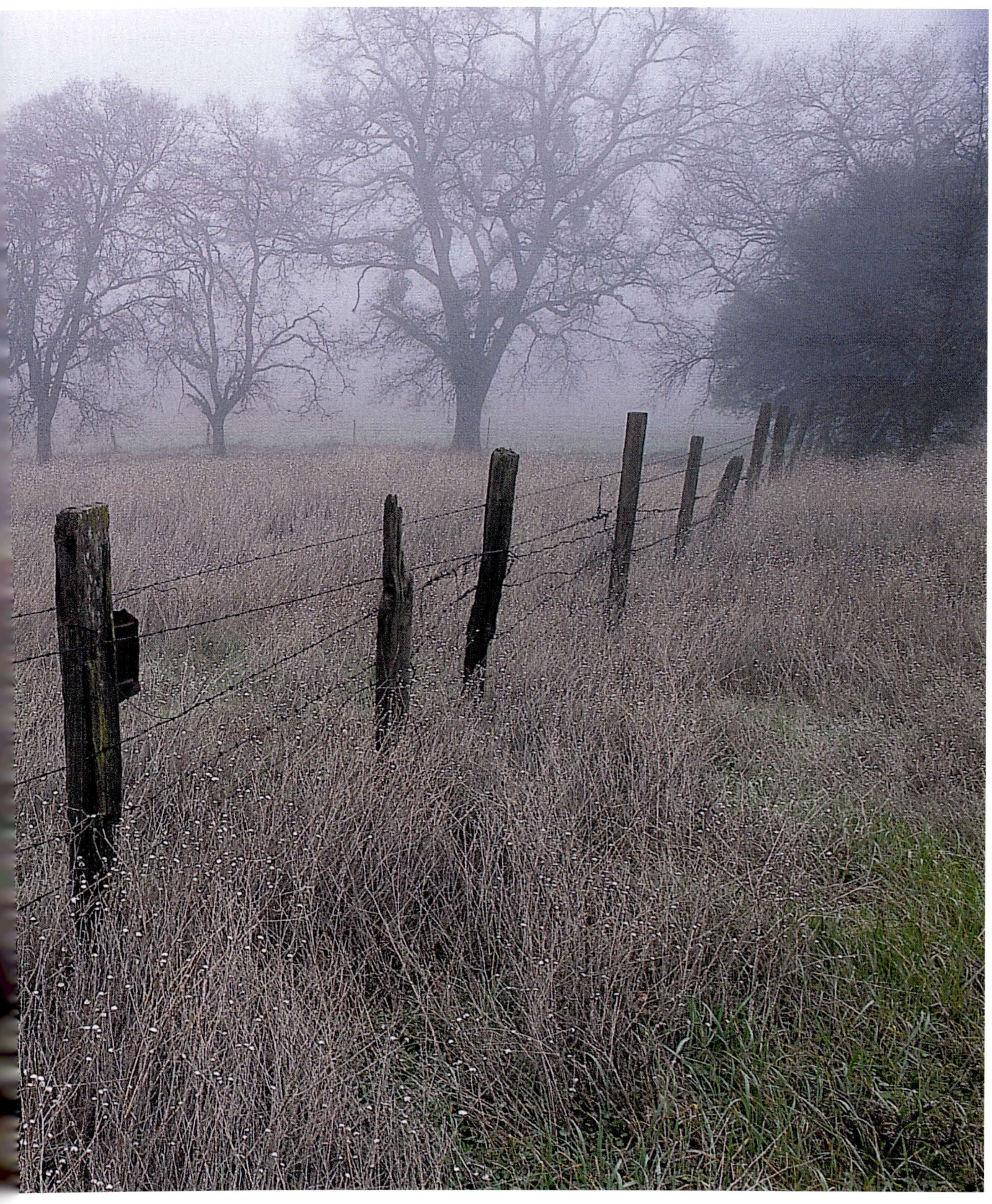

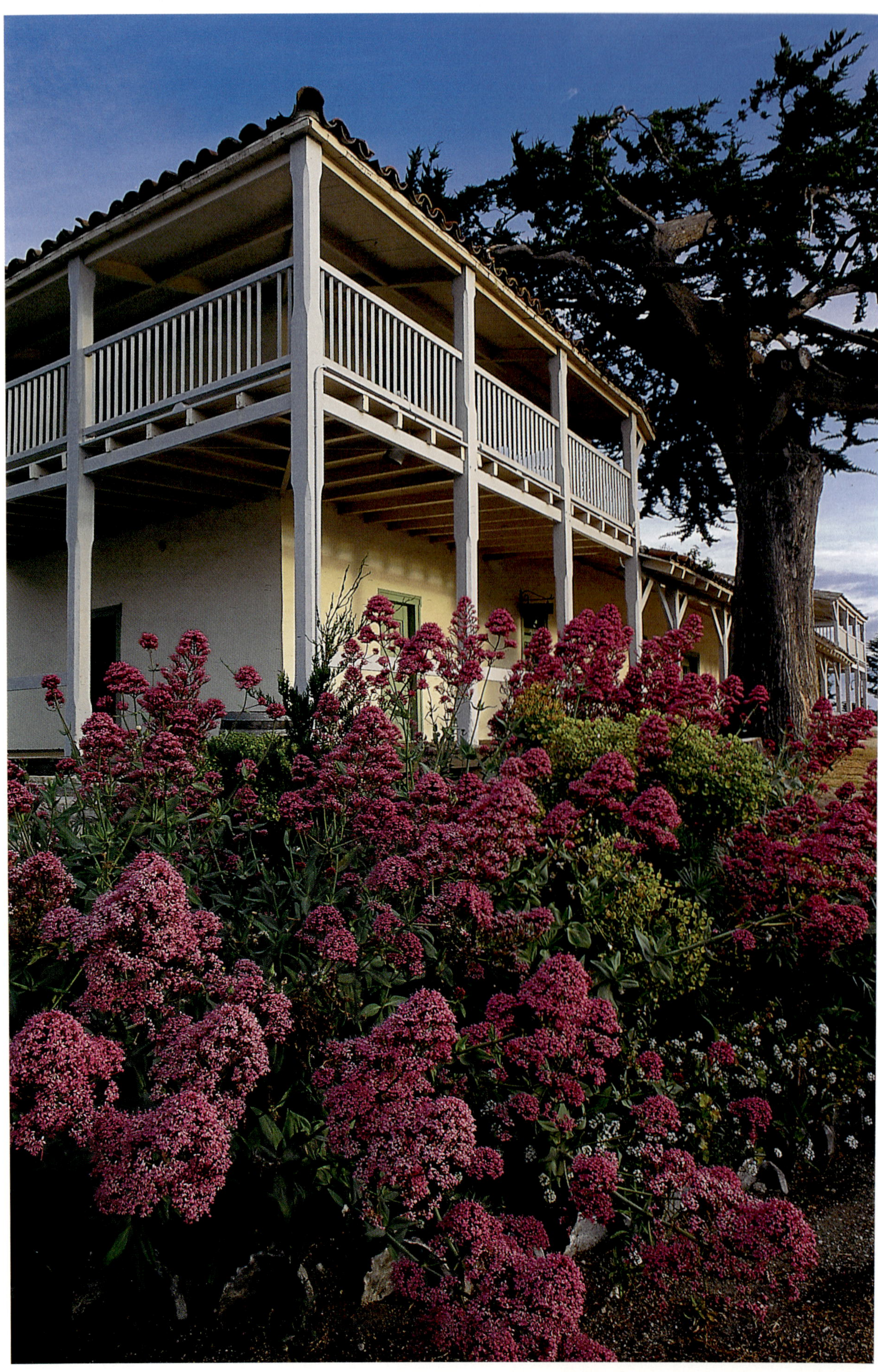

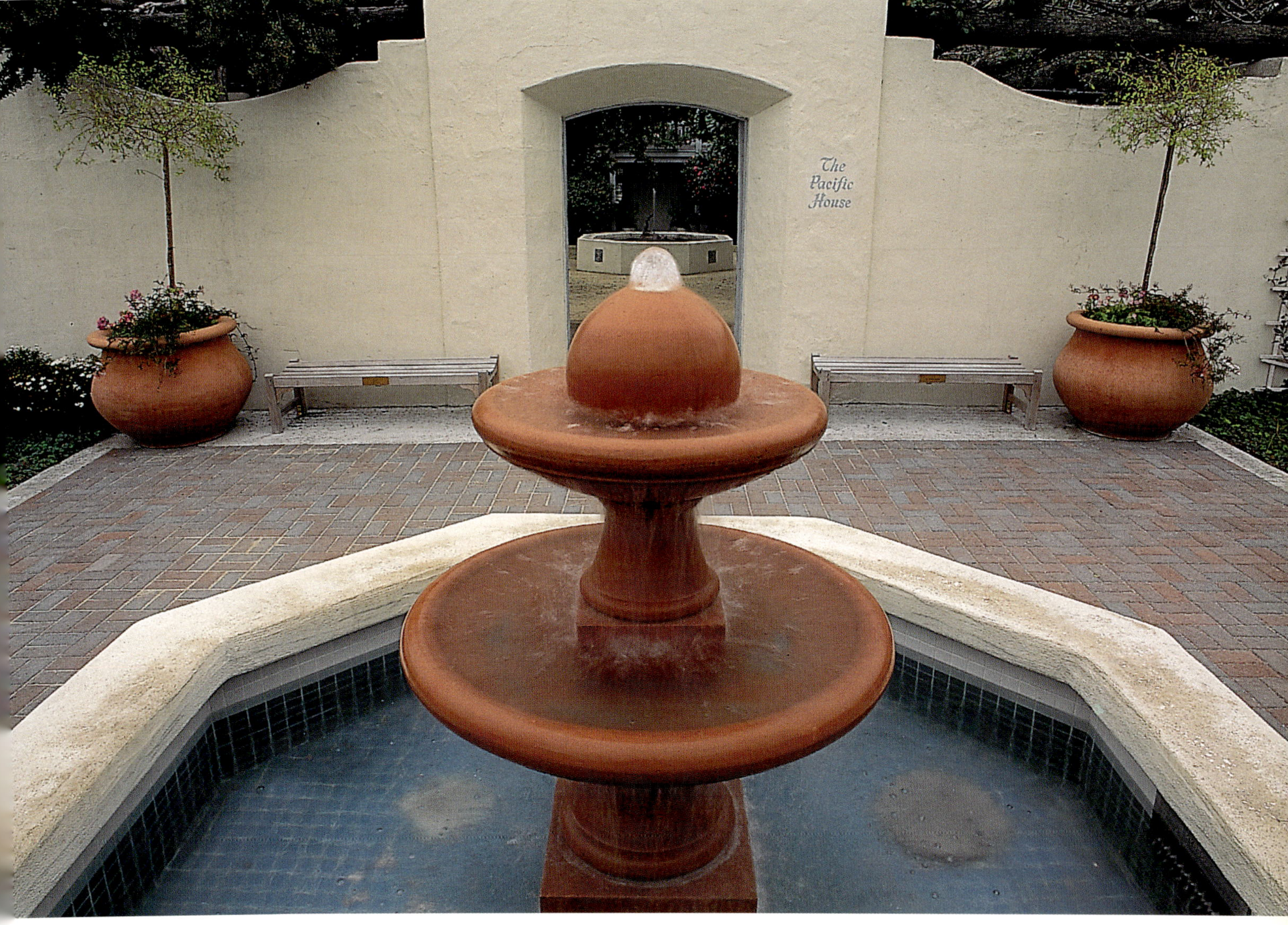

◄ *Monterey's Path of History features Custom House and other old adobes with balconies and colorful gardens.*
▲ *Exhibits at Monterey's 1847 Pacific House profile the city's early days and the area's Native American past.*

3. THIRTY-FIRST STAR

While California's first state legislators were spending these months crafting the details of state government (first in Vallejo, then San Jose again, and finally in Sacramento, as the state capital was shuttled among these towns), the scene of California's destiny had shifted across the continent to Washington, D.C.

The drafters of California's constitution and its elected officials for a year after the signing of the state's constitution had operated in a legal vacuum, a political twilight. They had formed a state government and operated as such; they had elected representatives to the two houses of Congress; and they had done this without the prior knowledge or approbation of the federal government.

Even before early 1850 when California's elected representatives reached Washington, D.C., and called upon the president, the vice president, the justices of the Supreme Court, and prominent members of both houses of Congress, President Zachary Taylor had informed Congress that California had formulated a constitution and would be seeking admission to the Union. He recommended that it be admitted. On January 29, 1850, Henry Clay proposed a series of compromises that would accept California as a state.

Then the elected senators and representatives from California arrived in Washington with certified copies of the state's constitution and the news of the organization of a civil government that was seeking to be admitted to the Union as a state.

But the thirty-first Congress, which had assembled in December 1849, was locked in a great sectional battle. Led by John Calhoun, one of a band of great senators who had dominated the Senate and United States politics for more than three decades, the Southern congressmen fought fiercely to protect the balance between the free and the slave states. Fearful of the growing population and economic power of the North, the Southerners saw that the admission of California as a free state would end that balance in the Senate, and thus the ability of the South to ward off threats to slave-holding and its agrarian way of life. Calhoun predicted the end of the Union should California be admitted to statehood; and he was fiercely backed by such Southern firebrands in the Senate as Jefferson Davis.

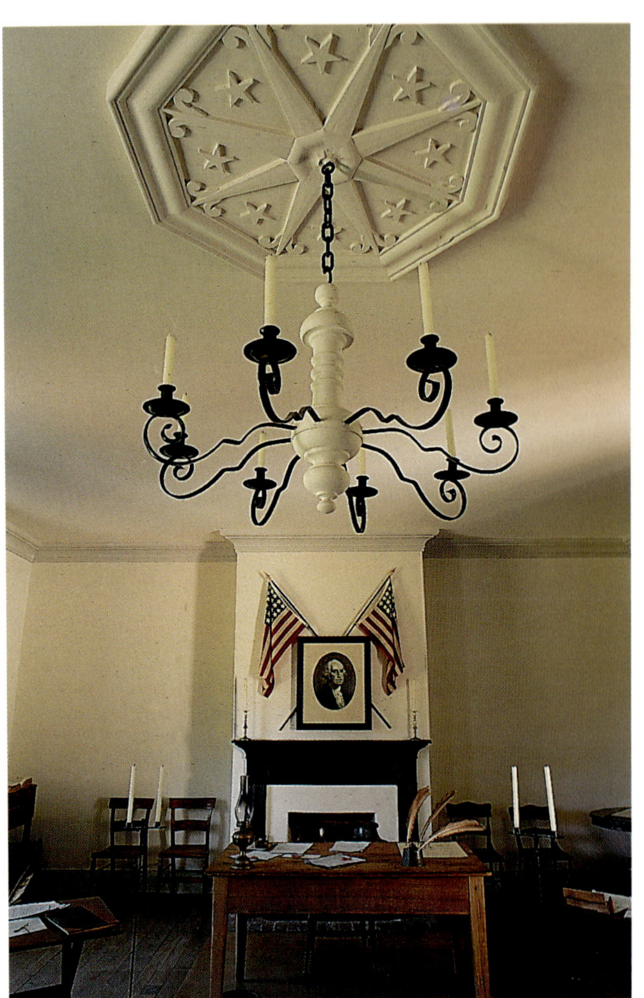

▼ At Colton Hall, delegates wrote a constitution banning slavery and protecting women's property rights.

There was, however, a group in Congress that was passionately devoted to the preservation of the Union and in favor of admitting California as a state. This group, led by elder statesmen Henry Clay and Daniel Webster, constructed an elaborate set of compromises that allowed for both admission of California as a state and retention of the Union.

William Gwin, one of the senator-designates from California, was of great help in garnering support for the compromises. A Southerner with splendid connections in the Congress, blessed with brilliant political acumen, and eager to begin his career as a United States senator, Gwin was able to influence a number of Southern congressmen to vote for the compromises.

Finally, on August 18, 1950, Senator Stephen A. Douglas's bill to admit California to the Union passed by a vote of 34 to 18, after several attempts to amend it failed. It went on to the House, where it passed 150 to 56. President Millard Fillmore signed the bill on September 9, 1850, thus making California the thirty-first state of the United States. On September 11, the California delegation to the Congress—two senators and two representatives—were sworn in.

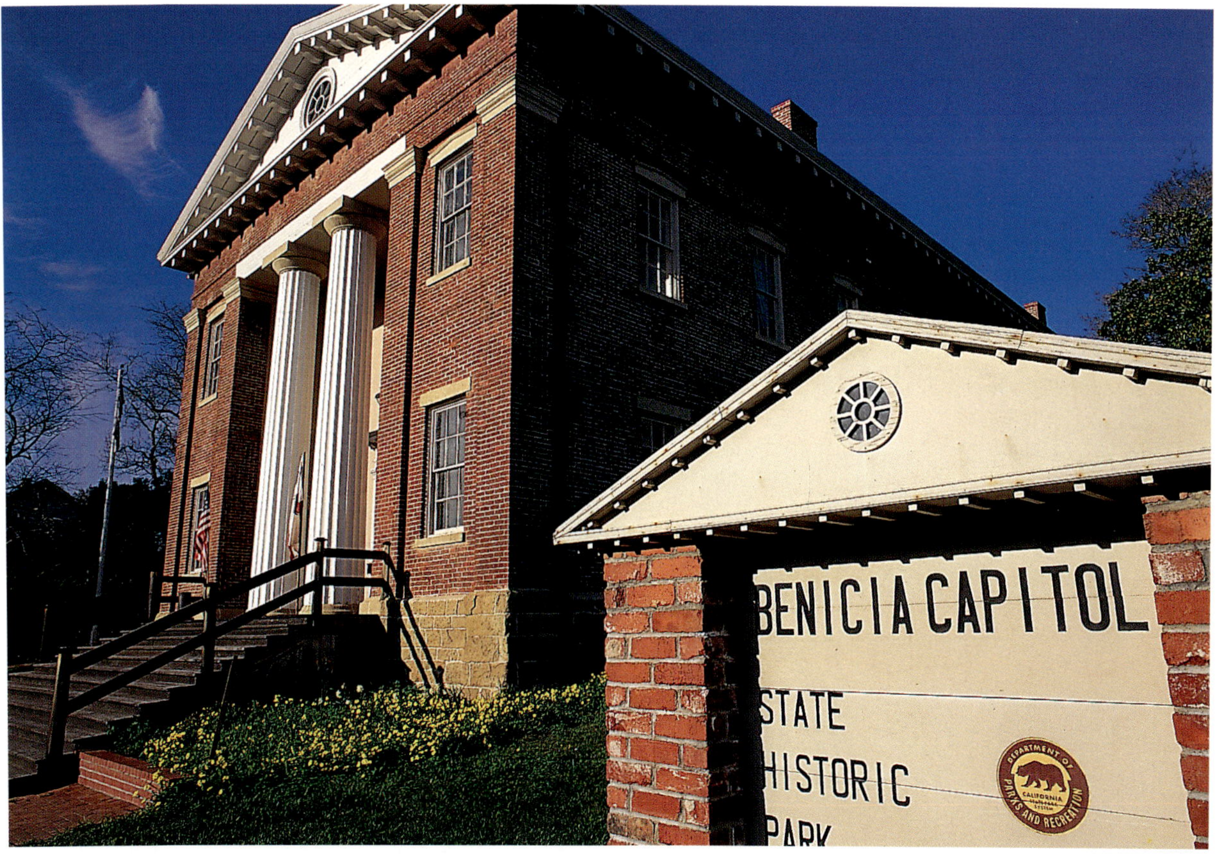

▲ *The state saw several early capitals, including Benicia. California's oldest existing capitol (1853-54) now stars as a state historic park.*

About five weeks later, on the morning of October 18, the news arrived aboard the mail steamer *Oregon*. The ship entered the harbor of San Francisco bearing two banners, each with the inscription, "California is a State." A diary entry by Charles E. Huse reports the effect of the *Oregon*'s dramatic news:

At 11:00 o'clock A.M., the Oregon *came up the harbor, draped in flags from stem to stern, while her guns thundered out to tell Californians "California is admitted." This is glorious news. A salute was soon after fired in the Plaza, and the flag, with another star of paper pinned on was run up on the lofty staff, which a Yankee climbed to read the hal- yards at the cap. A general discharge of small arms and firing of crackers, with now and then the booming of a hoarse mouthed cannon kept up till after midnight, proclaimed the joy with which the glad news was received.*

A holiday was declared. Citizens congregated in Portsmouth Plaza to congratulate each other. United States flags flew everywhere—on the ships in the harbor and on the buildings in the city. Guns were fired. Bands played. Processions formed. At night, bonfires were lighted. Then, on October 29, the city of San Francisco held a formal celebration. A parade of floats and numerous ethnic organizations and other groups snaked through the dirt and plank streets of this frontier city. At Portsmouth Plaza, music, orations, and poems memorialized the important event.

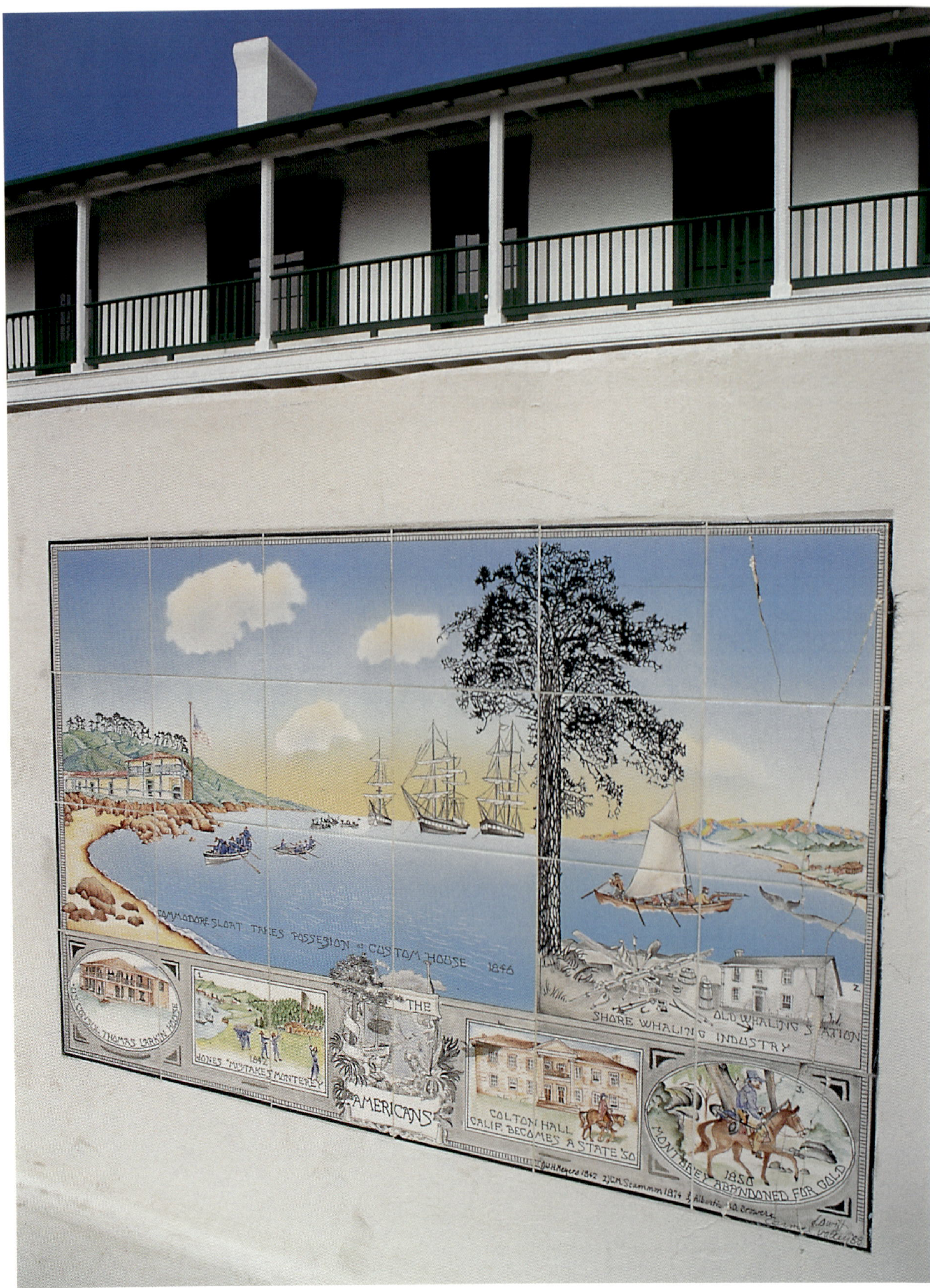

California had become a state. A bit more than four years after Sloat, Montgomery, Stockton, Frémont, and others had wrested California from Mexico; two and a half years after the discovery of gold brought tens of thousands of migrants to California; and less than a year after forty-eight disparate men had written and signed a state constitution in Colton Hall in Monterey—California had become a full-fledged member of the great confederation of the United States.

The compromise that had been fashioned in Congress, allowing for California's admission to statehood, managed to hold the Union together for another ten years before it broke apart, leading to the tragedy of the Civil War. When this cataclysm did take place, California remained resolutely in the Union.

Neither on the day Millard Fillmore signed the bill admitting California to statehood nor on those October days of 1850 when Californians learned of this event and celebrated it with such enthusiasm, could anyone envisage what triumphs, what glories, what further economic advances, what development California would undergo during the next century and a half.

◄ *A mural fronting Pacific House in Monterey State Historic Park illustrates the U.S. period of California's past.*
▼ *Monterey's Fisherman's Wharf was the site of a stone pier built in 1846 for trading vessels.*

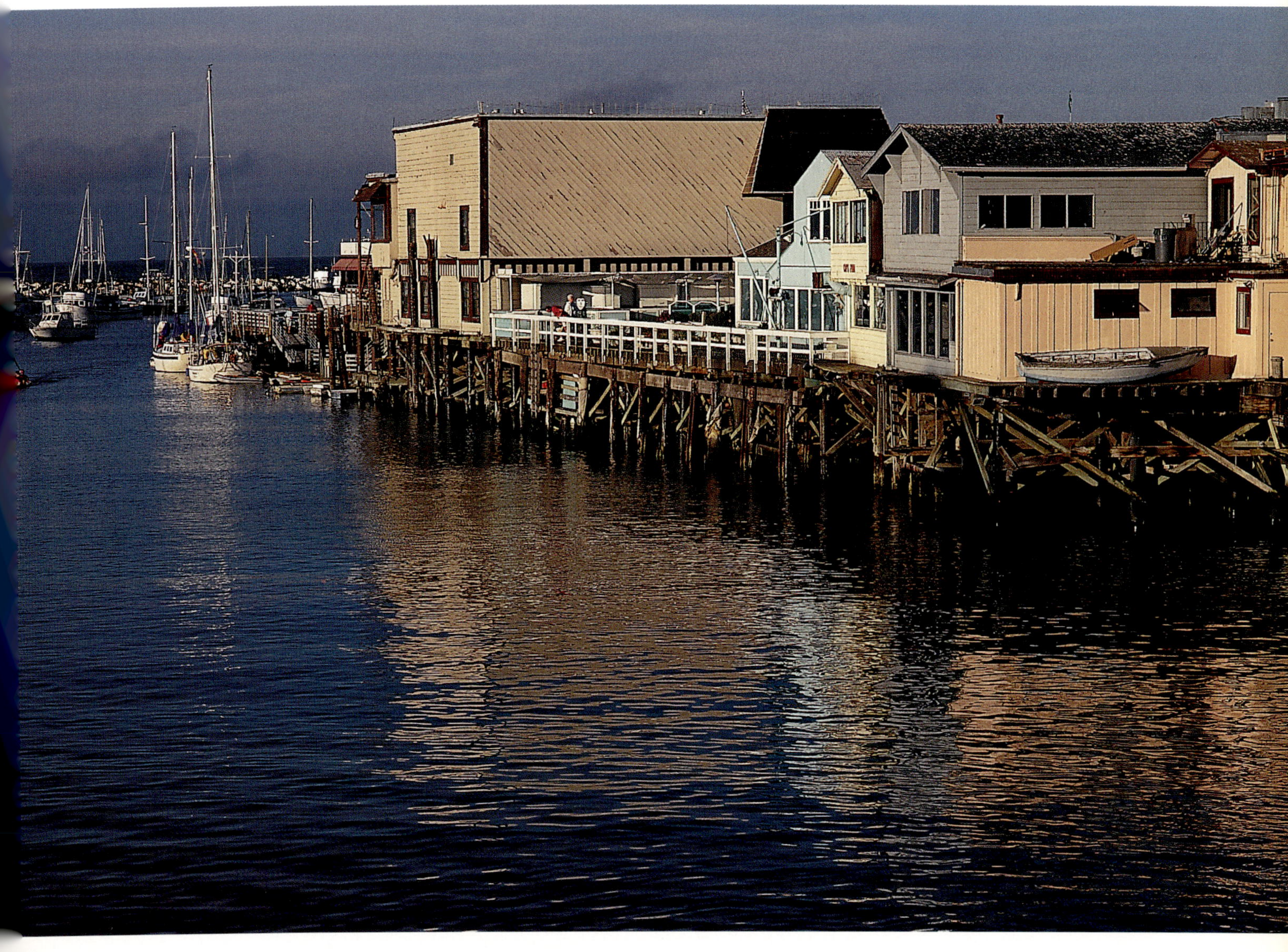

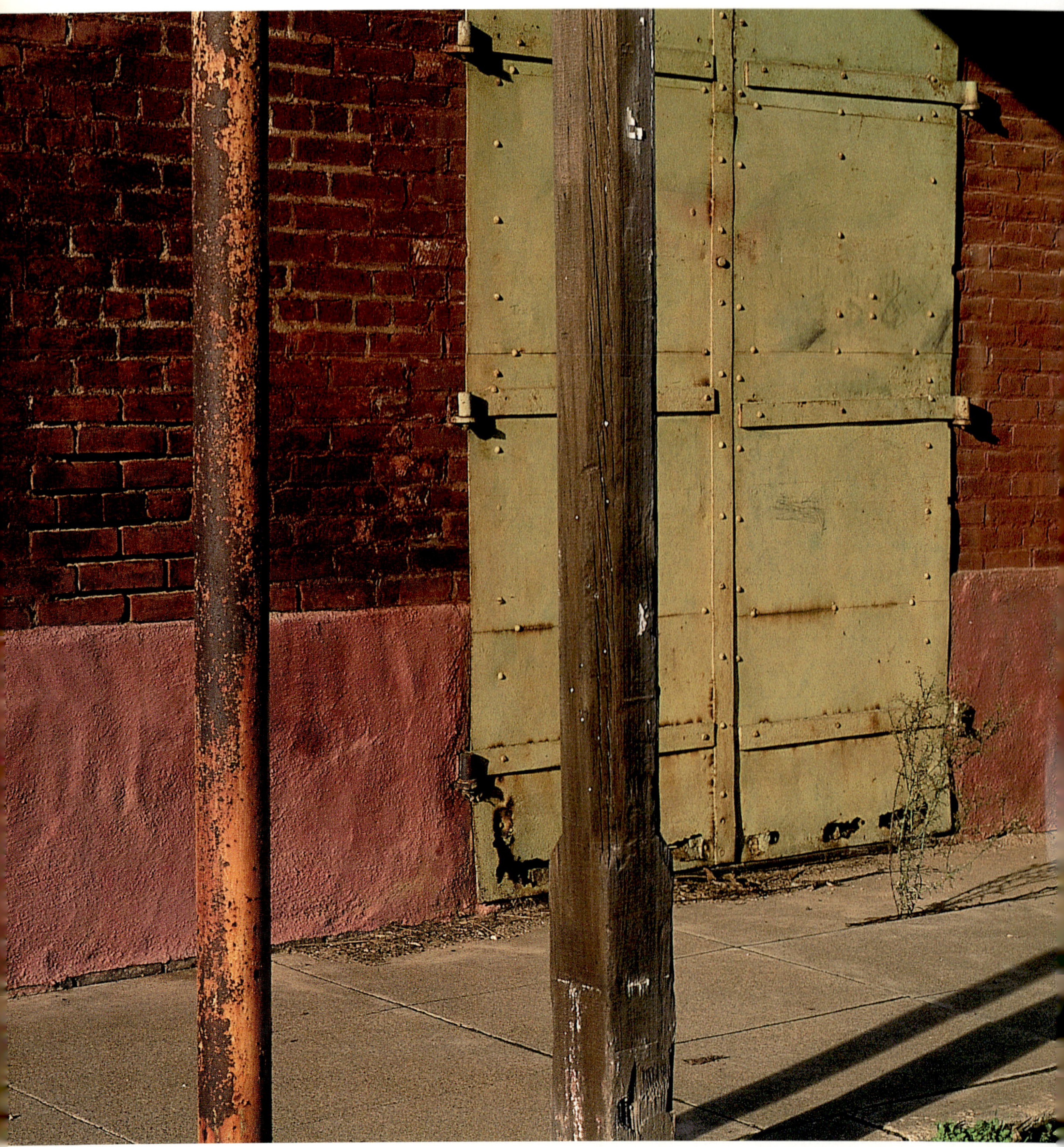

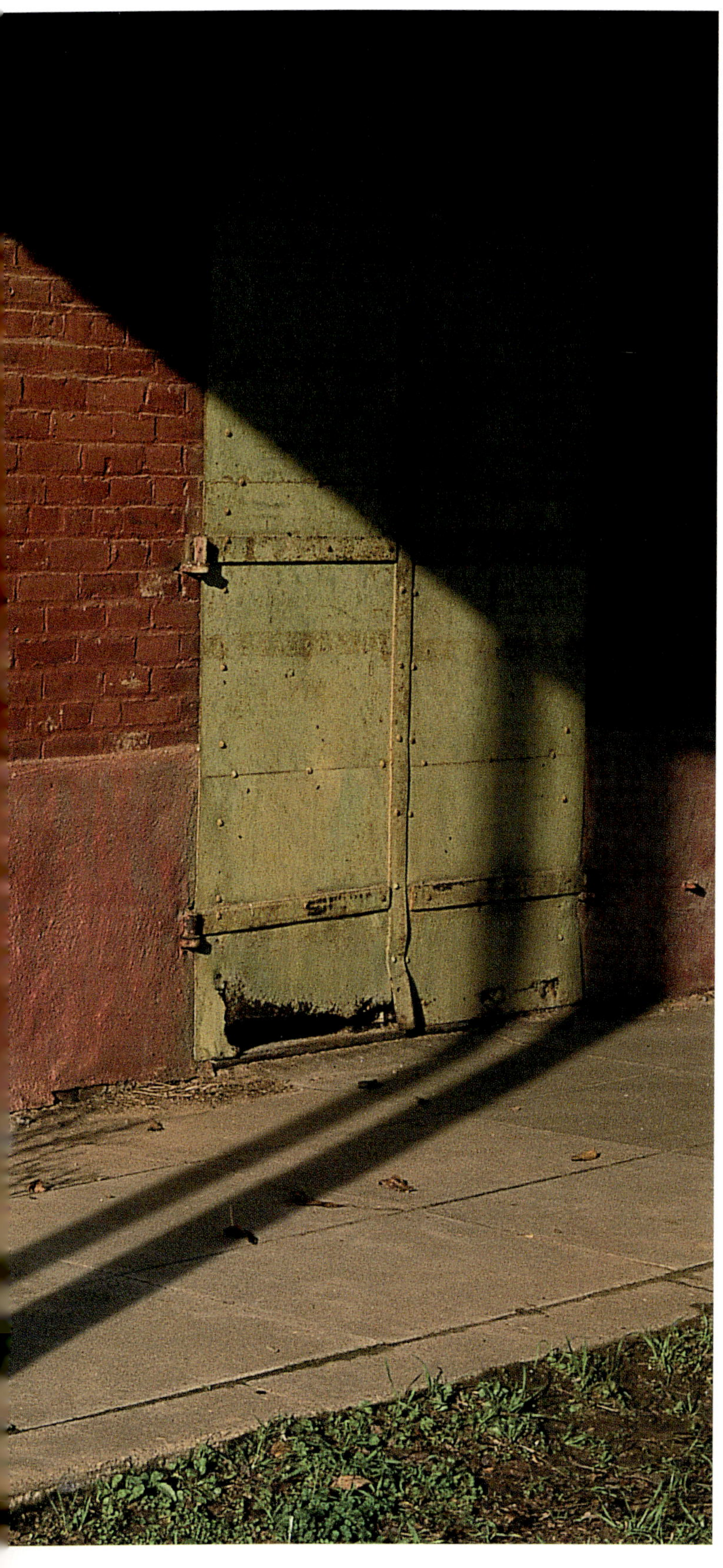

THE ECHOES CONTINUE

1. REVERBERATIONS OF HISTORY

California: The Golden State. The Golden Land. Gold Mountain. Around the globe, from the poorest village in the most backward country to the most cultured city in the most technologically advanced nation, that name evoked—and continues to evoke—dreams of a land filled with boundless opportunity.

California's motto, *Eureka!* (I have found it!), borrowed from the Greek philosophers' exclamation of excitement at a mathematical discovery, echoes the spirit of the discovery of gold in 1848. Whether or not a gold seeker found his fortune in the gold fields or stayed to build a life in the flourishing towns or in the rich countryside, he had, indeed, found it.

Those who formed this state were bold people, somehow having found the resources for the long, arduous journey to an unknown land, enduring the dangers of the journey, then engaging in back-breaking labor at what was often a profitless task.

The disheartened, the discouraged, and the homesick returned to the homes they had left

◄ *Hornitos was a reputed hideout for the notorious bandit, Joaquín Murieta.*

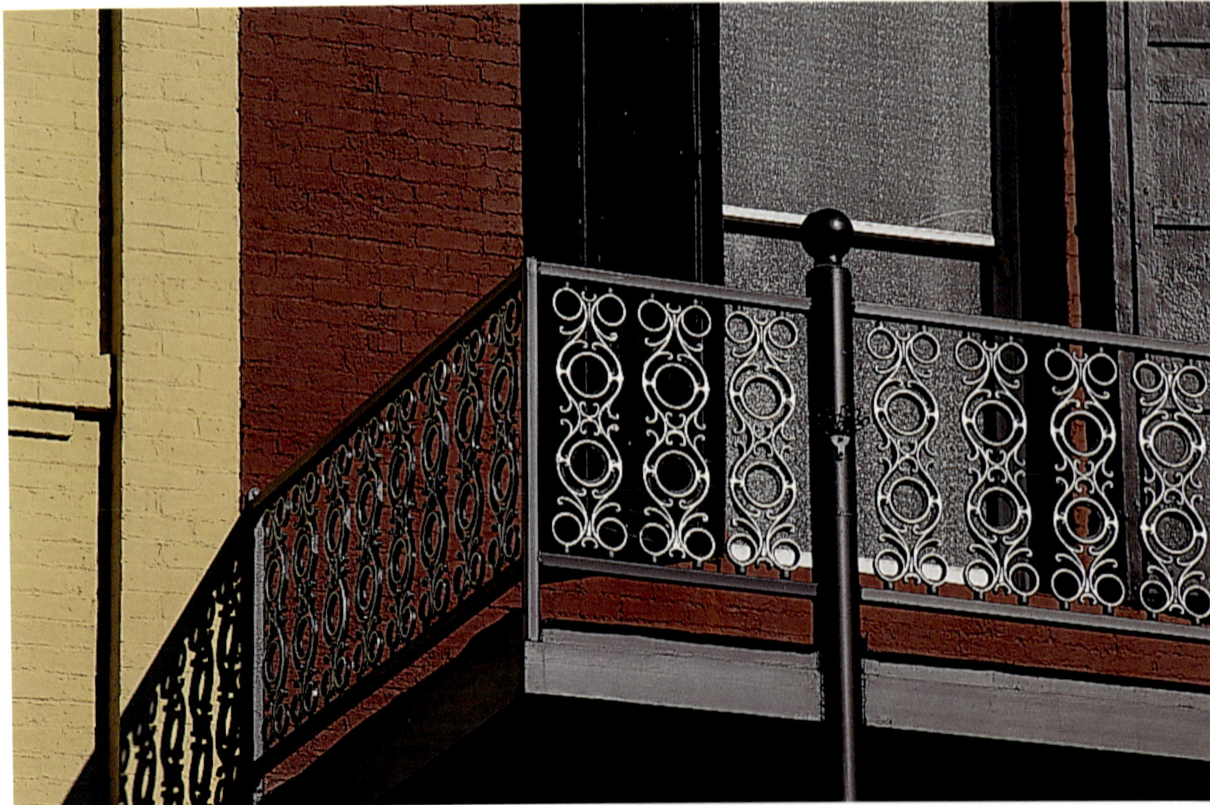

▲ *Nevada City retains its picturesque Gold Country charm, featuring a brick downtown, as well as steepled churches, Victorian houses, and fall foliage.*
▶ *The aptly named Highway 49 passes right by this wall painting in tiny Drytown north of Sutter Creek.*

with high hopes such a short time before. Most, feeling deeply their failure to gain the riches California had held out, would try to pick up the shattered pieces of their lives. The ones who continued to dream of the golden opportunities that might be found in California stayed and turned to other work. None ever forgot the epic adventure of which they had been a part. And all played a role in transforming a sleepy province of Mexico from a pastoral backwater into a dynamic area, the focal point of attention of much of the rest of the world—a land whose name has become synonymous with new beginnings.

Thousands of California's immigrants, far from the influence and constraints of their homes, managed to craft self-governing communities and towns out of the chaos and anarchy of the mining camps. They somehow conspired to establish an orderly, albeit often raucous, society.

In the year following the discovery of gold, a comparatively small group of serious-minded men gathered in California's Mexican capital city of Monterey and were able, within a few short weeks, to draft a progressive state constitution, without the permission or even the knowledge of the federal government. The constitution they crafted received the approval of the United States Congress when California was actually admitted to statehood as the thirty-first state in the Union.

Untrammeled by the strictures of historical development, surging with the ambition, imagination, and vitality that brought them to California, these adventurers set a new pace, envisioned new lives, and created a new society that remains unique.

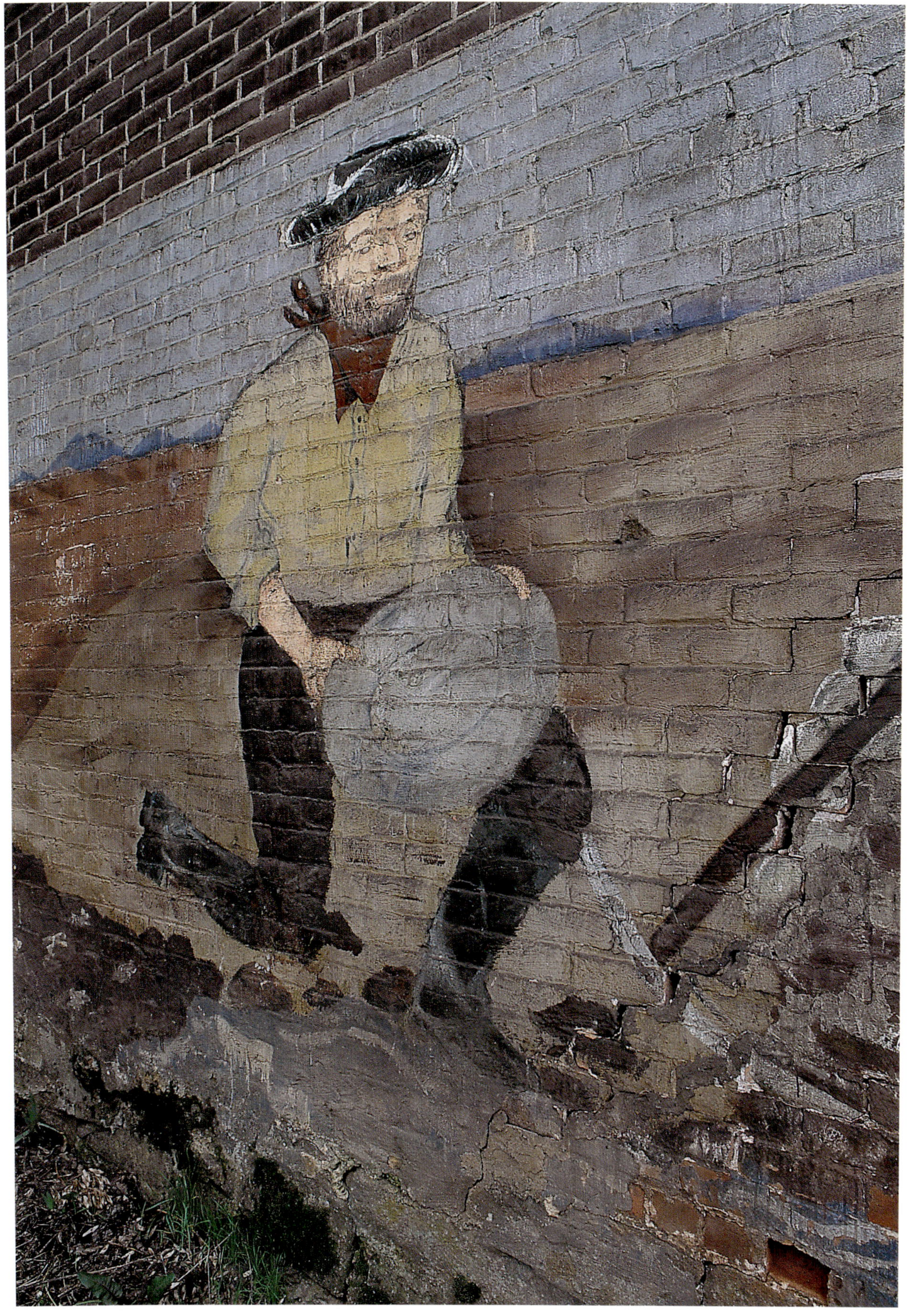

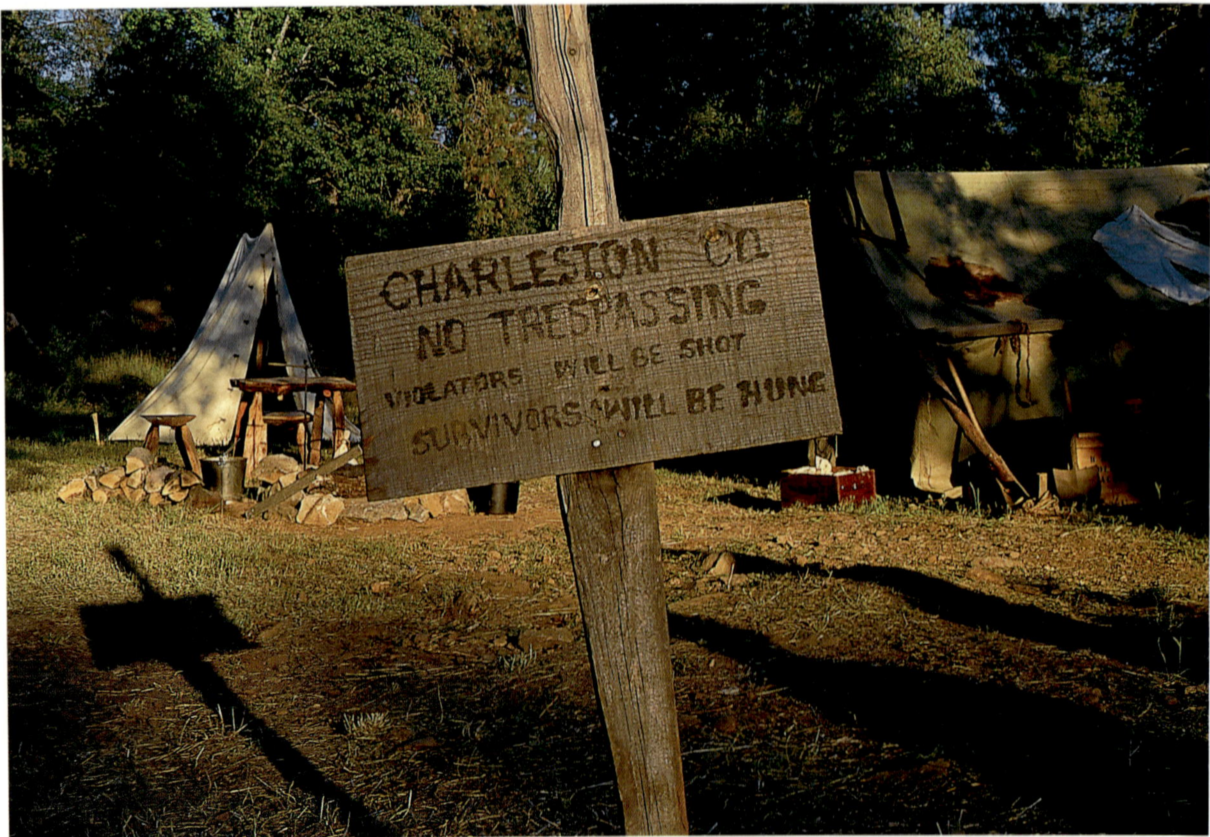

▲ *This re-created mining camp at Columbia and other Gold Country scenes—restored towns, historical museums, state parks, reconstructed Indian villages and living-history programs—help visitors understand the turbulent and romantic California Gold Rush.*

2. THE ECHOES REVERBERATE

California has an ability to fascinate the imagination, to challenge, to mystify, to stimulate, and to beckon dreamers from all around the world. The diversity and dynamism of this Golden State both exasperate and gladden observers.

It has contributed new energy, new solutions, and new perspectives to the country that conquered it in 1846. As the economic cornerstone of California, gold has given way to silver, oil, agriculture, aeronautics, entertainment, and technology. Tourism and a constantly expanding population have made California real estate some of the most valuable in the world.

But in the century and a half since the discovery of gold, although changed and transformed by time, California remains the child of the Gold Rush: for it was the impact of the discovery of gold that forged this distinctive society, that inaugurated its own brand of government, and created the Golden Land that has become today's California.

And always, the echoes of the beginnings of this land continue to reverberate, helping to shape its future. The Golden Land that formed untold millenia ago continues to attract new waves of argonauts who have come to pursue their own Golden Dreams.